A Natural History Guide

GREAT SMOKY MOUNTAINS NATIONAL PARK

Rose Houk

Photographs by
Michael Collier

HOUGHTON MIFFLIN COMPANY
Boston   New York

For information about permission to reproduce
selections from this book, write to Permissions,
Houghton Mifflin Company, 215 Park Avenue South,
New York, New York 10003

Library of Congress Cataloging-in-Publication Data

Houk, Rose, 1950-
    Great Smoky Mountains / Rose Houk ; photographs by Michael Collier.
        p.   cm. — (National parks natural history series)
    Includes bibliographical references.
    ISBN 0-395-59919-9 (cl.). — ISBN 0-395-59920-2 (pa.)
    1. Natural history—Great Smoky Mountains (N.C. and Tenn.).
2. Natural history—Great Smoky Mountains National Park (N.C. and
Tenn.).   3. Great Smoky Mountains (N.C. and Tenn.)   I. Title. II. Series.
QH105.N8h66 1993
508.768'89—dc20   93-9270
                                                                         CIP

Printed in the United States of America

AGM 10 9 8 7 6 5 4 3

To my family

Acknowledgments

I owe great debts of gratitude to many people who have given aid and support throughout this project. First, to Paul Schullery, an intelligent man dedicated to the values represented by our national parks. His encouragement and reviews of the manuscript were indispensable. To Jeremy Schmidt and Wendy Baylor, friends, compatriots, and incredibly talented souls. And to all the enthusiastic and incisive folks at Houghton Mifflin, especially Harry Foster, Susan Kunhardt, and Lisa White. Thanks to Rick Balkin for guiding me through the process.

As always, the kind people who work at Great Smoky Mountains National Park responded generously to my many requests. Naturalist Don Defoe supplied initial ideas and a thorough review of the manuscript. Kitty Manscill, Glenn Cardwell, Keith Langdon, Janet Rock, Sue Powell, Leon Konz, Bob Miller, Nancy Gray, Steve Moore, Ed Trout, Kim DeLozier, and Mike DeMunn gave their time and knowledge. Steve Kemp, publications director of the Great Smoky Mountains Natural History Association, deserves a special thank-you for ideas and good coffee. James Renfroe and John Peine and the Uplands Research Laboratory in the

Smokies kindly shared the results of their work, and Nicki McFarland graciously supplied publications.

Chris Lucash of the U.S. Fish and Wildlife Service shared his observations and philosophy about red wolves. Thanks also to Professor Kiisa Nishikawa at Northern Arizona University, who enlightened me with her work on salamanders, and to Paul Delcourt at the University of Tennessee for permission to use information and illustration from his research on paleoecology. Mig Gallagher at the Cornell Laboratory of Ornithology and Don Wick at the Tennesseee Wildlife Resources Agency were most cooperative in help with photographs.

Words will never adequately convey my gratitude to two special people. Park librarian Annette Evans was always there with her friendship and love of the Smokies. Michael Collier, my husband, contributed most of the photographs that grace the pages of this book. I thank him for all the magical times he spent with me on the trails and around campfires in the Great Smokies.

CONTENTS

Introduction

The Earth and sky were tones of green, much as the planet must have seemed in primordial days. The air was saturated with moisture. Although a storm was imminent, I needed to escape the overhanging canopy that closed off my view of the world.

I picked up a walking stick someone had left at the trailhead and started up the trail alongside the Little River in the Smoky Mountains in east Tennessee. A few spatters of rain started to fall. Other hikers were running back down the trail, but I had no desire to turn back. The rain provided welcome, refreshing relief from the intense summer humidity.

As the rain fell harder, I felt every pore in my skin open to soak it in. I stepped back off the trail and took shelter under the trees, the leaves overhead layered like big outspread hands. I watched and listened as the rain thundered down, turning the leaves a glossy green. I could feel their pores opening as mine were, gratefully accepting the gift of moisture.

I had been on this trail many times in many seasons. I knew the instant solace these verdant forests and high mountains can bring to a soul strung taut with the day-to-day concerns of living. And on each visit, I saw new wonders. Once, on a fern walk, someone in my group found a gametophyte, a tiny, translucent, heart-shaped structure critical in the reproductive life of ferns. It was a marvel of creation. On another day early in spring, I observed the tender pinkish leaves of a budding yellow buckeye. The other leaves and flowers had not yet opened or bloomed, but the buckeyes were delicately announcing the glad tidings of spring in the Smokies.

Such sights are probably not the main attractions that draw the millions of people to the park each year. They come to see trees, flowers, waterfalls, bears, and majestic mountain vistas. These are indisputably good reasons, but for me the small, unexpected sights and discoveries are what almost always make a trip to the Smokies memorable.

It happened again that day as I walked along the Little River. After the rain let up, I left the trail and stepped down among the roots and the boulders along the riverbank. The sound of my approach was drowned out by the roar of the stream, and I startled a pair of deer browsing a few yards away. I sat quietly and watched the thin mist thread over the stream. The deer soon returned to their munchings, occasionally casting wary eyes in my direction but not running away.

A spider on a branch in front of me silently spun an invisible web. It hung in midair over the stream without apparent support. For some time I watched the spider diligently connecting its web to the branch. Time became suspended in midair too; I began to feel as much a part of the forest as the deer, the spider, the trees, and the river.

Such contentment seems too rare in our lives. We can be thankful that there are places like the Great Smoky Mountains where we can still find it. Every day the natural world here provides something to see and learn, constant surprises and wonders and mysteries. Like the colorful blackchin red salamander that came out from under a leaf on a rainy morning; the uncanny sound of barred owls calling in a dark cove forest in midafternoon; the pink catawba rhododendrons on Noland Divide that took my breath away when I came around a curve and saw them; and the rare whorled pogonia blooming in camouflaged colors beside a bench along a popular trail.

The natural history of the Smoky Mountains is an infinite story, and any book on the subject can only be a chapter or a page in that story. Thus, this book is a selective natural history. Rather than a guide or comprehensive list of all the components of the natural world, it is a sampling of the communities and the interactions of a few of their members.

The underpinnings of the story rest with the Great Smoky Mountains themselves, the rock they are made of and how they came to be here. The plants that grow in the Smokies are due in large part to that geologic foundation. The topographic relief and varied climates, along with plentiful moisture and warmth, have created immense vegetational variety.

Deciduous forest, including the unique cove hardwoods, clothes the greatest portion of the mountains. Northern hardwoods, the highest elevation broad-leaved forests in the East, grow near the small but significant spruce-fir forest of the highest elevations. Curious grass and heath areas known as balds are also present in the Smokies, and ecologists still debate their origins and maintenance.

All of these habitats sustain a diversity of life virtually without equal in temperate forests anywhere in the world. Although the Smokies have received an immense amount of study, species of plants and animals are still being discovered. The diversity of some creatures, such as the salamanders, reaches such richness that they are known as Smokies specialties.

The 800 square miles of Great Smoky Mountains National Park appear green and natural, protected and renewed since the devastation of logging in the early 20th century. But as with natural communities everywhere, the Smokies are not immune to threats that come mainly from the outside.

Introduced animals and diseases have destroyed some of the park's major plant species, such as the American chestnut and the Fraser fir. The wild boar, for example, has caused extensive damage to certain plant communities. Boars also compete with native animals for a limited supply of food. They have created an ongoing management problem in the park and have taken up a great deal of time, money, and attention for nearly three decades. Other exotics are being watched closely as they move in, and attempts are being made, within the realm of environmental reason, to protect the park from these onslaughts.

Some native species, meanwhile, have become extinct, while others teeter on the brink. There are signs of hope, though, in the park's present inventorying and monitoring of rare plants and invertebrates and reintroductions of the red wolf, the river otter, the peregrine falcon, and a fish called the madtom.

Although we consider our own species the most advanced on Earth, our understanding of the complexities of places like the Smoky Mountains is primitive. We know only a little of the interactions going on each day in the woods and streams. But we do have the tools to know more. The question is whether we have the will to use them not only to continue to preserve the Smoky Mountains, but also to save other valuable places that can teach and show us things we may not yet know to ask.

KEY TO SYMBOLS

Throughout this book, symbols in the margins will help you quickly find information on the subjects that interest you most. Watch for symbols for the following subjects:

 Birds

Trees

Wildflowers

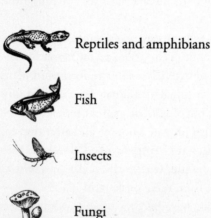 Reptiles and amphibians

Fish

Insects

Fungi

 Geology

Part One
The Land

1
The Foundation
Geology of the Great Smokies

I nestled into the fluted rock at the base of the Chimneys, contentedly munching cheese and crackers and gazing out on the undulating ridgelines of the Great Smoky Mountains. Stretching rank upon rank into the distance, the mountains looked furry and gray in their leafless winter garb.

The Chimneys are a pair of sharp pinnacles the Cherokee Indians called *Duniskwalguni,* "forked antlers." The English name comes from the natural hole or "chimney" that has formed in the rock. But I didn't make it all the way up to peer into the chimney. Instead, I stopped a mere 50 feet short of the top, watching as others gingerly inched their way along the tilted, knife-edge exposure. I had passed some of them, a bit too smugly, perhaps, on the steep walk up the trail. Though I can hold my own on the steady plodding part, death-defying heights reveal my basic lack of courage.

I was happy to be just where I was, perched on rock half a billion years old called the Anakeesta Formation. I had come to the Chimneys not only to stretch my legs and lungs but specifically to gain a closeup view of the Anakeesta, to run my hands over its surface, worn smooth by hundreds of millions of years of rain and hail and ice. On this pleasant Sunday afternoon in December, I had embarked on a personal geology field trip.

Winter is a good time to view the skeleton of the mountains, when the leaves are gone and the rocks' twisted, contorted darkness whispers their old age. So ancient and so cooked are the rocks of these mountains that they hold no signs of life.

The Great Smokies are not especially famous for their geology. Most visitors come to gaze at the trees and flowers and streams and waterfalls. Smokies geologist Philip King knew that the rocks were only occasional objects of interest: "Only now and then, when the visitor's trail through the forest must circuit a rough ledge of rock, can he realize that the forest and the soil on which it grows are a mere veneer — a thin cover over the ancient rocks of the mountains."

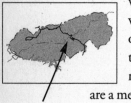

Chimneys

My fellow hikers at the Chimneys that day did not seem particularly fascinated by the rocks either. One was curious, though, about our altitude. I told her we were seated at 4,700 feet above sea level, 50 feet shy of the official Chimney Tops. Over the two miles of trail, we had ascended 1,350 feet, and we appreciated the fact that it was downhill all the way back. Gravity would be on our side.

After a 30-minute skip back down the trail, I rested on a damp, cold boulder beside the Little Pigeon River. I peeled an orange and thought about the Earth. The skin of the orange could be compared to the Earth's thin crust (though the crust is really more like the skin of a peach in relative thickness). The Anakeesta Formation and all the other rocks in the Smoky Mountains, both visible on the surface and invisible beneath me, are part of that crust. The greatest portion of my orange represented the rest of the Earth, the mantle and the core, the parts we never see.

Laying Down the Rocks

First you have to make the rock. Seated on my boulder chair, I contemplated the thousands of feet of solid rock that stretched beneath me. (It would take a *fast* elevator eight hours to descend through the thickness of rock!) This is the unshakable and reassuring foundation, the "basement rock," of the Smoky Mountains. It is hard rock with a crystalline

Great Smoky Mountains N. P.

The Chimney Tops in winter. These sharp pinnacles, a popular hiking destination and landmark on the Newfound Gap Road, consist of Thunderhead Sandstone and are topped by the ancient Anakeesta Formation.

texture: gneisses, schists, granites. Geologists cannot say for certain when these basement rocks originally formed. They will say that the rocks metamorphosed, or changed, from sandy, shaly sediments about one billion years ago in the Precambrian, the first era in Earth's history. In contrast, the Earth is about four and a half billion years old, and the oldest rock known is 3.8 billion. Without so much as a wink, geologists speak of millions, even billions, of years. For many of us, such magnitudes of time are beyond comprehension. We can only trust.

About the only place to see exposures of crystalline basement rock in the Smokies is on the southeast edge of the park, up Ravens Fork and Big Cove; around Dellwood and Maggie Valley, North Carolina; and in a few isolated places around Bryson City. To see them is to see a hint of their unfathomable lives, the great heat and pressure that changed them from one rock into another. To the north and east of the Smokies rise the Blue Ridge Mountains, almost entirely made up of these old, old basement rocks.

Atop the basement complex sits the core rock group of the Smokies, the Ocoee Supergroup. This collection of rocks was named in the 1850s for the Ocoee River, on the southern boundary of Tennessee. The Ocoee Supergroup started life as pebbles, sands, and muds eroding off a landmass onto the continental shelf of a relatively shallow ocean. About 50,000 feet of sediments accumulated and were compressed into rock.

These sediments were only lightly metamorphosed, and the bedding planes, or lines of the individual layers, can still be seen. Thus, attached to the basic sedimentary name of the Ocoee rocks is the prefix "meta-," as in metasiltstone or metasandstone. The Ocoee was laid down in late Precambrian time, a billion to 600 million years ago. Though some life forms are known from the late Precambrian, none has been fossilized in Ocoee rocks.

Molten rock, forced under great heat and pressure into "basement" rock, formed this quartz intrusion. The metamorphic basement rock, the oldest exposed in the park, is nearly a billion years old.

The Ocoee Supergroup is subdivided into several groups. Reading from bottom to top (oldest to youngest), first comes the Snowbird Group, found in the Pigeon River valley on the east side of the park and in the foothills just north. Next is the Great Smoky Group, the core of the

core, the main mass of the mountains. A quick glance at the geologic map of the park (a map that provides hours of enchantment) reveals a nearly unbroken swath of peach color from east to west. That peach color represents the Great Smoky Group.

Geologists typify the Great Smoky Group as a "thick monotonous mass of clastic sedimentary rocks, pebble conglomerate, coarse to fine sandstone, and silty or argillaceous rock." All the rock you see along the transmountain highway from Sugarlands to Newfound Gap and down to Smokemont on the North Carolina side belongs to the Great Smoky Group. Members of the group include the fine-grained Elkmont Sandstone, the coarse-grained Thunderhead Sandstone, and the "silty or argillaceous" Anakeesta Formation. The original grains of rock were poorly sorted, suggesting that water currents deposited them fairly rapidly.

The somber, gray, thickly bedded Elkmont and Thunderhead sandstones are made up mostly of quartz and feldspars. The resistant Thunderhead is the rock responsible for most waterfalls in the park. So far, the streams have not had the muscle to erode the hard sandstone, and for now must simply flow down it when it stands in their way. The rusty and dark gray slates, schists, and phyllites of the Anakeesta Formation are exposed not only at the Chimneys but also on famous Charlies Bunion. The formation is named for Anakeesta Ridge, "place of the balsams," about a mile north of Newfound Gap. For its high sulfide content, the Anakeesta is often called "acid rock." Sometimes pyrite, or fool's gold, can be found in it.

On top of the Great Smoky Group, still part of the Ocoee Supergroup, is the Walden Creek Group. It is found to the northwest in the foothills overlooking the Appalachian Valley. The Walden Creek Group is a hodgepodge of several kinds of rock: shales, siltstones, conglomerates, and sandstones, along with some quartzites and limestones. One of the best things about the Walden Creek Group is the colorful names of two of its members — the Sandsuck and Licklog formations.

The early settlers in the mountains had their own descriptive names for the rocks. The truck-sized boulders spattered with sulfurous yellow lichens and festooned with green rhododendrons were graybacks. The hard quartzites were flintrock, the mudstones dirtrock. They knew the common limestones too, for they offered the best — and flattest —

farmland. The Anakeesta Formation, the rock of the Chimneys, to them was slaterock.

When geologists look at the structure of the Walden Creek Group they see great disarray, rocks that have been bent, broken, folded, and crumpled "nearly everywhere." When rocks break, the result is called a fault. The culprit of the deformation in the Walden Creek Group is the Great Smoky Fault, one of four such major faults in the Smoky Mountains (the Greenbrier, Gatlinburg, and Oconaluftee are the other three.)

These faults have turned the rocks literally on their heads. The Great Smoky Fault is a thrust fault, formed when one rock mass is pushed over another at a low angle. Often, the one pushed over is older than the one below, violating the geologic maxim of "younger on top of older" and greatly complicating the detective work of geology. The direction of thrust in the Smokies is predominantly toward the northwest. The thrust faults are impressive in their force and extent, with one rock mass shoved over another, like tiles on a roof, over the course of many miles.

Most of the rocks in the Great Smoky Mountains date to the Precambrian, the dimmest period of Earth's history. A small percentage are younger sedimentary rocks, dating to the early days of the Paleozoic Era, about 300–500 million years ago. Notable examples are the limestones and sandstones found in and near the long Chilhowee Mountain, which trends northeast-southwest on the northwest edge of the park. The sandstones reflect their origin as sands deposited on a continental shelf, while the limestones were carbonates laid down in deeper, quieter waters farther out in the ocean.

By the time of the Paleozoic, marine life was flourishing, and fossils in these rocks record that life. Cylindrical tubes made by the borings of worms have been found. The remains of marine creatures such as three-lobed arthropods called trilobites and clamlike brachiopods have also been found in the limestones in Cades Cove. Cades Cove is a geologically intriguing place. The limestones in the cove were exposed when the older Precambrian rocks that were thrust over the younger limestones eroded away. In geomorphology, these are known as "windows"; other windows have been opened at nearby Tuckaleechee, Miller, and Wear coves. These isolated, flat valleys are usually oval in shape and occur between 1,200 and 1,800 feet elevation. Found also in these limestone areas are sinkholes and caves created by chemical weathering of the rock. They provide unique habitats for plants and animals not found elsewhere in the park.

From Look Rock on Chilhowee Mountain you can see far to the west, to the rolling foothills of the Appalachian Valley, part of the neighboring Ridge and Valley geologic province. The Smoky Mountains, in fact, represent a geologic transition. They sit midway between the younger Ridge and Valley Province, what has been called "New" Appalachia, and the highly metamorphosed, uniformly hard rocks of the Blue Ridge Province to the east, "Old" Appalachia.

Crumpling and Raising the Rocks: The Big Squeeze

> "It is a strong faith that our globe, like the totality of creation is a great organism . . . all the parts of which are purposely shaped and arranged."
> — Arnold Henry Guyot

Arnold Henry Guyot, a Swiss-born meteorologist, glaciologist, and natural scientist, has been called the "geographic discoverer and definer" of the Appalachian Mountains. In the summer of 1859, Guyot rode horseback on the newly cut trail over the summit of the Great Smokies at Indian Gap. Guyot's intent was to measure and record the elevations of the major peaks in the Smokies and to outline their geography.

Guyot's definition of the beginning of the Smoky Mountains on the eastern edge was this:

> To the South-west of the gorges through which the Big Pigeon [River] escapes from the mountains, the chain rises rapidly in high pointed peaks and sharp ridges, up to a remarkable conical peak called Luftee Knob 6,220 feet. This is the beginning of the Smoky Mt. chain proper, which by general elevation both of its peaks and its crest, by its perfect continuity, its great roughness and difficulty of approach, may be called the master chain of the Appalachian System.

Tracing the mountains to the west, Guyot described sharp rocky ridges covered with a dense growth of trees and laurel. Beyond Road Gap, the chain rises to its highest point, Clingmans Dome, at 6,643 feet. Then it gradually drops down, sending "a long and powerful ridge called the Forney Ridge to the South-west, to the Little Tennessee [River], while the main range continues due west."

With only a fragile barometer, Arnold Guyot made remarkably accurate measurements of the highest peaks in the Great Smokies. The range, the "master chain of the Appalachian System," contains some of the highest peaks in the eastern United States, with more than 16 rising more than 6,000 feet above sea level. As he (and others) knew, the Smokies were part of that system of mountains called the Appalachians, which extend for nearly 2,000 miles south from the Gaspé Peninsula in Quebec to central Alabama.

The Smoky Mountains form a clenched fist on the border between eastern Tennessee and western North Carolina, their crest marking the boundary between the two states. Though their majestic heights render them clearly a range unto themselves, the Smokies are considered part of the greater Unaka chain. The Unakas in turn are an offshoot of the Blue Ridge Mountains of Virginia and North Carolina.

Guyot's pioneering contributions to Appalachian geography were of inestimable value. As a product of his times, though, his work was necessarily descriptive. He established the geographic location of the mountains, and no doubt he also perceived patterns and perhaps wondered why the mountains were here. In Guyot's century, geologists thought mountains resulted from the contraction of the Earth's crust as it cooled. Their model was the skin of a dried apple, whose wrinkles and folds represented mountain ranges.

Guyot probably would have been greatly excited by discoveries a hundred years later, discoveries that try to explain the how and why of mountains. These discoveries are encompassed by the grand theory called plate tectonics, which tells a tale of an Earth in constant motion and change. Plate tectonics theory describes mountains as signs not of a shrinking crust but of the growth of the crust.

Here is the basic plate tectonics story. The surface of the Earth is made up of six to eight major plates. These plates, composed of crust

Lichen and moss cover blocky Ocoee Supergroup rock, exposed along the Little River Gorge. The layers of the original ocean sediments are still visible.

and part of the mantle, average about 90 miles in thickness. The rigid plates float or slide on a partly fluid layer farther down in the mantle, like blocks of wood on water. Driving the plate movements are convection currents set up by sources of heat deep in the mantle. The currents are created when magma is heated, expands, and rises towards the Earth's surface; as the magma gets farther from the hot core, it cools and then sinks again. Though the rates of plate movement are slow, they are measurable — on average, the plates move about two inches a year. In this giant shell game, entire oceans open and close and whole continents shift about, all, of course, over thousands of millions of years.

On this continent, we are citizens of what is called the North American Plate. Our next-door neighbors include, to the west, the Pacific Plate, to the east the Eurasian and African plates, and to the south the

South American Plate. Where now we are separated from our Eurasian and African neighbors by 3,000 miles of water, when the southern Appalachian Mountains formed we were all united in one gigantic land-mass called Pangaea, meaning "all Earth."

Plates basically interact in three ways. They are pulled apart, or rift-ed, at places called spreading centers. This process is happening today in the middle of the Atlantic Ocean and in the Red Sea. Plates also shear, or slip past one another, as on the San Andreas Fault that causes so much trouble in California. Or they converge, or collide, one diving down beneath another at what is called a subduction zone, seen at present in the Himalayas. Using the pre-sent as the key to the past, most geologists favor this last alternative as the best model for the formation of the Appalachians.

Cades Cove is a large limestone valley in the western part of the Smokies. It is a "win-dow" of younger rock, opened when the older rock that forms the sur-rounding hills and mountains eroded away.

As John McPhee writes in his book *In Suspect Terrain,* "Figuring out the Appalachians was Problem 1 in American geology, and a difficult place to begin, for it is scarcely a matter of layer-cake legibility, like the time scale

in the walls of the Grand Canyon. It was a compressed, chaotic, ropy enigma four thousand kilometres from end to apparent end, full of over-turned strata and recycled rock, of steep faults and horizontal thrust sheets, of folds so tight that what had once stretched twenty miles might now fit into five."

Some geologists have concluded that the Appalachians have actually seen at least four major mountain-building pulses, or orogenies. The first was the Grenville, followed by the Taconic and Acadian, which were most significant in the New England portion of the range. In the early Precambrian a continent rifted open, creating a proto-Atlantic Ocean called Iapetus. Iapetus remained open for a long time but began to close 330 million years ago. As it closed, the African Plate moved westward toward the North American Plate and finally collided with it by about 270 million years ago.

The oceanic crust dove down, or subducted, underneath the conti-nental crust, bringing the continents together in a crash. In McPhee's words, that crash was "no less brutal than slow — a continent-to-conti-nent collision marked by an alpine welt, which has reached its old age as the Appalachian Mountains." This final mountain-building episode, called the Alleghenian, created the ancestors of what we now know as the Smoky Mountains.

The intense, incomprehensible compression caused by these collisions has been invoked to explain the large-scale metamorphism of the Precambrian rocks and the major thrust faults that have destroyed any kind of orderly rock record in the Smokies.

Though some geologists still point to the Appalachians as a classic model of continent-to-continent collision, others remain unconvinced. The grand explanation of plate tectonics seems to work best when applied to oceans rather than to continents. Research to test the tectonic mod-els in the Appalachians yields ever more complicated reconstructions. And a big piece of the puzzle is missing. The primary evidence for the collision — fragments of the colliding continent and a suture at their junc-tion — is not obvious or exposed.

Shooting a big hole in the continent-to-continent idea has been evi-dence recovered from beneath the surface. Though the rocks cannot be seen, they can be heard through use of seismic-reflection profiles. Vibrations are sent down into the Earth. When rock of a different density is encountered or the speed of the sound waves changes, the reflections that come back record these changes. The method is rather like a CAT scan of the human body.

Seismic profiles taken in the southern Appalachians in the late 1970s showed that beneath the metamorphic rocks of the surface are horizontal sedimentary rocks down to about 11 miles. The presence of sedimentary rocks in windows like Cades Cove supports this, as does the fact that the reflections are similar to those of the sedimentary rock of the coastal plain. These findings suggest that about 475 million years ago a big, subsurface fault began to transport the metamorphic surface rocks as a thin sheet for at least 160 miles over the edge of the continent that was to become North America.

In the absence of pieces of Africa or a suture, geologists are looking for an alternative explanation to an eyeball-to-eyeball continental collision. Some have turned to the idea of "suspect terranes." In other parts of the world, islands and smaller pieces of land broken off larger plates have been found plastered onto the edge of continents. Had such islands been in the proto-Atlantic Ocean as the plates moved westward toward North America, they would have been swept along, like cars in a chain reaction accident on an interstate, and stuck onto the edge of North America. These "suspect terranes," used to explain the formation of the great mountains of the West Coast, might also work for the East. A microplate then, rather than a whole continent, might also have slammed against the continent and caused the compression that buckled the land and made the Appalachian Mountains.

Tearing Down the Mountains

The geologic story, whichever one turns out to be true, does not stop with the raising of the Great Smoky Mountains. As soon as mountains are built, they begin to wear away. The Smoky Mountains today are a product of another 200 million years of Earth history.

After the Alleghenian orogeny, supposedly the last, things quieted down for a dozen million years or so. Then, about 200 million years ago, the present-day Atlantic Ocean began to open. Africa and North America broke up, or "decoupled." Rivers started to establish their courses. Over millions of years, water wore down these old mountains into the awesome series of peak, deep valley, peak, deep valley that we now feast our eyes upon. And though the Smokies are undeniably steep and rugged, they have been ravaged by erosion for so long that their contours are relatively gentle compared to much younger mountains like the Rockies or the Sierra Nevada. The Smokies have reached a stage topographers call "subdued," with peaks rounded into domes, and bare, craggy rockfaces rare.

Erosion is normally a slow, invisible process, but not always. Sometimes it can be swift and catastrophic. Ninety percent of the Smoky Mountains land area consists of slopes of 10 degrees or greater. Such steep terrain receiving prodigious quantities of rainfall is given to landslides and debris flows. The type of landslide most common in the Smokies is called wedge failure. In 1984 such a failure occurred about four miles from Newfound Gap, and the rocks that careened down the hillside blocked the transmountain highway for hours. The V-shaped, barren scars left by these slides are easily seen from the highway.

Their topography finally established, the Smokies had only to wait for another, more recent geologic period, the Pleistocene, which would again significantly shape them, though more indirectly. The Pleistocene, or "Ice Age," began 1.8 million years ago. The Ice Age actually consisted of at least a dozen rhythmic cycles of glaciation followed by interglacial periods; each cycle has lasted about 100,000 years. Seventy to eighty thousand of those years were a deep freeze, while about 10,000 years were warm. The last glacial period, which ended about 10,000 years ago, is called the Wisconsin. Its interglacial period, in which we now live, is called the Holocene.

Glaciers covered a good portion of North America during the Pleistocene with as much ice as is in Antarctica now. They gouged out much of the landscape of New England and the Midwest. Although glaciers never quite reached the Smokies, they did approach within 75 miles of Tennessee.

The profound effects of the glaciers can be seen everywhere, from the landforms to the way plants are distributed in the Smokies. From 16,500 to 20,000 years ago, when glaciers were last at their maximum extent, ground in the southern Appalachians was frozen year-round. In

Long-term landscape changes on Mount LeConte over the last 20,000 years. From "Dynamic landscapes of East Tennessee: an integration of paleoecology, geomorphology, and archaeology." University of Tennessee, Knoxville. Department of Geological Sciences, Studies in Geology 9: 191-220. Courtesy of Paul Delcourt .

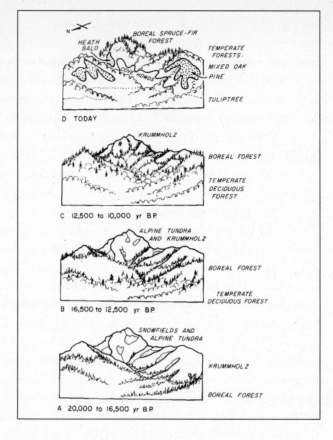

patches, the subsurface soil was solidly frozen as permafrost. Alpine tundra landscape features such as stone polygons, stone stripes, block fields, and boulder streams resulted from continuous freezing and thawing and heaving up of the rocks. These characteristic tundra ground patterns have been mapped throughout the Appalachian region as testimony to this time. A line of stunted trees at about 5,000 feet elevation marked tree line. Above that grew tiny alpine tundra plants.

About 16,500 years ago, things started to warm a bit. Mean annual temperatures at high elevations increased from 18 degrees to 32 degrees Fahrenheit. The warmer temperatures allowed spruce and fir trees to move up the slopes and mingle with the alpine tundra. But the mountains were still in the grip of intense freeze-thaw cycles. Evidence of the heaving of the land again shows in the stone polygons and stripes. As warming continued, boulders and soil started creeping downslope in a process called solifluction, creating major disturbance to the landscape and preventing trees from becoming established on hillsides. Those big boulders, the lichen-splotched graybacks, still pose on the hillsides where they came to rest during the Pleistocene.

By 10,000 years ago the glaciers had receded northward, and the erosional forces of flowing streams began to do their work in the Smoky Mountains. Likewise, the distributions of plants and animals in the mountains began to assume their modern-day aspect. Cold-loving alpine plants could no longer live so far from glaciers and became locally extinct or restricted to the highest elevations. The spruce and fir forest clung to the summits of the highest peaks, and, in a major change, the temperate deciduous forest replaced the open coniferous forest at middle and lower elevations. The warming trend continued until about 6,000 years ago, and since then climate in the southern Appalachians has been cooling once again.

Animal life changed dramatically too. Several species of small mammals, among them one species of beaver, present in the late Pleistocene became extinct or restricted in their ranges. Large mammals such as the mammoth, mastodon, dire wolf, giant short-faced bear, Jefferson's ground sloth, and stag-moose also disappeared. Most of the large mammals were grazers, living off the grasslands of the open parklands of the boreal forest. As the conifers found refuge on the highest slopes and deciduous forest moved into the lower elevations, the grasslands shrank and with them the ranges of the big grazers, until they were pushed out onto the Plains or became extinct.

One recent finding strikes at a long-standing idea about the evolution of the forests of the Great Smokies. That idea holds that these mountains have been around so long — about 260 million years — that plant and animal species have had a great deal of time to develop their present incredible richness. The cove hardwood forests, in particular, were believed to have sought refuge on the Cumberland Plateau just west of the Smokies during the Pleistocene. As the climate warmed, the deciduous forest then radiated out to assume its present range throughout the eastern United States.

But researchers say that the species-rich cove hardwood forests could have developed no earlier than the Holocene. Before that time, cold temperatures and ground disturbances in the southern Appalachians would have prevented their establishment. During glacial times, the

Sunset from Cliff Tops on Mount LeConte. Millions of years of erosion have created the Great Smoky Mountains' present topography of ridge upon ridge with deep valleys between.

deciduous forest species took refuge in the warmer coastal plain region, spreading northward into the southern Appalachians only in postglacial times. The deciduous habit, dropping leaves in winter, was the adaptation that has allowed these temperate trees to survive the low temperatures of winter.

        ஐ   ஐ   ஐ

Although another geologic chillout may be just around the corner, for now the climate of the Smoky Mountains can only be described as temperate. The normal maximum temperature is no more than 84 degrees Fahrenheit in June and July. Normal minimums are usually only 25 degrees Fahrenheit in January. Occasionally a frigid "Siberian Express" storm will roll in from the polar regions, but ordinarily winters are fairly mild, especially at lower elevations, with flowers sometimes blooming in January and frogs croaking in February.

The mountains wring great amounts of precipitation from the atmosphere. In summer, warm, moist air flowing northward from the Gulf of Mexico is lifted over the mountains. When this air reaches the higher elevations, it cools, and the moisture in it condenses and falls as rain, frequently in afternoon thunderstorms.

Even the fog that often veils the mountains supplies a surprising amount of water, not as direct rainfall but through an interesting interaction with the forest. Smokies hikers are well aware of the drenching that can result from walking in a cloud. The small moisture droplets in the fog and clouds are too light to fall to the ground. Instead they are carried on air currents and blown against the leaves and branches of the trees. The droplets collect and grow until finally they are heavy enough to fall to the ground as measurable precipitation. In the spruce-fir forests of Vermont's Green Mountains, a botanist estimated that at least five inches of water could collect on an acre each year from this combing of the clouds by trees.

With an elevational range of 850 feet to 6,643 feet from the bottom to the top of the Smoky Mountains, temperature and precipitation vary widely. As a rule of thumb, temperature decreases two to three degrees Fahrenheit for every 1,000-foot increase in elevation. Precipitation ranges from an annual average of 55 inches in Gatlinburg to 85 inches — near rain forest proportions — on the highest peak, Clingmans Dome. Precipitation is fairly evenly distributed throughout the year, though April–May and September–October can be dry periods. March is usually the rainiest month.

A central aspect of the climate of the mountains is the four distinct seasons. Spring can arrive two months before the actual vernal equinox.

Mountain Wisdom

Appalachian Mountain people have their own ways of predicting the weather. Thick spider webs, hornet nests close to the ground, and dogwood trees loaded with berries are all signs, they say, that you better get out an extra quilt, for a cold winter is coming on. About the time the blackberry bushes bloom in May, mountain folk expect a cold spell to interrupt the warmth of spring. They call it blackberry winter. There's also snowball winter, which arrives with the blossoming of the viburnum, or snowball bushes. Laurel winter is a chilly time in July when the mountain laurel blooms in the higher elevations. And huckleberry showers, ground-soaking rains, come with the wild huckleberries in summer.

With it comes unpredictable weather. In early spring, below-freezing nighttime temperatures can be expected, and savvy hikers headed for the high country know not to gauge their gear by conditions in Gatlinburg. By April the weather is generally mild. This is when spring sweeps through the mountains like a green firestorm. Bees swarm, flowers bloom, and ramps — malodorous, onionlike plants — ripen. A cold snap can still come in May, when the dogwood trees have put out their starched white blossoms. Mountain folk call it "dogwood winter."

Summer days are hazy, warm, and humid, a good time to head for the hills and sit in a creek. Summer nights are filled with the flickering of fireflies and the throaty croaking of bullfrogs. Warm days and cool nights are typical of September and October. Monarch butterflies, assembling for their southward migrations, flutter in the air like falling leaves. The deciduous trees adorn themselves in the breathtaking yellows, golds, and crimsons of autumn. In some years, acorns rain down from the oaks.

Winter is a quiet, restorative time in the mountains. In the lower elevations, the deciduous trees are bare, their anatomy fully revealed. Chalky white sycamores raise ghostly arms along the river banks, and dark green rhododendrons and Christmas ferns stand out against the brown ground. Though winters are generally fairly mild, extreme temperatures are possible, especially at the higher elevations.

Not uncommonly, visitors at Sugarlands can look up and see the hulk of Mount LeConte dusted with snow or hoarfrost. By November, snow can visit the high country. A foot or two of snow can fall in a winter storm in the mountains, but normally snowfall is measured in inches. Florida license plates are common at Newfound Gap when the snow flies, the occupants of the vehicles shrieking and throwing snowballs.

What does all this geology and climate have to do with the natural history of the Great Smoky Mountains? The rock has made this land what it is, what author Edward Abbey called the "Land of the breathing trees, the big woods, the rainy forests." The shape, chemistry, and character of the bedrock determine where water flows, the quality of that water, what the soil consists of, what plants can grow on that soil, and what animals can live with those plants. It is an intricate and subtle intertwining. The brook trout that swim in the pure cold streams depend on the shade of the rhododendrons, which in turn thrive on the acidic soils created partly by the bedrock.

2
Green Mansions
The Deciduous Forest

G reen, everywhere green. The very air is diffused with the color, and the sense of things growing is nearly palpable. Whenever I enter the forests of the Smoky Mountains, an image flashes from somewhere deep in my mind of W. H. Hudson's novel *Green Mansions*, a book I read as an impressionable child. I think of Rima the Bird-Girl, a mysterious young woman who lived among the moss, ferns, and dense foliage of the "glad green forest."

What is most remarkable about the Great Smoky Mountains, for me and for many others, is the magnificent forest. More than 80 percent of the park's land is classified as part of the complex Eastern Deciduous Forest Ecosystem. It consists of broad-leaved trees that drop their leaves in winter — oaks, elms, hickories, maples, beech, birches, basswoods, ashes, walnuts, Carolina silverbell, sweetgum, sourwood, sycamore, tuliptree, hawthorns, hackberries, and magnolias, to name a few.

In the Great Smoky Mountains, nearly 130 species of trees and well over a thousand species of shrubs, vines, and herbs create a boggling tangle of growth that is at once a naturalist's dream and nightmare. The range of altitudes in the Smoky Mountains, the abundant precipitation, and relatively mild temperatures mean even greater complexity in the deciduous forest ecosystem.

Communities within it are defined by the predominant tree species — ranging from northern hardwoods at high elevations to oak-pine stands on dry ridges to the luxuriant cove hardwood forests in moist, protected valleys. Knowing where you are in the deciduous forest — botanically, that is — is not always easy. The pattern of growth in this forest is a patchy mosaic rather than clearcut zones. Boundaries between plant communities blur with even slight changes in temperature, moisture, and soils.

Although it is obvious to all that the forest is made up of trees, we might first ask what a tree is. Botanists and foresters define a tree as a large (at least 15 to 20 feet tall), woody plant with a single stem or trunk and a well-developed crown. Trees live comparatively long lives and are among the oldest and largest plants on Earth. In the Smokies, the trees are so tall that they can often be identified only with the aid of binoculars to allow a close look at their leaves.

Trees have advantages over other plants. Its woody nature lets a tree grow taller and get the lion's share of light; a tree can display its flowers to the wind or animal pollinators first; and it can disperse seeds over a greater distance. But there are some disadvantages to this prominence. A tree's height subjects it to natural hazards like wind-throw, fire, lightning, and, in recent decades, pollution. The large amount of "dead" material in trees, mainly in the form of heartwood in the center of the trunks, makes them vulnerable to disease and insect attacks.

The forest is arranged in layers, beginning at the top with the tree canopy. Beneath that is the understory of smaller trees and shrubs, closer to the ground is the herbaceous or field layer, and finally, at ground level, are the mosses and leaf litter. Because trees tower over all others and cast shade, they influence what can grow beneath them.

In a forest as dense as the Smokies, plants must compete not for water but for light and space. A percentage of the sun's light is reflected off the canopy, part is absorbed as heat, and most of the rest is used by the trees in photosynthesis. Only a small percentage is left for underlying layers of plants. For this reason trees are sometimes called sun plants, while the plants growing beneath them are shade plants.

In the Smokies, shade-tolerant ferns, such as woodferns, southern lady fern, and Christmas fern, grow profusely beneath the trees. Another example of a shade plant is the may-apple. Abundant chlorophyll and oversized, deep green leaves with a thin outer covering, or cuticle, are the may-apple's adaptations to the dim forest environment.

The big leaves of may-apple, a plant adapted to the shady floor of the deciduous forest. The white flower of the plant appears in May, tucked beneath the leaves.

In their effects on the soil, trees also exert a major influence on what grows in the understory and herbaceous and ground layers. Trees produce most of the leaf litter that, as it decomposes, dictates soil chemistry, depth, and nutrient composition.

Deciduous trees first evolved with other flowering plants about 150 million years ago, in the Cretaceous period. The deciduous forest developed largely in response to climate, specifically the seasonal distribution of rainfall and the length of the growing season. Cold winter temperatures prevent these warmth- and humidity-loving trees from growing farther north. Westward, there is not enough precipitation, and grassland takes over. Southward, there is no requisite winter dormant season.

The Cove Hardwood Forest

In a place outstanding for diversity of forest types, one type, unique to the southern Appalachians, stands out as the richest of the rich. It is the cove hardwood forest, the forest primeval, one of the most diverse plant communities in the world. The word *cove*, when used with hardwood forest, refers generally to a sheltered valley, sometimes flat and sometimes steep, below 4,500 feet elevation. Cove soils are deep and moist.

The presence of certain trees says "cove hardwood forest." Though others may be present, the trees that make up 80 to 90 percent of the canopy include yellow birch, beech, basswood, buckeye, tuliptree, Carolina silverbell, sugar maple, magnolia, hickory, and an evergreen, the eastern hemlock. These trees of the rich, cool coves consort together, says naturalist Donald Culross Peattie, "like the kings they are."

The buckeye (specifically yellow buckeye, *Aesculus octandra*) belongs to the horsechestnut family. This is the only tree in the park with a distinctive five-part, palm-shaped leaf. Buckeyes bear clusters of yellow flowers, and in spring their succulent new leaves uncurl from pink-tinged clusters. The seed capsule holds two shiny brown seeds, which bear a pale scar. That scar looked to people like the eye of a buck, hence the tree's common name. The seeds are poisonous but can be eaten after several days of leaching.

Another cove hardwood species is white basswood *(Tilia heterophylla)*, also called the linn from its family, the linden. When the wind ruffles them, basswoods take on a silvery appearance because of the hairy undersides of the leaves. Bees especially seek the nectar of the tiny white flowers that appear on basswoods in June and July.

The mountain or Carolina silverbell *(Halesia carolina)*, also known as peawood, opossum wood, or snowdrop tree, is another "indicator tree" of the cove hardwood forest. The silverbell's euphonious name comes from the lovely, white, bell-shaped flowers that cover the tree in April and May. Donald Culross Peattie's feelings are shared by all who see a silverbell in spring in the Smokies. Wrote Peattie, "He who has seen this tree in the Great Smoky Mountains . . . will never forget his first sight of it in bloom . . . and he will say to himself with pride that he once beheld one of the rare and noblest hardwoods of the North American continent."

The tuliptree *(Liriodendron tulipifera)* joins this arboreal variety show. It is one of the most abundant trees in the Smokies. Large, four-lobed leaves and yellow tuliplike flowers that bloom in May distinguish this member of the magnolia family. Tall, straight trees, tuliptrees sometimes grow in nearly pure stands on lands in the park once logged or cultivated. Though a common second-growth species, some giant virgin tuliptrees also grow in the Smokies. This tree is commonly called tulip poplar, though it is not related to true poplars. Nearly any mountain person you talk with will mention the "big poplars" up some trail.

The understory beneath the 150- to 200-foot-high closed canopy of a cove forest includes some small trees that add breathtaking beauty to the mountains in spring: redbud, serviceberries, and flowering dogwood. Common shrubs include hydrangea, doghobble, mountain laurel, and rhododendrons. One shrub is easily identified in autumn, when red and orange fruits pop out of their capsules. Most people know *Euonymus americana* as hearts-a-bustin' or strawberry bush. The herbaceous layer of the cove hardwood forest consists of an incredible

The delicate white flowers of fringed phacelia cover acres of ground along the Cove Hardwood Nature Trail in spring.

Second-growth tuliptrees grow pencil-straight in nearly pure stands in many parts of the park that were logged in the early part of the century.

profusion of ferns, impressive-sized creeping and climbing vines, and wildflowers unequaled in abundance and variety.

Along with simply knowing what the plants are, a daunting enough task in the Smokies, plant ecologists are also interested in features of the forest above the individual level. They attempt to take the measure of higher levels of the pyramid — communities, populations, and ecosystems. A striking contrast in species diversity is seen between cove hardwood forests and spruce-fir forests of higher elevations. In about a quarter acre of cove hardwood forest, one can find some 40 to 60 species of vascular plants (all those other than mosses, fungi, and algae), compared to only about eight in an area of equal size in the spruce-fir forest.

This well illustrates a major generalization of biogeography, the study of what grows where when. That maxim states that species diversity of plant communities increases as you go to lower elevations and warmer climates. This can be seen on a global scale from the Arctic to tropical rain forest and coral reef. In the Smokies, it can be seen as you go from

The leaf of the tuliptree is distinctive among the hardwoods.

Clingmans Dome, 6,643 feet above sea level, to Gatlinburg, at 1,500 feet elevation.

Along with astounding diversity, the cove hardwood forest exhibits another extremely significant attribute, productivity. This is the rate at which organic matter is created by photosynthesis. The importance of productivity for any ecosystem can hardly be overstated — it is the basis for all life activity. Ecologists often look at "net productivity," what's left after plants have respired. They measure it in grams per square meter per year.

One researcher estimated a net productivity of 1,390 grams per square meter per year for a cove hardwood forest in the Smokies, contributed mostly by trees. In comparison, the lowest net productivity, only 250 to 400 grams per meter per year, is found in tundra and deserts where cold, drought, or nutrient deprivation are limiting factors. Coral reefs and marshes, the most productive ecosystems on Earth, net 3,500 to 4,000 grams per square meter per year.

The Northern Hardwoods

Another community within the deciduous forest of the Smokies is the northern hardwoods. Here the main trees are yellow birch and beech, along with yellow buckeye, white basswood, and mountain and striped maple. Beech and yellow birch and buckeye sometimes grow in almost pure stands bordering the spruce-fir forests and grassy balds. Where it does not compete with spruce-fir, in the southwest section of the park, the northern hardwood forest reaches its prime. This Smokies community is unique; it is the highest elevation broad-leaved forest in the East.

Beneath the northern hardwoods grow grasses, ferns, and wildflowers such as coneflowers, skunk goldenrod, and Rugel's ragwort. Spring-beauties and fringed phacelia are common in the herbaceous layer of beech stands. On south-facing exposures, sedges dominate. Shrubs such as hydrangea, witch-hobble, and alternate-leaf dogwood are most common. Relatively deep, rich, well-drained soils

The stilt roots of this birch tree formed when the seedling grew on a fallen "nurse log," which later decayed, leaving the tree seeming to stand in mid-air.

lacking a deep litter or peat layer contribute to the persistence of the northern hardwood type.

Yellow birch *(Betula alleghaniensis)* trees can reach heights of 80 feet and are common in cold ravines and northern slopes. Though deciduous, yellow birches show adaptations to the cold, windy climate of high elevations. Their supple branches bend, and their waterproof, papery bark helps ward off drying winds.

Birches often appear to stand on stilts. These prop roots begin to grow when a birch seed falls onto a rotting, moss-covered log. The seed germinates, and as the seedling grows the roots are anchored to the "nurse log." Eventually the nurse log decays and disappears, leaving the birch supported on roots that reach out like the arms of an octopus. This interesting habit is almost epiphytic. Epiphytes are most common in trees in the tropics, where they can survive because of the high humidity and special adaptations that allow them to remove and store water and nutrients from the air. The incredible moisture of the high elevations in the Smokies lets these young birches survive up off the ground. Elsewhere such a habit would lead to excessive water loss, and the tree could not live.

Beech *(Fagus grandifolia)* shares dominance with yellow birch in the northern hardwood forest. The dull brown leaves of beech remain curled on the branches throughout the winter and provide a good means of identification. Varieties of beech (white, red, and gray) have been named that correspond with elevation and color of the wood. Recently, however, botanists have lumped the varieties under the single species *grandifolia.* Beech reproduce vegetatively by sending up abundant sprouts from shallow roots.

Beech trees were cut to make charcoal, for firewood, and for turning on a wood lathe. Besides its wood, the tree is valuable for its beechnuts. These spiny-husked fruits open with the first frost to release a brown, triangular nut. Grouse, turkey, mice, and squirrels eat them, as do black bears and deer. Beechnuts were also a favored food of the now-extinct passenger pigeon, so plentiful in the 19th century that they gave their name to the Pigeon River. Hollow beech trees make good dens and nest cavities for some mammals and birds.

An introduced species, the beech scale insect, causes a disease of the bark of beech trees. The insect allows a fungus to infect and finally kill the tree.

The disease was known only as far south as Pennsylvania until it was identified in beeches along the Appalachian Trail in the Smokies in 1986.

Beech trees often grow in pure stands in gaps, or low places, on south-facing slopes near the tops of the highest ridges in the mountains. Two well-known places in the Smokies, Newfound and Indian gaps on the Tennessee-North Carolina line, were beech forests before they were cleared many years ago. The boundary between "beech gaps" and the spruce-fir forests is sharp, creating islands within islands. Though they account for a very small amount of the acreage of the park, beech gaps, also locally known as beech orchards, are unique communities in the park. They remain one of the vegetative mysteries of the Smokies. Studies of the beech gaps suggest that wind might be an extremely important factor in establishing and maintaining them. Wind funnels through the gaps and is stronger there than in the adjoining forests. Many small, twisted beech trees evidence the severe damage wind causes.

Some naturalists have wondered why red spruce has not invaded beech gaps. Although spruce seeds reach the soil of the beech forests, they fail to germinate. That may be partly due to the fact that soil temperature and moisture are higher in the beech forest. In addition, decomposing beech leaves have been found to contain natural toxins that inhibit germination of spruce seeds. Animals may also eat a great many spruce seeds. An interaction of all these factors, rather than one alone, may offer the best explanation.

A Glorious Awakening

The word *deciduous* means "letting drop." The autumn leaf fall is central to the ecology of the deciduous forest. It means that light reaches the forest floor in winter and early spring. This fact is critical to the growth of herbaceous plants, most notably wildflowers. The flowers, mostly perennials, have coevolved with the trees. They have become essentially sun plants, timing their growth and blooming to take advantage of the light, before the tree canopy fills out and pitches them into darkness.

There is a glorious awakening of the land in these old mountains in spring. The perennials have remained underground, as rhizomes, corms,

The thin layers of glossy bark are characteristic of the yellow birch, a common tree of the northern hardwood community.

Rose Houk

and bulbs, through the short, cold days of winter. In response to the longer days and warmer temperatures of spring, a chemical alarm clock goes off in the plants. The "spring ephemerals," as they're known, break through the layer of moist leaves covering the ground, bloom, and form next year's buds in a very short time. Each species follows its own timetable.

The earliest are the "prevernal" flowers — the hepaticas, spring-beauties, bloodroots, and Dutchman's-breeches — that appear in March while the trees are leafless and sunlight on the forest floor is at its maximum.

Then the big show follows as the trees begin to bud out. The forest now is decked out in uncounted shades of mint, lime, and chartreuse. The trees bloom now too but are often overshadowed by the showy beauties at their feet. Triumphant trilliums in white, yellow, and maroon, sweet white violets, wild geraniums, acres of white fringed phacelias,

Solomon's-seal, bleeding-heart, irises, orchids, dogwoods, and mountain laurel continue the procession. It doesn't stop until June, when the trees are fully leafed out and the flowers can no longer get sun.

Wildflowers have evolved extremely specialized refinements that relate directly to the animals, mostly insects, that pollinate them. Flower shapes, colors, fragrances, petal markings, and blooming times are all designed to lure the bee, beetle, butterfly, or moth that will carry the pollen to another receptive flower, letting the species produce fruit and seed. The insect in turn reaps a food reward in the form of nectar or pollen.

Consider one spring ephemeral, the trout-lily, a lemon-yellow wildflower widely distributed at lower elevations of the park. The plant's mottled green and brown leaves have reminded some people of the speckled body of a mountain trout. Another common name, fawn lily, has been applied for similar reasons. Trout-lily is known by other names too, including adder's-tongue and glacier lily, as well as the misnomer dog-tooth violet, referring to the white, tooth-shaped underground corm. *Erythronium americanum* is its scientific name.

Several species of bees and large flies act as pollinators of trout-lilies. The mining bee is one that depends on the pollen of the trout-lily to feed her larvae. Queen bumblebees also methodically visit trout-lilies, dangling "upside down like Quasimodo, while gathering pollen or sucking nectar," as one botanist wrote. The queen bumblebee scrapes pollen grains from the anthers of the flower and packs them in a basket on each hind leg. When she visits another flower, the sticky mass is deposited on a waiting stigma, and fertilization can occur. The flowers' sugary nectar provides energy for her and, when added to the pollen, makes sweet, nutritious morsels for her brood.

The early-blooming trout-lilies provide an essential early link in the forest ecosystem. The cold-hardy bumblebees, in their "fur coats," are out earlier in the spring than most other insects. Thus they will pollinate the trout-lily and continue to do their good deeds with other flowers into summer and autumn.

Moths and butterflies are important pollinators too. Moths are equipped with long, sucking mouthparts that allow them to pollinate funnel-shaped flowers such as jimsonweed and evening-primrose. Their nocturnal lifestyle fits with the white or yellow night-blooming flowers they pollinate. The Io moth *(Automeris io)* is one species that inhabits the deciduous forests of the Smokies. Uncoiling a long "tongue," the Io moth dips into the blossoms and draws out nectar as if through a straw. The larval stage of the Io is a caterpillar armed with extremely irritating spines, a good defense against predators, primarily birds. The adult moth shows another defense, prominent dark "eyespots" on the hind wings that when flashed tend to startle away a predator. The beautiful luna moth *(Actias luna),* in the same family as the Io, is identified by its transparent, light green, tailed wings. The caterpillar larvae of the luna eat leaves of hickory and sweetgum trees, but when they become adult moths they eat nothing. Their sole aim during their two weeks of adulthood is to find a mate. The male luna locates the female by means of his sensitive feathery antennae that are loaded with organs for smell. The female emits a pheromone that the male can detect from some distance.

The Tree Dwellers

In early spring the Smokies forests resonate with a most distinctive bird song: *zee zee zee zoo zay,* this bird whistles in monotonous repetition. Upon hearing that song, one visiting ornithologist responded, "That's the Smokies." The bird is the black-throated green warbler, a summer resident of the park. Black-throated greens arrive in late March and stay through October. Along with many other warblers, it is in the genus *Dendroica,* which means "tree dweller." This yellow-cheeked wood warbler nests and lives in the forest canopy, taking to evergreens in general, especially the eastern hemlock in lower elevations.

Another bird of the canopy is the red-eyed vireo, which some consider *the* bird of the deciduous forest. Based on censuses in the Appalachians, in 1948 ornithologist Roger Tory Peterson reported that the red-eyed vireo was one of the three most abundant birds in the deciduous forests of eastern North America, along with the ovenbird and the redstart. By the 1960s, however, many observers noted that in some places the red-eyed's population had crashed and the bird's future was uncertain.

Red-eyed and yellow-throated vireos and a number of other forest songbirds, including thrushes, warblers, orioles, flycatchers, and tanagers, are called neotropical migrants. They spend winters in the Caribbean,

Latin America, and South America, returning to the eastern woods in spring and summer to breed. On their epic migrations these birds usually fly at night to escape predators, and like sailors they use the stars for navigation.

Neotropical migrants have become creatures of great concern, for surveys have shown drastic population declines in some species over the past few decades. Since 1978, more than 70 percent of migrant species have declined in the eastern United States. The reasons are several. The birds are losing wintering grounds in Central and South America because of deforestation, and their forest breeding grounds in the eastern U.S. are becoming fragmented and lost to development. Parasitism of their nests by other birds, notably the brown-headed cowbird, is another threat.

The Great Smokies provide an important laboratory where possible causes of these population declines may be discerned. Long-term censuses of breeding bird communities are underway in the park. The Smokies program is part of a larger interagency and international effort called Partners in Flight. Costa Rican biologists will study the wintering habitats of birds in their country as well. So far, censuses using mapping, point counts, and mist-netting of birds have been carried out in the Smokies in an old-growth cove hardwood stand in the Roaring Fork area, in a second-growth cove hardwood site in Cherokee Orchard, and in an old-growth spruce-fir forest on Mount Collins (now mainly spruce since the die-off of Fraser fir from insect attack). One early finding is the high diversity and density of birds in old-growth cove hardwood forests, made up mainly of neotropical migrants.

Perhaps because the Smokies are the largest remaining tract of protected deciduous forest in North America, red-eyed vireos are still common and abundant. They usually arrive in the park by April and stay until October, inhabiting the forest canopy below 4,500 feet elevation. If you ever actually see this bird in the dense summer foliage, look for the distinctive ruby-red eye with a dark stripe. More likely you will hear it, for the vireo sings its heart out all day. The song consists of phrases with pauses that can be rendered as *look up. . . see me. . . over here. . . higher. . . .* This penchant for song has earned it the nickname preacher bird. In fact, one especially vocal red-eyed may hold the North American record for most frequent singing — it sang 22,197 songs over 10 hours one summer day.

Great Smoky Mountains N. P.

The red-eyed vireo feeds on moths and caterpillars. A favorite is the cankerworm. Vireos will also eat beetles, wasps, bees, ants, cicadas, treehoppers, and even berries and other fruits. A vireo takes another place in the food chain if a sharp-shinned hawk should grasp one in its talons.

The bushy-tailed gray squirrel is a valuable resident in the deciduous forest because it inadvertently plants many trees while burying nuts.

Interacting closely with the vireo is the brown-headed cowbird, cousin to blackbirds, grackles, and bobolinks. They make up the Troupial family, all of which move in large flocks or troupes. Cowbirds are notorious for their practice of social parasitism; they are, in biological jargon, "obligate brood parasites." In fact, their scientific name, *Molothrus ater*, means "black parasite." Red-eyed vireos are among the cowbirds' most frequent hosts. Female cowbirds lay their eggs in active vireo nests. Vireos incubate the cowbird eggs alongside their own and feed and nurture the foster nestling until it fledges and joins its own kind.

The ovenbird occupies approximately the same elevational range as the red-eyed vireo but builds its nest and spends most of its time on the forest floor. This diminutive wood warbler, olive brown with pink legs, is a common summer resident in the park. The song is a rising *teach, teach,* described by some as the sound of stones ringing together. Ovenbirds are more often heard than seen. They spend much of their time walking along the forest floor, wagging their tails and poking among the leaf litter looking for snails, earthworms, crickets, and spiders.

The ovenbird's name comes from the unique shape of its nest. With grasses, leaves, stems, and mosses, a female ovenbird erects her nest in a depression in the ground. The nest takes on the shape of a miniature Dutch oven. Though ingeniously hidden under a roof of dead leaves, the nest and its eggs are heavily preyed upon by snakes, skunks, and weasels. As do other ground-nesting birds like the killdeer, the female ovenbird employs what is called distraction display, putting on a crippled-bird act to divert a predator's attention away from her young.

A mammal that spends a good deal of time in the trees is the eastern gray squirrel. Unlike many smaller mammals that burrow in the ground or frequent roadsides and meadows, the gray squirrel is closely tied to the deciduous woods, depending on trees for food and shelter. Acorns, beechnuts, and walnuts are favorite foods, along with the large winged seeds of silverbell in late summer and fall.

With the disappearance of chestnuts from the Smokies forest by 1940, squirrels were forced to rely more on acorns. They are selective about acorns, eating white oak acorns first and burying red and black oak acorns for later consumption. The red and black oak acorns have a higher tannin content, which makes them less desirable as food. The fortunes of gray squirrels are tied directly to acorn abundance. If the acorn crop fails, as it does in certain years, squirrel populations drop.

In winter, several gray squirrels have been seen denning together in cavities in the trees. They breed in winter and again in late spring. The stomach contents of timber rattlesnakes in the park show that gray squirrels are a major prey of the snakes.

The Brown Earth

We often don't see the soil for the trees in the deciduous forest. But within and beneath the leaves, twigs, and branches of the forest floor exists another community carrying out its daily life largely unseen by our eyes. The soil is a dynamic part of the ecosystem, supporting the community even as the community shapes the characteristics of the soil.

The main factors involved in soil formation are climate, parent rock, vegetation and associated organisms, topography, and time. The soil of temperate deciduous forests, called simply "brown earth," is characteristic of relatively wet, warm climates. These conditions, as well as the thinness of deciduous leaves, hasten decomposition; more than half of the litter layer decomposes within only a few years.

Like the forest above it, the soil consists of layers, or horizons. The thin uppermost layer is composed of newly fallen dry leaves. Beneath this is the moister humus, called mull in the deciduous forest. This grades down into the subsoil layer and finally to weathered or unweathered "parent" rock material, which in the Smokies is mainly the metamorphosed sandstones and shales of the old Ocoee Supergroup. Chemically, deciduous forest soils are alkaline or neutral.

The number of organisms in a square foot of forest floor may be four times as great as Earth's human population. Among them are bacteria, as many as 30 billion in one pound of forest litter. In a single day these bacteria can decompose a hundred to a thousand times their weight in matter.

Assisting the bacteria are algae and various microscopic animals, called cryptozoa, including protozoa, rotifers, roundworms, flatworms, and algae. In the next rank in the soil food chain, larger animals such as slugs, snails, pillbugs, millipedes, ants, beetles, termites, and earthworms take over the decomposition chore.

Earthworms are the workhorses of the deciduous forest soil. Gardeners know them well as tillers of the ground and value their presence. In the late 19th century Charles Darwin, the father of evolutionary theory, wrote his final major treatise on these lowly creatures and acknowledged their worth: "Long before man existed the land was regularly ploughed and continues to be ploughed by earthworms." Another author says earthworms "literally eat the earth and everything in it." Material in mull has probably passed at least once through earthworms. Through their almost constant tunneling, earthworms also actively help drain and aerate the soil, and their castings become food for smaller decomposers.

Earthworms perform their labors in the cool of the evening, hence their other well-known name, night crawlers. With muscular, segmented

*Jack-in-the-pulpit, a
member of the arum family.
The striped spathe forms a
cap for "Jack," the spadix.
This plant appears in spring
in the lower elevations of the
deciduous forest.*

bodies, they can burrow in the ground. They emerge from their burrows to harvest dead leaves, which are crushed, dissolved, and mixed in
their digestive systems along with the soil. Some of the material is
taken into their systems, and the rest is eliminated. Earthworms seem
to have a sweet tooth; when given a choice between sugar maple or oak
leaves, they select sugar maple. They show an aversion to acidic soils,
which explains why they are usually not found in the soil of coniferous
forests.

Thus, in this hidden but incredibly busy world of the forest floor and
the soil, some organisms eat litter itself, while others eat bacteria and
fungi that eat litter.

In the deciduous forest of the Smokies, an estimated 500,000 tons of
leaves drop from the trees each autumn. In addition to this incredible
amount of leaf litter, the forest floor is also covered with a host of woody

plant parts — twigs, broken branches, even whole logs. All are destined to become part of the soil.

The decay of wood is initiated substantially by one insect: the termite. Though termites are not popular in our homes, they provide unending benefits in maintaining the flow of energy and nutrients in forest ecosystems. Termites are one of only four animals (the others are some snails, wood-boring beetle larvae, and goats) that can digest cellulose, a key ingredient in wood.

But termites don't digest wood by themselves. Living in their guts are protozoa and bacteria that ferment cellulose and convert it to a form the termite can eat. The termite reciprocates by feeding the cohabitant. So highly evolved is this mutual relationship that each species of termite has its own species of protozoa or bacteria. Without its protozoan, a termite will still eat wood but won't be able to digest it and will eventually starve. The protozoan culture is passed down from one generation to the next when the young eat from the anuses of the adults. Termites in a colony also obtain food by licking waxy secretions off one another.

Distant cousins of the cockroach, termites are relatively primitive insects. But like ants, bees, and wasps (to which they are not related), termites are social insects. Their society is regimented, with strict roles for all to observe in the interest of maintaining the colony. The highest in the caste system are the primary reproductives, the king and queen; beneath them are the supplementary reproductives; next come worker termites, the perpetual adolescents of the group; and at the bottom are the soldiers. The queen lays the eggs, the workers look after the queen and her eggs and larvae, and the soldiers defend the colony. Those waxy secretions that serve as food may also contain chemicals that prevent worker termites from becoming sexually mature.

Although snails are basically aquatic animals, some kinds of snails are able to survive in the damp environment of the deciduous forest floor. Land snails eat decomposing leaf litter and also other animal carcasses. Walking along the Bull Head Trail one summer day, I found a snail attached to the ear of a dead mouse lying on the trail. The snail appeared to be trying to eat the mouse, but the process was very slow.

Millipedes are frequently seen on the ground, eating dead leaves and decaying wood. They have two pairs of legs per body segment, distinguishing them from centipedes, which have only one pair. To deter predators, millipedes emit strong substances from scent glands. One of these substances, hydrocyanic acid, smells like bitter almonds. Another creature commonly seen crawling about on the leaf litter is the red velvet mite.

One of the most crucial components of woodland soils are fungi. They are what give soil its characteristic earthy odor. We know fungi best when parts of them appear aboveground as mushrooms or toadstools. But many other fungi are never seen, except through a microscope.

Fungi serve all kinds of purposes — they cure disease, leaven our bread, ferment our fruit, and kill our crops. Despite being known to the ancients, they remained so poorly understood that for some time many were grouped by mycologists only as *Fungi imperfecti*. Now they have a kingdom all their own, made up of about 50,000 species, separate from green plants, animals, and bacteria.

Some 2,000 species of fungi are known in the Smoky Mountains. Their functions in the forest are absolutely essential. Saprophytic mushrooms decay wood and return billions of tons of carbon to the atmosphere in the form of carbon dioxide. For many plants of the forest, underground fungi are essential to survival.

The basic structure of fungi consists of tiny filaments called hyphae grouped together in a bundle called a mycelium, or spawn. The mycelia are the networks of whitish veins seen underneath leaves and rotting logs. Special branches of the mycelia produce spores, the reproductive organs of the fungi. By the agents of wind, rain, the digestive systems of certain animals, or the touch of a human finger, billions of the dustlike spores are liberated and dispersed.

The fungi we usually notice are the often bizarre and wildly colored mushrooms, actually the above-ground fruiting bodies produced by mycelia. The forests of the southeast United States probably contain more kinds of mushrooms than any region of comparable size in North America. In the Smokies a few appear in spring, like the tasty morel, which favors old orchards. But autumn is prime mushroom time in the deciduous woods.

If we can divert our eyes momentarily from the spectacular leaf colors, we find the ground dotted with a plethora of polypores, puffballs, chanterelles, and earthstars. One you may smell before you see it is the stinkhorn. These phallic fungi emit the odor of decaying flesh from a slimy substance, called the gleba, that contains the spores. Much as wildflowers attract pollinating insects, the stinkhorn's scent draws flies. On their feet the insects carry off the slime (and the spores) to fertile ground.

Some mushrooms, like the jack-o-lantern and the honey mushroom, glow in the dark. The jack-o-lantern, which grows mostly from decaying oaks, is a widely distributed poisonous mushroom. The gills beneath the orange cap give off a greenish light at night. Mountain people call the glow "foxfire," which they say is a sign that cold weather is just around the corner.

Mushrooms are the group of fungi that decompose woody plant material. These saprophytes lack their own chlorophyll and live off decaying plants. For a long time this valuable function was believed to be the only service they render. But fungi don't just passively decay woody material. They are also predators, trapping and gobbling up all kinds of animals in diabolical ways that could provide material for a fantastic science fiction movie. The carnivorous habit seems to be one that

The fly agaric mushroom (Amanita muscaria) is pretty but poisonous. It is one of 2,000 species of fungi in the park.

Great Smoky Mountains N.P.

Bloodroot is one of the earliest flowers to bloom in spring, before the trees have leafed out. Its delicate white petals fall off the flower after only a few days.

fungi can shift to — Jekyll and Hyde style — to get necessary nitrogen.

Hundreds of species of fungi, says one researcher, "employ a remarkable arsenal of weapons," to "lure, trap, lasso, paralyze, colonize, or enzymatically dissolve multitudes of live victims." One example, the net fungus, will suffice. It traps nematodes, or roundworms, by producing on the hyphae an adhesive that sticks like glue. The captured nematode is helpless against it. The fungi's hyphae then enter the body of the worm, paralyze it with toxins, and digest it.

Also part of the dark soil world are another type of fungi, mycorrhizae. The name means "mushroom-root." Mycorrhizae form sheaths over roots in what is a highly specialized, mutually beneficial relationship between plant and fungus. The fungus stimulates growth of many branches on the root, making it far more efficient at gathering water and minerals, especially nitrogen. In turn the fungus receives food from the roots, and the result is a beatiful example of mutualism. Fossil mycorrhizae have been identified on roots 400 million years old. Almost all plant families form mycorrhizae; they are believed to be nearly universal among trees in older woodlands and essential to woody plants' survival. Orchids are especially dependent on mycorrhizae.

Beyond the mechanical act of breaking down the litter layer and working the soil, all these decomposers — the fungi, bacteria, and soil animals — perform another essential task. They keep the Earth's limited supply of nutrients cycling through the forest ecosystem. Basic elements such as carbon, hydrogen, oxygen, nitrogen, iron, calcium, phosphorus and others all enter the system from the environment and are used by the producers (green plants), which are eaten by the consumers. When plants and animals die, the decomposers release the nutrients in them back to the environment in an endless cycle. Compared with the spruce forest, the deciduous forest has a richer nutrient economy, a larger nutrient stock that turns over more rapidly, and a larger fraction of nutrients in the soil than in plant tissue.

Nine trillium species grow in the park. This one, Trillium erectum, *is often called wakerobin. It may also be red or purple.*

Where to See Wildflowers

For more than four decades, plant enthusiasts have come to the Smokies on the last weekend in April. They stand in lines two blocks long at seven in the morning, poring over their dog-eared copies of *Great Smoky Mountains Wildflowers.* From the Gatlinburg Convention Center, they fan out on the trails to the Sinks, Rainbow Falls, or Clingmans Dome to see the real thing. The woods resound with exclamations as yet another delicate blossom is found.

All have come for the Spring Wildflower Pilgrimage. Many of the pilgrims are veterans, here to see old friends, not of the human but of the botanical variety. Their common love is the riot of wildflowers that erupts in the Smokies in spring. With some 1,300 species of flowering plants, the park has duly earned its reputation as a mecca for flower pilgrims.

The Smokies are so famous for their vernal wildflower display that park rangers couldn't keep up with all the inquiries. Now, the *Bloomin' Report* lets people know of the progress of the flowering. Starting in late March and continuing through the last of May, the weekly report, available at the Sugarlands Visitor Center, provides Smokies visitors with information about where and when species are blooming in the park.

Here are a few recommendations from the *Bloomin' Report*, for people who want to see the greatest wildflower show on Earth: The Chestnut Top Trail near the Townsend entrance is always a good place to see flowers in early spring. By the first week of April, a walk up Porter's Creek in the Greenbrier area will show rue and wood anemones, bishop's cap, chickweeds, and four kinds of violets. Up Ash Hopper Branch, look for bloodroot, hepatica, and toothwort. For spring-beauties, try the Noah 'Bud' Ogle place on Roaring Fork.

Later in April, when the bloom is hitting its peak, nearly any trail in the park in the lower elevations (below 3,000 feet) will yield many flower "finds." Look for the showy orchis along the Cosby Nature Trail — showy in name only, for this is a timid little flower. The unusual yellow or nodding mandarin blooms along the Rainbow Falls Trail, and dwarf iris can be found along the Little River at Metcalf Bottoms. Along the way to Metcalf, watch along the roadside for a few clumps of beautiful pink bleeding-hearts and abundant red columbines.

Try Abrams Falls Trail and Elkmont Nature Trail to see the creamy white flowers of trailing arbutus. The crowning glory of wildflower viewing must be the Cove Hardwood Nature Trail, leading from the Chimneys picnic area. It winds through a veritable garden of flowers — huge white trillium, fringed phacelia, and the tiny flowers of Solomon's-seal. Huskey Gap, Cucumber Gap, Grotto Falls, and Hen Wallow Falls are other trails to try.

In May, flowers begin to bloom at the higher elevations. Along the Balsam Mountain Road, which opens in mid-May, you will see hordes of spring-beauties and trout-lilies. The Appalachian Trail is good too, beginning in early May.

Beware: This wildflower quest can become an addiction. No matter where you live, you may find yourself, each April, longing for the sight of a trillium in the Smoky Mountains. Don't fight it, life's too short. Just join the pilgrims.

WILDFLOWER CHECKLIST

Wild Ramps	*Allium tricoccum*
Wood Anemone	*Anemone quinquefolia*
Rue-anemone	*Anemonella thalictroides*
Filmy Angelica	*Angelica triquinata*
Columbine	*Aquilegia canadensis*
Hercules-club	
(Devil's walking stick)	*Aralia spinosa*
Jack-in-the-pulpit	*Arisaema triphyllum*
Rugel's Ragwort	*Cacalia rugelia*
Blue Cohosh	*Caulophyllum thalictroides*
Pink Turtlehead	*Chelone lyoni*
Striped Pipsissewa	*Chimaphila maculata*
Carolina Spring-beauty	*Claytonia caroliniana*
Rosebud Orchid	
(Spreading Pogonia)	*Cleistes divaricata*
Virgin's-bower	*Clematis virginiana*
Bluebead Lily	*Clintonia borealis*
Squawroot	*Conopholis americana*
Yellow Lady's-slipper	*Cypripedium calceolus*
Jimsonweed	*Datura stramonium*
Cut-leaved Toothwort	*Dentaria laciniata*
Squirrel-corn	*Dicentra canadensis*
Dutchman's-breeches	*Dicentra cucullaria*
Wild Bleeding-heart	*Dicentra eximia*
Yellow Mandarin	*Disporum lanuginosum*
Trailing Arbutus	*Epigaea repens*
Trout-lily	*Erythronium americanum*
Heart's-a-busting	*Euonymus americanus*
Joe-pye-weed	*Eupatorium maculatum*
Common Strawberry	*Fragaria virginiana*
American Columbo	*Frasera caroliniensis*
Galax	*Galax aphylla*
Teaberry	*Gaultheria procumbens*
Stiff Gentian	*Gentiana quinquefolia*

Wild Geranium	*Geranium maculatum*
Appalachian (Mountain) Avens	*Geum radiatum*
Rattlesnake-plantain	*Goodyera pubescens*
Sharp-lobed Hepatica	*Hepatica acutiloba*
Little Brown Jug	*Hexastylis arifolia*
Bluets	*Houstonia caerulea*
Common St. Johnswort	*Hypericum perforatum*
Stargrass	*Hypoxis hirsuta*
Pale Jewelweed (Touch-me-not)	*Impatiens pallida*
Crested Dwarf Iris	*Iris cristata*
Whorled Pogonia	*Isotria verticillata*
Mountain Laurel	*Kalmia latifolia*
Sand Myrtle	*Leiophyllum buxifolium*
Dog-hobble	*Leucothoe fontanesiana*
Turk's-cap Lily	*Lilium superbum*
Cardinal-flower	*Lobelia cardinalis*
Wild lily-of-the-valley	*Maianthemum canadense*
Bishop's Cap, Miterwort	*Mitella diphylla*
Common Evening-primrose	*Oenothera biennis*
Showy Orchis	*Orchis spectabilis*
Common Wood-sorrel	*Oxalis montana*
Ginseng	*Panax quinquefolium*
Purple Phacelia	*Phacelia bipinnatifida*
Fringed Phacelia	*Phacelia fimbriata*
Creeping Phlox	*Phlox stolonifera*
Yellow Fringed Orchid	*Platanthera ciliaris*
May-apple	*Podophyllum peltatum*
Rose Pogonia	*Pogonia ophiglossoides*
Smooth Solomon's-seal	*Polygonatum biflorum*
Flame Azalea	*Rhododendron calendulaceum*
Catawba Rhododendron	*Rhododendron catawbiense*
Rosebay Rhododendron	*Rhododendron maximum*
American Elder (Elderberry)	*Sambucus canadensis*
Bloodroot	*Sanguinaria canadensis*
Michaux's Saxifrage	*Saxifraga michauxii*
Fire Pink	*Silene virginica*

Blue-eyed Grass	*Sisyrinchium angustifolium*
False Solomon's-seal	*Smilacina racemosa*
Skunk Goldenrod	*Solidago glomerata*
Star Chickweed	*Stellaria pubera*
Foamflower	*Tiarella cordifolia*
Wakerobin	*Trillium erectum*
White Trillium	*Trillium grandiflorum*
Yellow Trillium	*Trillium luteum*
Painted Trillium	*Trillium undulatum*
Bellwort (Wild Oats)	*Uvularia sessilifolia*
New York Ironweed	*Vernonia noveboracensis*
Witch-hobble	*Viburnum alnifolium*
Sweet White Violet	*Viola blanda*
Birdsfoot Violet	*Viola pedata*

3
Children of Boreas
The Spruce-Fir Forest

The day is clear and cold. The wind blows furiously at Newfound Gap, a mile above sea level. Shivering sightseers take a quick look at the vista and hurry back to the warmth of their vehicles. I think seriously about doing the same, but instead don coat, hat, and gloves, and wish I'd brought my windbreaker.

The Appalachian Trail crosses the transmountain highway here. I start eastward on the trail, hoping the trees will break the wind. Instantly I'm glad I didn't follow my first instinct. This famous footpath, which can become a clogged wilderness highway in summer, is all mine on this magnificent morning.

Soon I stop to look at some strange-looking white crystals along the trail. They resemble a mineral, slivers of asbestos or gypsum, but on closer examination turn out to be ice crystals growing like some ghostly plant from the soil. On the north slopes, the trail is a solid sheet of ice; I step carefully from boulder to exposed root and back to boulder. As I turn a corner, a blast of wind causes me to curl under as the leaves of the rhododendron do.

Beside the trail are the gaping roots of the carcass of a toppled giant spruce. The trunk of a dead tree leans against a neighbor, creaking in the wind like old bones. As cold as it is, I begin to perspire as I work my way uphill, but I know I can't stop for long in this wind.

At the junction of a side trail, I choose a comfortable log in a sunny clearing, where I can sit and take off my gloves long enough to write in my notebook. Such clearings are uncommon in this closed boreal forest, in Russian called the taiga. The term *boreal* appropriately derives from the name Boreas, Greek god of the north wind. Boreas prevails here in this slice of northern climate. Two kinds of trees dominate at this rarefied altitude: red spruce and Fraser fir. It is a unique forest community found above 5,500 feet elevation along the highest crests in the northeast portion of the Smokies. The spruce-fir forest ends only a few miles west of here, around Clingmans Dome.

"Rhodies" in Bloom

When people ask, "When do the rhododendrons bloom?" they're usually referring to the Catawba rhododendron. This large shrub opens breathtaking purple flowers in late June on ridges in the high mountains of the Smokies.

A southern Appalachian endemic, *Rhododendron catawbiense* distinguishes the southern spruce–fir forests from the northern ones. The profusion of bloom is unpredictable; some years are heavy, while others are light.

These stately evergreens are reminders of a time when the Smokies were much colder than they are on this day. The trees are relicts, leftovers from the time when glaciers to the north exerted their chilling effect on the southern Appalachians. As the glaciers retreated, so did the spruce and fir trees, not only to Canada and the Arctic, but also to the highest peaks of the southern mountains.

The spruce-fir forest occupies only about 13,000 acres in Great Smoky Mountains National Park, a little more than two percent of the park's entire land area. Though small in area, this forest is extremely important biologically, for it is the southernmost spruce-fir forest in eastern North America and contains the most extensive old-growth stands in the southern Appalachians. Elsewhere in the southern Appalachians, logging and fires between 1880 and 1930 removed about half the spruce-fir stands. But because the stands were inaccessible, and because a national park was created here in 1934, most of the spruces and firs of the Smokies were saved from logging.

A keen awareness of the spruce-fir forest has been raised of late because of two imminent threats to it. In the past three decades, an introduced insect and environmental problems have highlighted the importance of this rare forest community.

A distinction can be drawn between the northern and southern boreal forests. Spruce-fir forests extend unbroken from Alaska eastward over a huge portion of Canada, and are distributed in a narrow swath down the spine of the Appalachians. But that southward extension is, in fact, disconnected (botanists would say "disjunct") both from the true boreal forest of the northern latitudes and from other nearby stands as well. Spruce-fir forest grows in 10 isolated high-mountain areas in the southern Appalachians. The Great Smokies are one of these areas.

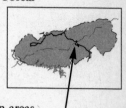

Appalachian Trail,
Newfound Gap

The geographic restriction of the southern boreal forest has led to unique biology. The isolation creates an "island" effect; and like islands, each of these scattered sections of spruce-fir forest develops its own set of native species. This helps explain why so many species here are rare and endemic, ones found on these peaks and nowhere else.

Spruce-fir is also the dominant forest of the headwaters of mountain streams in the Smokies, thus influencing water quality and aquatic life downstream. From a purely aesthetic viewpoint, this forest is important to the thousands of backpackers and hikers who pass through it each year along the Appalachian Trail.

Because they enjoy a moister climate and warmer winters than conifers to the north, spruce and fir in the southern Appalachians grow faster and bigger. With only two dominant large trees, this is a relatively simple ecosystem, compared with the cove hardwood forests, for example. But the mere presence of the spruce-fir forest adds yet another measure to the already incredible diversity of the Smokies. Its cool, moist darkness shelters plants and animals that would otherwise never be found at this latitude. Certain lichens, mosses, wildflowers, "northern" birds, amphibians, and small mammals find suitable habitat here and only here.

The Spruce-Fir Community

In the 18th century, and certainly by the 19th, the southern Appalachian Mountains became internationally known among botanists. Competition was keen among these men and women for discoveries of new species. Among the earliest was an exuberant Frenchman, Andre Michaux. He is well known for a climb to the top of Grandfather Mountain in North Carolina in 1794. Upon reaching the summit, Michaux belted out the

With its blunt-tipped needles, Fraser fir is one of the two dominant conifers of the high-elevation spruce-fir forest. The resin-filled blisters gave it the name "she-balsam" among mountaineers.

Marseilles Hymn and exclaimed, "Long live America and the French Republic!"

Accompanying Michaux on one trip was Scotsman John Fraser. As legend goes, Michaux feigned lost horses and sent Fraser ahead. Michaux's motive was his desire to lay sole claim to any botanical discoveries. Much to Michaux's chagrin, Fraser proceeded to discover a new species of fir tree that would bear his name.

Fraser fir *(Abies fraseri)* is a southern Appalachian endemic, found only in the mountains of Virginia, North Carolina, and Tennessee, where it replaces the balsam fir of the northern boreal forest. As with all firs, Fraser's is distinguished from spruce by cones that stand upright on the branches. The purplish cones mature and then disintegrate in autumn, leaving a spikelet on the branch. Red squirrels eat the small papery-winged seeds held within the bracts of the cones.

The evergreen needles on Fraser fir are flat and blunt-tipped, arranged on either side of the twigs. Where they are attached, the needles are expanded and leave a noticeable round scar on the twig. To the people of the southern mountains, the whitish, resinous blisters on the bark of Fraser fir appeared to be filled with milk; they called the tree "she-balsam."

Above 6,200 feet, Fraser fir grows in almost pure stands. The extreme climate on the summits stunts the trees' growth, kills seedlings, and makes for a sparse undergrowth, except for mosses and lichens. Ecologist R.H. Whittaker described these pure fir stands as a "dwarf" conifer forest that "on a fair day has a charm of its own but at other times, with the summits involved in cloud and a raw wind whipping fog through the firs, assumes the bleakness of the climate in which it lives."

Below 6,000 feet, red spruce shares the southern boreal forest with Fraser fir. *Picea rubens* bears spiny, four-cornered needles. The cones are said to be pendant, hanging down from the branches. Red spruces prefer moister places in the Smokies, and along streamcourses some grow as low as 3,500 feet. Giant old spruces have been located in the park; 300-year-olds are known, and many tower more than a hundred feet high. Spruce was in great demand during World War I for construction of airplanes. During those years, some 50 million board feet of spruce were cut in the Smokies, mostly between Mount Collins and Double Spring Gap and in the Smokemont area.

Both spruce and fir are conifers, trees that belong to a large, ancient group of plants called gymnosperms. The fact that they reproduced by seeds, rather than water-dependent spores, let gymnosperms triumph over their predecessors, horsetails and club mosses. The other major group of plants that would evolve were the flowering plants, or angiosperms. Gymnosperms bear "naked" seeds, while the seeds of angiosperms are enclosed and protected in ovaries. The abundant pollen produced by gymnosperms is spread fairly indiscriminately by the wind. Flowering plants have become much more specialized and successful, coevolving tight relationships with birds and insects that are their pollinators.

As flowering plants (including all the grasses, wildflowers, and deciduous trees) colonized the Earth, conifers were often left with only the highest, coldest elevations. They have had to adapt to stay alive. The trees' conical shapes and flexible branches let them bear the weight of snow without breaking. Evergreen needles likewise are an adaptation that allows conifers to carry on photosynthesis whenever conditions are right, without having to sprout new leaves each year as deciduous trees do. (In truth, evergreen trees also shed their leaves, or needles, periodically, but not annually or all at once.) The resin that flows through the conifers' veins acts as a sort of antifreeze, protecting them from very cold temperatures.

As with all forest communities, the spruce-fir forest is divided into layers. Beneath the shade of the canopy grows an understory of smaller trees and shrubs, including yellow birch, mountain-ash, pin cherry, thornless blackberry, mountain cranberrybush, red-berried elder, Catawba rhododendron, and hobblebush. The presence of an evergreen, broad-leaved shrub layer, especially of Catawba rhododendrons, on ridges and steep rocky slopes is another distinctive difference between southern and northern spruce-fir forests.

The northern hardwoods, yellow birch and beech, grade into the spruce-fir as elevation increases. Though deciduous, the yellow birches, like their evergreen companions, are adapted to the cold, windy climate of the high elevations.

The herbaceous layer of the spruce-fir forest consists of lush growths of moss, ferns, and wildflowers. Two kinds of ferns are especially successful, the mountain woodferns in the genus *Dryopteris* and the northern lady ferns in the genus *Athyrium*. Relatives of the ferns include the ancient group called club mosses. One species, the shining club moss, grows in bright green tufts over the ground in the spruce-fir forest.

Club mosses are among the most primitive vascular plants. They evolved 350 to 400 million years ago on land and, like ferns, reproduce by means of spores. Along with ferns and horsetails, club mosses virtually ruled the plant world on land for about 65 million years. Some attained the stature of giant trees.

Club mosses have only one kind of spore, neither male nor female. They propagate by relying on the wind to distribute these tiny spores, by extending the rootstock from which new plants generate (giving some the name running pine), or, as in the case of the shining club moss, by producing little bulblets on the ends of the leaves that fall to the ground and start a new plant. The incredibly abundant, dustlike, flammable spores of club mosses have served many uses: as pill coatings and soothing powders, in photographic flashbulbs, and even for fireworks.

Casting more emerald green over the ground are the mosses, which along with liverworts are known collectively as bryophytes. The group is startlingly abundant and diverse in the spruce-fir forest — more than 280 species have been counted, and new ones are still being discovered. Among

Red spruce, the second dominant evergreen of the spruce-fir community. Unlike the erect cones of the Fraser fir, spruce cones hang down from the branches.

the most common are the haircap, windblown, and sphagnum mosses. Several grow only on the bark of Fraser fir, either living trees or dead and downed ones, and depend solely on the fir for their growth. Scientists speculate that mosses may act like wicks that trap moisture from fog and as sponges that hold moisture and nutrients in the forest floor.

Along with the mosses are the ground- and tree-hugging pioneers of the forest, the lichens. One man, at least, has found ultimate solace in the lowly lichen. For people who find the "chant" of politicians "hollow and old," writes lichenologist Daniel McKinley, and for those who do not want "too quickly to worship the artifices of man, I recommend the lichen." Lichens are a combination of algae and fungus living together harmoniously in one plant — algae provide the food and fungus the structure. They often gain footholds in the cavities of the roots of windthrown trees and splash their greens, silvers, and rusts across the gnarled gray branches of the beeches.

An easy lichen to identify is usnea, or old man's beard, a smaller lookalike of Spanish moss that hangs from trees in the warmer lowlands of the

South. (Spanish moss, however, belongs to the bromeliad family and is not a moss at all.) A bird of the spruce-fir forests, the Blackburnian warbler, may incorporate usnea into its nest.

One of the greatest services lichens perform in the plant world is helping build soil. They can grow on bare rock, secreting acids that begin to weather the rock. Once even the smallest pocket of soil has formed, a self-fulfilling prophecy occurs. More soil gathers, until finally enough has accumulated for the seedling of a one-day mighty spruce or fir to establish itself.

Soils of the spruce-fir forest are different from the loamy mull of the deciduous forest. A distinct, undecomposed layer of evergreen needles forms a topmost humus layer called mor. In some places a grayish bleached mineral layer underlies this organic material. The soil is thinner and more acidic, partly because of the chemistry of the conifer needles and partly because of the parent rock material. All the soils of the higher mountains in the spruce-fir region have been described as "extremely" acid. Despite the abundant moisture, the litter layer at these altitudes is slower to decay. The acidity level slows decay by slowing the growth of soil microorganisms. The cold also retards decay. While the litter layer of a deciduous forest may decompose in a year to a few years, it can take 10 years for conifer needles to decay.

Fungi, along with tiny animals that tenant the soil, especially springtails and mites, play a large part in decomposing the mor. Earthworms, however, are rarely found in mor; they are unable to stand the acidity. Springtails, exceedingly abundant wingless insects, feed on fungi and bacteria. Bacteria live in the gut of some springtails and help digest cellulose. Mites, eight-legged relatives of spiders, are nearly as abundant in the soil as springtails, on which they prey.

With its acidic soil and nearly constant shade, the spruce-fir forest is less conducive to wildflower extravagance than the deciduous forest. There is no time in early spring when the sun can shine through the canopy, so those flowers that do bloom beneath the spruce-fir must be able to tolerate shade. Their names, such as Canada mayflower and *Clintonia borealis* (bluebead lily), tell of their northern affinities.

One flower that is characteristic of this forest is the lovely wood-sorrel *(Oxalis montana)*. Large, green shamrock leaves make this plant

Shining club moss is common on the floor of the spruce-fir forest. Club mosses are not true mosses.

unmistakable. Single, dainty white flowers with pink stripes bloom in May and June. Mrs. William Starr Dana, in her 19th-century classic *How to Know the Wildflowers,* wrote of the wood-sorrel that "at the very name comes a vision of mossy nooks where the sunlight only comes on sufferance." Despite such poetic description, wood-sorrel is loaded with an acrid substance called oxalic acid, giving it another common name in the mountains, sour grass.

Visitors to Europe, Asia, and Africa might recognize wood-sorrel as well, a situation that has fascinated botanists for some time. Often termed the "Asian connection," this similarity between the flora of the southern Appalachians and Eurasia can be explained by looking back into geologic time. Two hundred million years ago, the continents of North America, Eurasia, and Africa were one land mass. A continuous swath of broad-leaved forest covered this span. Wood-sorrel was one of many plant species that evolved here. When this supercontinent split apart to form the modern-day continents, the plants were separated. Millions of years later, when a land bridge formed in the Bering Sea, these cousins were rejoined temporarily, but were again torn asunder when the bridge was severed after the last ice age.

Curiously, early botanists such as Andre Michaux scoured the highest peaks elsewhere in the southern Appalachians but never entered the Smokies. Not until the middle to late 19th century did botanists start to work here. Their collections have taken interesting twists and turns, providing 20th-century botanists with some detective work.

One such curiosity is a "lost" plant of the spruce-fir forest, the twinflower. Its scientific name is *Linnaea borealis*, for the great Swedish botanist Carolus Linnaeus, who had first found it in Finland. Linnaeus so loved the plant he had his portrait made with it. Its common name comes from the pair of delicate pink blossoms that hang from the stalks.

Old-man's beard, or usnea, is a lichen that adorns birch and conifers.

On August 13, 1892, Albert Ruth, superintendent of schools in Knoxville and an amateur botanist, noticed the

flowers and put a piece of the plant in his tin collecting box. Ruth, however, misidentified the plant and did not precisely note where he had found the sample. When University of Tennessee botanist A.J. "Jack" Sharp purchased some of Ruth's pressed plant specimens in the 1930s, his alert eyes saw one he identified as the elusive twinflower. Searches for twinflower in the spruce-fir forests of the Smokies then and during the 1980s have been unsuccessful. Botanists speculate that the plant may now be extinct in Tennessee, or perhaps Ruth's sample was actually one sent to him by someone in the north.

Other vegetative rarities of the southern Appalachian spruce-fir forest range from the ground-hugging prostrate bluets to the five-foot-tall filmy angelica. One endemic, known only from the high Smokies, is Rugel's Indian plantain. It is named for Ferdinand Rugel, a Swiss-German expatriate who was one of the earliest botanists to explore the Smokies in the mid-19th century. Because of its isolated, specialized, and highly limited habitat, Rugel's plaintain *(Cacalia rugelia)* is officially listed as a threatened species by the states of Tennessee and North Carolina. Though botanists say there are no immediate threats to the plant in the park, the species will be closely monitored for a long time to come.

Rugel's plantain, also known commonly as Rugel's ragwort, is a member of the composite family, a giant group that includes all the sunflowers, asters, and daisies, some 19,000 species worldwide. Rugel's plantain does not produce especially striking flowers — they are tiny and cream to reddish in color, clustering on tall stalks and blooming from June to September. Their odor, however, is memorable — they smell like skunk.

Birds that live in the spruce-fir forest are, not surprisingly, also found farther north and in higher elevations. Among them are red-breasted nuthatches, red crossbills, veeries, golden-crowned kinglets, winter wrens, black-capped chickadees, brown creepers, Blackburnian warblers, and northern saw-whet owls.

The scientific name of the saw-whet owl, *Aegolius acadicus*, hints at its north country home. The species name derives from Acadia in Canada, where the first specimens were collected and identified. Saw-whets can be heard in the woods on clear, moonlit nights in April and May when they are courting. Their whistled song sounds like the sharpening, or whetting, of a saw. They have been known in the park since 1941, but reports of saw-whets nesting here are unverified.

The most nocturnal of all owls, saw-whets become active at night as they hunt for mice and other small mammals. Owls possess extremely keen sight and hearing, which helps them in night-hunting. Their arresting large, golden eyes are set in "facial disks." These disks serve acoustical functions, focusing sound. Soft feathers around the ear openings further funnel sound. Owl wing feathers are adapted for nocturnal predation — soft leading edges on the flight feathers let air pass silently over, so their prey do not hear them coming. Saw-whets are the smallest owls, ranging only about seven to eight inches long. They nest in cavities in trees, sometimes selecting abandoned woodpecker holes. They are remarkably tame birds.

Small songbirds such as the red-breasted nuthatch and red crossbill are at the southernmost limit of their breeding ranges in the Smokies spruce-fir forest. Their primary food is the seeds of red spruce and Fraser fir. Equipped with needle-sharp bills, nuthatches wedge the seeds into small spaces in the bark of a tree, then peck them open. The year-round availability of seeds lets nuthatches remain in the spruce-fir even during winter. The success of the seed crop corresponds fairly closely with the nuthatch population, which varies widely each year.

Nuthatches are known for their unusual habit of spiraling upside down as they forage in the tree bark. Long, sharp claws on their toes help hold them to the bark as they walk headfirst.

On a climb up a 60-foot fire tower in the Appalachians one summer day, a naturalist noted the "layering" of birds in the spruce-fir forest. Juncos and winter wrens inhabited the ground level. Red-breasted nuthatches occupied the higher branches, while golden-crowned kinglets searched for insects on the outermost twigs. At around 30 feet Blackburnian warblers occurred, and in the tallest young spruces was an abundance of red crossbills.

Here the crossbills find the cones that bear the seeds on which they feed. With their crossed mandibles that act like shears, these birds can force apart cone scales and extract the seeds with their tongues. Crossbills, members of the finch family, are uncommon permanent residents of the park. Old Smokies mountaineers called them "salt birds" because they fed at salt licks put out for cattle on the grassy balds. Red crossbills have been seen at shelters along the Appalachian Trail between Tricorner Knob and Silers Bald, a former grazing pasture.

Rose Houk

Common wood-sorrel clings to wet mossy places at the base of trees in the spruce-fir forest. It flowers in the spring.

Another flying creature found in the southern Appalachians is a mammal rather than a bird. Flying squirrels actually glide rather than fly — bats are the only mammals that can truly fly. Flying squirrels are medium-sized animals that fly at night from tree branch to tree branch. The squirrels' "wings" are loose folds of skin, called patagia, that extend between their front and hind limbs. There are two species, the northern and the southern. Both are found mostly in spruce-fir and northern hardwoods, though southern flying squirrels are also found in deciduous forests in lower elevations. The northern flying squirrel depends more on lichens and fungi than on the seeds and nuts the southern flying squirrel eats. The two can be told apart by the color of the hairs on the stomach: the northern's are gray at the base, while the southern's are white.

Of the two species, the northern flying squirrel is much rarer in the Southeast. It is known from only three or four isolated places in North Carolina, Tennessee, and southern Virginia. Since 1958, no specimens of the northern had been recorded in Great Smokies National Park. But in

1987, a researcher trapped, positively identified, and released three northern flying squirrels on Clingmans Dome. Nevertheless, the northern flying squirrel remains a species on the brink in this area. Though it was never common here, the decline in its numbers is attributed to tree cutting outside the park, displacement by the more aggressive southern species, and possible problems from a parasite that may be transferred to it by the southern flying squirrel.

Like many inhabitants of the islands of spruce-fir forest in the southern Appalachians, the northern flying squirrel is isolated from the center of its normal northern range, making it more vulnerable to habitat destruction. Admittedly, that isolation is a factor that began at the end of the Pleistocene. Natural climatic changes are unavoidable, but protecting these animals from human activities is within our realm.

An amphibian, the pigmy salamander, can be added to the list of unique spruce-fir inhabitants. The first specimens of *Desmognathus wrighti* were found on Mount LeConte in 1936. Known primarily from the Smokies, pigmy salamanders are also found to the north on Grandfather Mountain in North Carolina and Whitetop Mountain in Virginia. This tiny lungless salamander lives underneath stones, logs, bark, and moss, usually above 5,000 feet elevation. The largest one ever found was about two inches long. They are so small that a park naturalist reported seeing an injured one being dragged by a black beetle on the Appalachian Trail.

Pigmies have light bellies and light tan or reddish bands on their backs. Many also have black marks on the back, in a herringbone pattern. Strictly a land animal, this salamander hides in the litter of the forest floor during the daytime. At night it emerges, climbing the trunks of spruce and fir trees in search of food.

All of these citizens of the unique spruce-fir forest are seeing great changes in their community. The most obvious is the loss of one of the two dominant trees of the ecosystem — the Fraser fir — to the depredation of an introduced insect. Less obvious, and only now being researched, are the complex effects of acid deposition and air pollution on the remaining red spruce. Some of those changes likely will include the extinction of some species. Will it be the lovely wood-sorrel? Or the diminutive pigmy salamander? Or a moss that has not yet been named by science? We do not know for certain.

4
The Treeless Places
Grass and Heath Balds

The fire boss sprinkled a few drops of fuel from the drip torch onto the slash pile. He struck a match and the pile ignited with stunning swiftness. The crew, dressed in yellow hardhats and Nomex jackets, scratched a fire break around the pile. With a device that looked like a large rubber fly swatter, the ranger smothered any disobedient flames that threatened to creep beyond the fire line. We stood and watched the wood burn, keeping an eye out for any spot fires that might flare up downwind. It was a cold day in April and we welcomed the warmth of the fire.

In about 20 minutes the orange flames had consumed most of the tangle of hawthorn branches. All that remained were smoldering gray ashes to be guarded until the rain, forecast for midnight, assured that the fire was extinguished. I had hiked up the six-mile Gregory Ridge Trail to observe this controlled burn on Gregory Bald, a large grassy meadow high in the mountains above Cades Cove in the west end of the Smokies. The slash consisted of wood that crews had cut and piled a season earlier. Cutting, burning, and mowing are all methods being used by the Park Service to restore and maintain Gregory and Andrews balds to their historic look.

In early spring, the mountain oat grasses on Gregory Bald are a tawny brown. By midsummer, the grassy bald is bright green.

Grassy balds are open, meadowlike areas in the higher elevations of the southern Appalachian Mountains. In the Smoky Mountains, they are found primarily on ridgetops between 5,000 and 6,000 feet in the western half of the park. In the northeast section of the park, grassy balds are replaced by another type called heath balds. About 20 grassy balds or old fields have been identified in the Smokies, ranging in size from four to about fifteen acres.

Because the Smoky Mountains are not high enough to have a true timberline, such treeless areas have attracted attention for a long time, for both scientific and aesthetic reasons. When a hiker tops out onto a bald, it is like seeing the curvature of the Earth. Their openness offers refreshing relief from the tunnel vision of the forest trails. In summer the flowering of mountain laurel, rhododendron, and azalea on the balds makes them a favored destination for thousands of hikers.

Grassy balds are like prairies in the forest. The predominant plant species is native mountain oat grass *(Danthonia compressa)*, along with some timothy and bluegrass. In this open, sunlit environment,

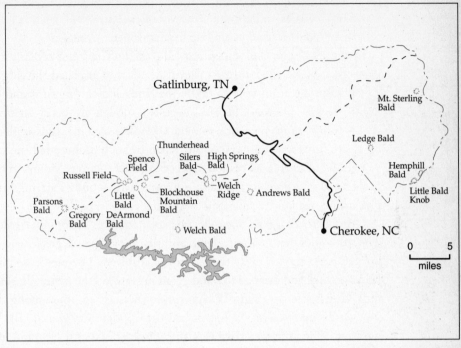

Gatlinburg, TN

Mt. Sterling
Bald

Ledge Bald

Thunderhead

Spence   Silers   High Springs
Field   Bald   Bald

Russell Field

Welch
Ridge

Blockhouse
Mountain
Bald

Andrews Bald

Hemphill
Bald

Little Bald
Knob

Parsons
Bald

Little
Bald

Gregory   DeArmond
Bald   Bald

Welch Bald

Cherokee, NC

0   5
miles

*Distribution of grassy
balds*

wildflowers such as asters, goldenrod, yarrow, angelica, St. Johnswort, and the rare purple-fringed orchid can grow. Red foxes, brown thrashers, timber rattlesnakes, and southern bog lemmings inhabit these grassland communities. Golden eagles and ravens soar above these prime hunting grounds, their sharp eyes searching for rodents and carrion. Where bald and forest meet, animals of both ecosystems can be found in a small area.

Balds have stimulated a great deal of debate among botanists. Under the rules of natural succession, when an opening occurs in high-elevation hardwood or spruce-fir forests, pin cherry, briars, and coarse weeds usually come in, eventually giving way to mature forest. What created grassy balds in the first place, and why did they stay open? Was it natural or human causes?

Early botanical explorers in the southern mountains failed to mention the balds. But in 1835 a naturalist described the bald on Roan Mountain in North Carolina as "a vast meadow, without a tree to obstruct the prospect; where a person may gallop his horse for a mile or two." In 1887 another author noted that "the absence of timber on the so-called 'balds' is perhaps due to waves of excessive cold; such at least, seem the naked trunks looming up here and there, to suggest."

In the 1930s, an ecologist proposed that the Cherokee Indians had created and used the balds. As they hunted, they traveled the ridges, 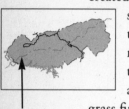 stopping at night to camp on the balds and cutting surrounding trees for firewood. He also suggested, though his theory does not receive much credence, that the Cherokee used the balds as places to lure game and as lookout stations. Such uses eroded the soil and allowed a succession of weedy species to grow. Mountain oat grass finally became established, outcompeting woody seedlings and preventing trees and shrubs from becoming established.

Gregory Bald

One Cherokee legend does offer an explanation for the origin of balds. The story goes that U'la'gu, a large bird that looked like a green-winged hornet, was carrying away the Cherokee children. The medicine men held a council and decided to stand guard in a line on the mountain summits. The first one to sight U'la'gu would shout, then others along the line would do likewise. Whoever had the opportunity would kill the monster. When the men tried this, they discovered that U'la'gu hid in a cavern in the Blue Ridge. Their prayers to Great Spirit to reveal U'la'gu were answered by a bolt of lightning that destroyed half the mountain and allowed them to kill their enemy. To reward their bravery, the Great Spirit declared that all high mountains would be devoid of trees so the Cherokee could always see their enemies.

Others sought more immediate explanations. One researcher, noticing that insects called twig gall wasps were killing trees, principally oaks, on southern balds, proposed that these insects were responsible for creating the balds. Another thought climatic exposure caused the balds. Still others looked to prevailing southwesterly winds and grazing as the causes. Some see the balds as products of the Pleistocene — specifically the grazing of ground sloths, caribou, musk-ox, bison, and other large mammals that inhabited the southern mountains during the ice age.

The balds appealed to the early mountaineers because such clearings, at a premium in the mountains, provided pastures in which they could graze their livestock. Taking cattle, sheep, and horses up to the balds in summer freed up precious cropland, eliminated the need to fence livestock out of the lowland fields, and provided cooler, insect-free places for grazing.

Russell and Spence fields and Gregory, Andrews, and Silers balds bear the names of the settlers who likely cleared the original forest, or who helped enlarge small natural areas by grazing or clearing. Descendants of these settlers have told how their families drove small herds from the valleys to the mountains, usually in May. Herders charged one or two dollars a head for cattle, less for other kinds of livestock. A herder would have under his care on one range 200 to 500 head of cattle, a few hundred sheep, and a few horses, goats, and mules. Former herder "Uncle" Jim Shelton, when he was 89 years old, said the reason for the balds was "very plain. That Smoky Mountain was so very high that thunder and lightning just played down on the ground" and prevented trees from ever growing.

In mid-September the livestock on the balds was rounded up and held in pens called "gant lots" for a few days, where the cattle would become gaunt from weight loss. The trip back down would be easier on the cattle, the settlers thought, if the cows were underfed for a few days. The livestock was then driven back down from the

Settlers drove sheep and cattle up to the grassy balds such as Thunderhead to graze in summer. Grazing is believed to have been one factor that kept the balds open.

Great Smoky Mountains N.P.

balds to market. Settlers feared that cattle would develop "milk sickness" if left on the range beyond September. This disease, likely caused when livestock ate white snakeroot, would sicken the cows and anyone who drank their milk.

Grazing ceased on some balds in the second decade of the 20th century; when Great Smoky Mountains National Park was created in 1934, all grazing stopped within the park boundaries. Only one year later, the grass on the balds grew knee high. Blueberry bushes, followed by serviceberry shrubs and beech trees, soon began to invade. Even then, people asked that certain balds be preserved as they were before the park was established. To many, it seemed apparent that grazing was a major reason balds had remained open and grassy.

In the absence of grazing, all the balds were (and are) being overgrown at varying rates. On Gregory Bald, for instance, less than half the original 15 acres were still grassy in the mid-1980s. Cades Cove, clearly visible in the 1930s from the top of Gregory, can no longer be seen clearly over the treetops. Despite this growth, the balds still contrast with the forests surrounding them. The rapid succession of trees is most evident to someone who saw the balds before the park was established.

The hawthorn slash piles being burned on Gregory Bald tell a big part of the story of the grassy balds in the Smokies. The profusely branching hawthorns have become the most aggressive invaders of the grassy area of Gregory, and the piles we watched burn represented perhaps 50 years of growth. If their encroachment continued, in another 50 years the bald might be completely overgrown. Thus, though the question of the balds' exact origin has not been settled to everyone's satisfaction, the Park Service decided in the 1980s to restore and maintain Gregory and Andrews balds. They were chosen, among other reasons, because these two balds are believed to have originated naturally, though they were maintained by livestock grazing.

Gregory and Andrews balds also possess scientific and aesthetic values. On Gregory, it is the famous flame azaleas. On his travels through southern Appalachia in 1775, William Bartram wrote that their reds, oranges, golds, yellows, and creams "cover the shrubs in such incredible profusion on the hillsides that suddenly opening to view from dark shades, we are alarmed with apprehension of the hill being set on fire." Botanists have declared the flame azaleas on Gregory Bald among the finest in the

Great Smoky Mountains N. P.

Hiking party on Gregory Bald in 1934. From the north-facing side of the bald, Cades Cove was fully visible.

world, and one of the attributes that easily qualified the Smokies as national park material.

On a return trip to Gregory Bald in late June, I saw the famous azaleas blooming in all their splendid glory. I could scarcely believe I was in the same place as on that blustery gray day in April when the grasses were brown and the shrubs bare. In late June, though, the bald was green. The air was scented like a tropical garden, and industrious insects buzzed from flower to flower. Sunday hikers strolled around the bald as if through an arboretum. I too walked from shrub to shrub, examining and photographing the spidery blossoms.

On many of the stems grew galls, which form when certain species of insects feed on plant tissue. These galls, I was told, were edible and tasted like watermelon. So I sliced one open and tried a small piece. It was surprisingly moist, and with some imagination I could detect the resemblance to watermelon.

Andrews Bald has its own floral attractions, including three species of fringed orchids as well as stunning Catawba rhododendrons. Also on Andrews is a small bog where carnivorous sundew plants grow.

The decision to restore the balds involved several specific considerations: to preserve healthy grass turf, prevent erosion, repair boar rooting, protect the hybrid azaleas on Gregory and retain a view of Cades Cove, leave a buffer zone around the bog on Andrews, and monitor woody plant encroachment, rare plant populations, and boar rooting.

Restoration of the balds would require some kind of periodic disturbance every two or three years. This would necessarily be a labor-intensive endeavor because the balds can be reached only by trail, and most work would have to be done by hand. After the pros and cons of many methods , including grazing, were examined, mowing, cutting out woody species, and burning the resulting slash were selected as the most feasible ways to restore the two balds.

Grassy balds support a community of animals as well. Slithering through the high grasses are timber rattlesnakes, one of the two venomous snakes in the park (copperheads are the other). A five-foot-long timber rattlesnake was found on Mount Sterling Bald, and rattlesnakes have been encountered on Andrews and Gregory balds. A researcher nearly stepped on a rattler on Gregory Bald, one she reported had especially striking coloration: "Just gold as gold could be, with light brown markings." Timber rattlers have two color phases, yellow and black, which old-timers mistakenly believed were males and females.

The timber rattler's scientific name, *Crotalus horridus*, embodies people's perceptions of it. With a little care, however, the odds of being bitten by a rattlesnake are very small. A Smokies naturalist noted that the snakes "don't go out of their way to bite you; they just sit there. They're gentlemen."

These carnivorous reptiles eat primarily chipmunks, mice, and squirrels. Rattlers are pit vipers: to locate their prey, especially at night, they use heat-sensitive pits between their eyes and nostrils. In daylight, rattlesnakes sense prey at a distance by ground vibrations, then use their eyes and the pits as the prey comes within closer range. To obtain food, rattlesnakes coil their bodies and employ a sit-and-wait strategy to capture prey that come within striking distance. Once the toxic venom has been injected through the snake's fangs into the prey animal, the snake swallows the dead animal whole.

The "rattles" on the end of the snake's tail are actually modified scales of hornlike material. Each time a snake molts or sheds its skin (one to

four times a year), a new segment is added to the rattle, until the snake reaches adulthood. Nonpoisonous snakes like rat snakes and corn snakes vibrate their tails in dry leaves as warning, but only rattlesnakes have evolved an anatomical adaptation to alert would-be predators of their presence. The rattles are used strictly for defense. The rattle probably evolved at a time when rattlesnakes shared

The view from Andrews Bald near Clingmans Dome in the 1930s. Grazing had stopped on the bald and shrubs were just beginning to take over.

habitat with numbers of large hoofed animals and other possible predators.

A small animal wary of timber rattlers is the southern bog lemming. With its short tail and thick body, this small rodent looks like a vole, but it has longer, coarser, darker hair. At one time these mammals were considered intermediate between voles of mid-latitudes and true lemmings of high latitudes. Now, however, mammalogists consider them lemmings. Though they are found around bogs, much of their range includes grasslands or damp, sedgy areas. Bog lemmings are active day and night, winter and summer, using runways in the grass that they build or that were built by other small rodents. The leaves, stems, seeds, and roots of grasses are their favorite food; neat piles of cut grass beside runways are signs of their presence.

Near the top of the food chain poses the red fox, ready to pounce on southern bog lemmings, cottontails, and other small mammals that frequent the grassy balds and the forest edges. Red foxes are adaptive, flexible animals, and their range is larger than any living terrestrial mammal except humans. Native to North America, they spread to the southeast United States and westward to the Great Plains in the 18th century.

This elegant member of the canine family is known for its hunting abilities. One biologist has written, "A hunting fox is a study in silent grace." As a red fox hunts, it moves quickly through its home range, sniffing at clumps of grass and brush. Catching the scent of prey, the fox arches and leaps in a surprise attack. To supply the pound of food it eats each day, a fox may be out hunting day and night. Though the fox prefers small mammals it is an opportunistic omnivore. A fox will eat berries and fruits, insects, earthworms, birds, and carrion, depending upon what is seasonally available. Two hikers once watched a fox carry away a wild boar piglet between Russell and Spence fields.

Red foxes are sometimes seen hunting rodents on the grassy balds.

Tennessee Wildlife Resources Agency

During breeding season in early winter, a male and female will hunt together, covering a home range of one to three square miles. The pair chooses a den site, usually a burrow on a sunny slope, bank, or good lookout, in which to raise their young. The male brings in food until the young are able to go out with the parents and hunt. In some social groups, nonbreeding female foxes will also help rear the pups. The fox family stays together until autumn of the first year, then the parents separate and the nearly full-grown young are on their own.

Because of their bushy coats, red foxes appear larger than they really are. An adult red fox may weigh about 15 pounds and attain a length of about three feet. The white-tipped tail of the red fox is a distinctive marking.

At Gregory Bald that morning in April, I watched a raven twirl off the edge of the Earth. I could have followed its aerobatics for hours. Balds are good places to see ravens, which are fairly common at higher elevations in the park. These blue-black birds are, surprisingly, classed as songbirds; with four-foot-wingspans, they are the largest songbirds. Their "song," however, is more like a croak or gargle. Members of the crow family, ravens can be distinguished from their cousins by their larger size and wedge-shaped tails. Also, crows tend to congregate in flocks, while ravens are usually solitary. The common raven has large nostrils, a heavy, arched bill, and feathers on its throat that lend a bearded, scholarly appearance.

Scavenging, ravens wheel over the grassy balds looking for dead animals. They eat other songbirds, insects, berries, and mice. One study in Maine revealed that ravens call others of their kind to join the feast when a food source such as a carcass is located. This behavior among ravens may have to do with attaining status and securing mates.

Heath Balds

When speaking about balds in the southern Appalachian Mountains, many people are referring only to grassy balds. But a distinction should be made between grassy balds and heath balds. Heath balds have received much less attention from botanists, perhaps because they are stable, self-maintaining communities not in need of active resource management. Yet the origins of heath balds are equally fascinating and obscure.

Like grassy balds, heath balds are treeless areas found usually at high elevations in the southern Appalachians. But the members of the plant community are different — they include Catawba rhododendron, mountain laurel, sand myrtle, blueberries, huckleberries, azaleas, and wintergreen. All are evergreen shrubs that belong to the Ericaceae, or heath family, better known in places like Scotland.

Heath plants have been described as tough, wiry species that thrive in extreme environments — "true mountaineers." Heath plants have adapted well to the adversities of the high-elevation climate. They assume dwarf forms that hug the ground. Their branches are tightly entwined and pruned to a uniform height by the wind. Leaves are small and thick, a defense against excess evaporation in such windy, cold places. The most striking characteristic of heath balds in the Smokies is the sudden change to an environment that feels like alpine tundra or seacoast chaparral. A walk through a fog-shrouded heath bald is like a walk through a Lilliputian forest.

Heath balds are most common on steep ridges on the west slope of the mountains. Their extent is greatest on the south- and west-facing slopes below those ridges, from Laurel Top along Sawtooth to Mount Collins, westward onto Mount LeConte, and southwest to the limits of the spruce-fir forest. Some heath balds are also found on lower, rounded summits like Brushy Mountain in the Greenbrier area of the park.

The incredibly dense growth of heath balds earned them the name "hells" from early mountain people, who found travel through them nearly impossible. The glossy leaves of heath plants also gave rise to another vernacular name, "slicks."

Why heath balds occur on certain ridges and not others is difficult to say. Fire is probably the most important factor in their origin, along with windfall and landslides. In clearings created by these natural disturbances, the heath plants already present in the forest closed in and prevented tree reproduction by their dense cover and the acidic, infertile soil they created. Because heath balds are subject to fire, some people have considered them simply a step in the natural forest succession that follows fire. Others think heath balds are themselves climax communities. The nucleus of many of the balds may be old shrub root systems that repeatedly regrow after fire. Heath balds may be considered self-maintaining, fire-adapted communities whose existence is favored by a

Heath shrubs on Cliff Tops glow with silvery light. Heath balds have been called "slicks" by mountain people.

combination of high elevation, steep slope, and exposure to prevailing winds.

Soils of heath balds may be bare rock outcrops with soil pockets, or peat, or what is called podsol. The brown, moist peat soil is frequently a foot or two deep, covered with a mat of sphagnum and other peat-forming mosses. Podsols, soils with a gray, leached layer beneath raw humus, develop where average temperatures are low and precipitation is high. The habits of heath shrubs make them especially well suited to podsol soils. The shrubs' shallow root systems spread horizontally and form a dense, intertwined mat of roots in the uppermost soil horizon.

Other plants of the heath balds include lichens and mosses. Herbaceous plants, though sparse, may cover 20 to 40 percent of the high, open balds, but they are often almost nonexistent in the closed heathlands at lower elevations. Like other plants of the heath, these generally are prostrate and evergreen. Teaberry, galax, and sometimes trailing arbutus are among them. When the shiny green leaves of galax turn red, the pioneers gathered the plant and sold it in markets at Christmas. The exquisite painted trillium may also grace the heath balds in moister, shaded places.

Rufous-sided towhees and indigo buntings, which prefer brushy tangles, are birds that may be seen on the heath balds. Another is the chestnut-sided warbler. By the middle of April, it has migrated north from Central America to spend the summer in the high elevations of the park. By mid-June this warbler has started nesting in the rhododendrons. Such low-growing shrubs are perfect for chestnut-sided warblers, which usually place their nests within four feet of the ground. The nests are constructed of fine strips of vines, shredded weeds, down, and fibers, lined with grasses and animal hairs. Caterpillars, moths, grasshoppers, and spiders make up their meals. A wide chestnut-colored stripe and yellow head mark this warbler. Its song is described as *please, please, pleased to meetcha.*

The chestnut-sided warbler is one bird that has actually benefited by forest clearing. It was considered rare in the 19th century; John James Audubon saw only one during his travels. But as virgin trees were cut in the East, its preferred shrubby, second-growth areas became more plentiful, and now chestnut-sided warblers are common.

There are many good reasons for preserving the enigmatic balds of the Smokies, aside from the intangibles they afford: a sense of freedom and breathing room not obtainable in the forest. They provide hunting grounds for ravens, rattlesnakes, and foxes. They are habitat for rare and endangered plants. And they provide a historical snapshot of the Smokies as the mountain pioneers knew them.

5

Going to the Water
Streams of the Smokies

The Cherokee Indians have a prayer called "Going to the Water." It is the focus of perhaps the most impressive of all their ceremonies, performed only on the most special occasions — birth, death, in preparation for the green corn dance, or in requests for a long life. The person who offers the prayer stands beside a flowing stream at dawn, facing east. The prayer is to Long Man, the personification of running water, whose origins are a water seep.

For worshipers of water, the Smoky Mountains are heaven. More than 2,000 miles of swift, clear streams, decorated with dancing waterfalls, course through the forests. The sight and sound of running water are never far away.

The streams sculpt the mountains, feed the forest, and sustain wildlife. They are the veins that carry more than half of the 890 billion gallons of water that fall on the Smokies each year. The remaining portion of the precipitation evaporates, seeps into the spongy ground to be stored as groundwater and to emerge as springs, or is taken up by plants and transpired from their leaves to help form the bluish haze that gives the Smoky Mountains their name.

The streams' erosive powers have inscribed the present ridge-and-valley topography of the Smokies. From spring-fed headwaters in the highest ridges, the streams tumble rapidly down the mountains, cutting deep valleys, or hollows, between the ridges. The drainage pattern of the Smokies has been described generally as "coarse," meaning the drainages are not closely spaced. From above, the park's stream systems form branches that resemble a tree, with each tributary a branch. This dendritic (treelike) pattern is most characteristic on the east side of the mountains. A second pattern, called trellis drainage, is evident to the west. Trellis drainage is characterized by streams that parallel the ridges, except in short stretches where they break through the ridges.

Different rock types have dictated these drainage patterns. To the east, crystalline rocks of uniform hardness are responsible for the dendritic pattern; to the west, the ridges are of sedimentary rocks, some soft, some hard. Streams have established their courses on the softer rocks and have cut gorges parallel to the ridges, setting up the trellis pattern.

Each stream drains a relatively small area, averaging about 200 square miles. But their gradients are exceptionally steep — in the headwaters some streams drop as much as 2,000 feet per mile. The gradient lessens through the middle courses of the streams, and by the time they reach flat lands, their gradient — and their flow — decreases considerably.

Forty-five watersheds have been identified within the boundaries of the park. The largest ones include Little River, which heads on Clingmans Dome and flows down the north side of the mountains and out of the park into Fort Loudoun Lake on the Tennessee River. The Big Pigeon River flows along the eastern boundary of the park. Abrams Creek and the East, Middle, and West Prongs of the Little Pigeon drain a significant portion of the Tennessee side of the park. The beautiful Oconaluftee River (from the Cherokee word *Ekwanulti*, "place-by-the-river") flows through the heart of the North Carolina side of the park. All the streams and rivers flow northwestward into the Tennessee, Little Tennessee, or French Broad rivers. Every drop of rain that falls in the Smokies eventually ends up in the Gulf of Mexico, to return one day in the form of rain or snow or fog from a gulf-born storm.

The word *stream* is a hydrologic term rarely applied to watercourses in these mountains. Here they are branches and prongs, with colorful names like Scratch Britches Creek, Gnatty Branch, and Fish Camp Prong. As important to the mountaineers as the branches and prongs are the springs. They treasure the "bold" springs, those that deliver a constant, pure supply of drinking water. And they know too which ones are "fittified," with unreliable flows. People who once called the Smokies home still come back to fill their jugs at the bold springs. The powers of that good, clear mountain water, many believe, can bring a person a long and healthy life.

The abundant precipitation that drenches these mountains also means that floods are a fact of life. Records in old family Bibles and notches on the pillars of grist mills furnish evidence of some of the big ones. One of the great floods of all time in East Tennessee came in 1867. Another occurred in 1875, and still another in 1928. And then there was the infamous flood of 1951. It had been a hot day, the first of September, and at 5:45 p.m. a cloudburst hit Mount LeConte. Four inches of rain fell in an hour. Marble-sized hailstones pelted the ground, and hikers were marooned overnight. The transmountain highway across the park was washed out in five places, the Alum Cave Trail was demolished, and landslides washed out two bridges in the Sugarlands area.

While newspapers report the immediate, disastrous damage wrought by floods, a longer-term view shows that periodic flooding is as much a part of the mountains as the trees and the flowers. The brown, foaming freshets scour the streambeds and deposit fertile floodplain soils. The organic debris delivered by spring floods may be especially well-timed. It is deposited in the streams just as the forest litter that entered the previous autumn has been exhausted.

The water quality in most Smokies streams is good. In a study in 1977 and 1978, most of the major drainages in the park were tested for a wide range of chemical and biological characteristics, among them pH (acidity), dissolved oxygen, temperature, discharge, and nitrate concentrations.

The study showed that seasonal changes in water temperature, an extremely important variable in any stream ecosystem, closely followed changes in air temperature. Water temperatures changed rapidly in April and October, with little change through summer and in midwinter. Stream discharge generally decreased through the summer, dropping to minimums in September and reaching maximums in March, the month of greatest rainfall.

Corresponding seasonal changes in water quality are probably related to changes in temperature and discharge. Summer, the growing season in the forest, is also the time of greatest evapotranspiration (water lost through evaporation from the soil and transpiration from plants). Water is retained longer in soil during this time, resulting in reduced streamflow and a lower water table. The more time water spends in the ground in contact with soil and bedrock, the longer there is for chemical reactions, and the more concentrated minerals become in the water. In contrast, when water flushes through the ground quickly, as with the high discharges at higher elevations or during floods, there is less time for chemical reactions to occur.

Geology has a great deal to do with water quality. The nature of the rock is critical to the dissolved minerals found in streams. Streams flowing through the Great Smoky Group, mainly quartz and feldspars that do not weather readily, have extremely low concentrations of dissolved minerals. The Anakeesta Formation, however, contains significant quantities of pyrite and other sulfides that dissolve to form sulfuric acid. Streams flowing through the Anakeesta, found at the higher elevations, thus are more acidic.

Geology also explains the near absence of lakes and ponds in the Smokies. Except for a few sinkholes and a couple of swamps and bogs, there is hardly a stationary body of water anywhere in the park. Because glaciers never reached these mountains, no depressions were gouged out to hold standing water.

The ecological dynamics of lakes and ponds differ distinctly from those of streams and rivers. In scientific terminology lakes are *lentic*, a word that means slow or calm. Streams are *lotic*, or moving. Streams change character as they move from higher to lower elevations. As streams pass through different forest types, the degree of shading by plants changes, which in turn affects water temperature. The standing water in a lake takes up heat, while the moving water of a stream dissipates it. Thus, lakes are warmer, streams cooler.

The animals and plants that live in streams have adapted to the movement of food and water. Stream animals tend to live on the bottom and have flattened or streamlined bodies. They anchor themselves by suckers, claws, or webs. Some species face into the current, so they can catch food drifting by. Aquatic insects may themselves become part of stream drift should they need to escape a predator. A large group of salamanders has adapted to the current by getting rid of lungs, which reduces their buoyancy and keeps them from floating away.

A stream and a forest have an intimate marriage that involves give and take on both sides. Streams not only carry things away from the forest, such as sediment, but they also give back minerals as organic matter decomposes in them. Unlike lakes, streams produce little food for the animals that live in them. Instead, the forest feeds the stream; bacteria, nutrients, and sediments wash in from soil, and insects and leaf litter fall in from overhanging trees. These provide detritus and food for aquatic animals. In autumn in the deciduous forest, there is a sudden influx of organic material into the streams in the form of millions of tons of leaves falling from the trees. Microorganisms, the base of the stream ecosystem, immediately attack this leaf litter, taking up nitrogen. This explains why autumn is the time of lowest nitrate concentrations in streams. The nitrogen in streams begins to increase again as decomposition progresses.

As in the forest and the soil, layers exist in a freshwater stream. On the stream bottom is rock, sand, gravel, silt, or boulders. The various sizes and character of this substrate determine the kinds of animals that can live and breed there.

After a long absence, beavers have returned to a few streams in the low elevations in the Smokies.

Dave Murrian, courtesy Tennessee Wildlife Resources Agency

Along with the animals of the substrate grow plants, mostly algae and mosses. Mosses, or bryophytes (from the Greek word for moss), likely evolved from algae. They are small green plants with tiny, leafy stems. Though they lack flowers and a network of veins or vascular bundles, mosses do make their own food through photosynthesis. Mosses are anchored not by true roots but by branched filaments called rhizoids.

Mosses require water for reproduction. The male and female organs are produced by a leafy green gametophyte, the moss plant itself. Sperm swim through water or moisture to reach the female egg and fertilize it. From this union, the stella and capsule of the sporophyte grow, depending entirely on the female gametophyte for nutrition. When the spores in the capsule are ripe, a raindrop or insect knocks off the capsule's protective cap, and a cloud of spores is released. These are then dispersed by wind or animals. When a moss spore lands on moist earth, it swells and bursts and puts forth a slender thread that quickly branches and spreads. Buds appear, which eventually develop into leafy shoots, and a new moss gametophyte is born.

Mosses are pioneers of the botanical world. They establish themselves where more complex plants cannot. Unlike flowering plants, which need sunlight, mosses do well in shade. Coolness and abundant precipitation are, in fact, conducive to their growth. If bare ground is temporarily exposed in a damp climate, mosses will appear.

Though mosses are largely terrestrial, some are confined to water. A group called the water mosses thrives in fresh water, attached to sticks, stones, or slender, floating stems and branches. Their spore cases are oval or cylindrical, with cone-shaped lids immersed in leaves at their base. The fountain mosses *(Fontinalis)* grow on rocks in cool running water. The golden or yellowish green flaccid stems, frequently a foot long, give these plants their name. Another, with the haunting name of torn veil moss *(Rhacomitrium),* lives around waterfalls or wet rocks in mountain streams. It grows on stones in tufts of close, flat patches. These mosses are dull, dark green above, and black or brownish near the point where they are attached to stones. The oblong or cylindrical spore case stands erect on the seta, the slender, bristly stalk that appears to be part of the stem.

A few species of beard mosses *(Grimmia)* are found in streams. These small, dingy plants form conspicuous gray tufts, growing in dense cushions or large mats. The leaves are usually tipped with white hairs. The aquatic apple moss *(Philonotis)* prefers places where water drips, runs slowly, or flows over shallow, rocky streamfed springs. Cedar mosses are water lovers too, and are found clinging to rocks in streams. Mud and sand collect in them, providing nutrients for the plant. Metallic green plume mosses *(Fissidens)* form mats on wet, shady banks and rocks or float freely in water. Their stems are simple or only slightly branched, and the leaves grow opposite each other along the stem. A many-branched plume moss called maidenhair grows in mats on moist, shady ground, on wet rocks, and around tree roots. Its sharply pointed leaves shed water.

Living the Aquatic Life

Hidden in the tangled strands of moss lurk aquatic insects, most commonly mayflies, stoneflies, caddisflies, dobsonflies, and dragonflies. Aquatic insects account for a large amount of biomass in streams and are key links in the stream food web — they convert plants for use by other organisms and serve as major prey for fish, salamanders, and other stream-dwellers. Their presence and abundance, especially mayflies, stoneflies, and caddisflies, signals extremely good water quality. They can live only in streams that are well oxygenated.

Aquatic insects, each with its own particular habitat needs, partition the stream habitat. Free-living mayflies live in the strands of mosses; stonefly nymphs hide in the leaf pack; larger, predatory stoneflies cling to the undersides of big, flat rocks; dobsonfly nymphs inhabit bigger, faster waters; and dragonfly nymphs burrow in the streambanks.

Many aquatic insects are primitive animals. Ancestors of the modern stonefly and mayfly date to Permian times, 280 million years ago. Even then both had an aquatic nymphal form, an adaptation that gave them an advantage over insects of land and air — they could escape competition and crowding, elude predators, and withstand sudden changes in temperature. But an aquatic life requires meeting one huge challenge — getting air.

All insects possess a network of small air tubes that branch throughout their interior tissues. These tubes open to the atmosphere through small holes called spiracles. Air is admitted through the spiracles and is pumped by expansion and contraction of the insect's body. This basic air-breathing system had to be modified by water-dwelling larvae. Some insects have evolved gills, others tubes that can be projected above the surface of the water like snorkels.

Turn over nearly any rock in a Smokies stream and a nondescript brownish insect will scurry quickly from the sudden light. Likely the immature form, or nymph, of a stonefly or mayfly, it breathes by means of wispy gills that strain out oxygen from water. Mayfly nymphs, for example, have seven pairs of flat gills lining both sides of its abdomen.

Mayflies live a parochial existence. They are restricted to the watersheds where they hatch, and the nymphs may live for several years there. They eat small bits of organic matter, and are in turn eaten by foraging fish, amphibians, turtles, birds, and other water insects, often dragonfly nymphs.

Mayflies finally emerge from the nymphal form as adults with large transparent wings netted with veins. Two or three long "tail" filaments are a distinctive trait of this insect. Mayflies are unique in that the first winged form is not quite an adult. They must go through one more molt before achieving full adulthood.

They emerge in legendary swarms, but live only briefly. The lifespan of an adult mayfly is one or two days at most. This ephemeral life has given name to the order of insects to which they belong, Ephemeroptera. Mayflies do live long enough to fulfill their highest function: mating. The nuptial flight usually occurs over water late in the day. As author Peter Farb describes this event: "From a cloud of males, one darts out and seizes a female. The female is a reproductive machine, filled with eggs from the tip of its abdomen to the rear of its head. These it casts upon the water, and then drops listlessly to the surface." The morning after a swarm is a sad sight — thousands of dead mayflies litter the shore. The eggs the female casts upon the water survive in the stream, however, with the aid of an adhesive disk at the end of fine threads.

Stonefly nymphs have long, flat bodies adapted to life in the stream current. Like mayflies, some stonefly nymphs possess gills, but they are at the base of the thorax near the legs rather than on the abdomen. Stoneflies lack the two- or three-part tails of mayflies, but have long cerci (sensory appendages) and antennae on their heads. When full grown, usually in summer, stonefly nymphs climb out onto a rock in the stream to molt. The empty husks of the nymphs' bodies commonly are found on rocks and in trees along the streams. Though adult stoneflies possess wings, they are poor fliers and don't go far from water. Those that appear in summer generally have weak mandibles and do not feed. As with mayflies and caddisflies, adult stoneflies are, in the words of one author, "just breeding machines."

Caddisfly larvae, which look like caterpillars, are the architects of the aquatic insect world. Many species build elaborate cases for shelter, and each species has its own style of case. First the larva wraps itself in a tube of silk, spun much as a moth caterpillar produces silk for a cocoon. The caddisfly larva then incorporates leaves, twigs, sand, or pebbles, glued or held together with more silk. The shapes of the cases are elegant: some resemble snails or trumpets, others look like fishing nets.

Body half out but securely attached to the case by its own set of grappling hooks, the caddisfly larva drags itself over plants and stones in the stream as it feeds. The net-builders point the wide end of the funnel-shaped net upstream to snare prey as it floats by in the current. Once a feeding territory has been staked out, the larva sits at the mouth of the net like a hockey goalie, defending its domain from intruders. Most caddisfly larvae eat plants, though some prey on mayfly and stonefly nymphs.

When the larva is full grown, it closes its case and pupates inside. When fully developed, the pupa cuts away the case, crawls onto a rock, and molts into an adult. The four-winged, mothlike insects are erratic fliers, moving about mostly at night.

One of the most commonly seen stream insects is the water strider. Most of its days are spent sculling on the surface of the water, usually in backwaters where it won't be swept downstream. Water striders winter underwater and surface in spring to mate. They lay eggs on rocks or logs under water. When they hatch, the nymphs must break through the surface film of the water before coming out to molt and feed. They undergo five molts, each lasting about a week, before becoming full-fledged adults.

I can while away hours watching water striders paddling on a stream. They can remain on the surface because of tiny water-repellant hairs lining the tips of their legs. In addition, their claws are located high on their legs where they will not break the surface tension.

The strider's movements are a slow glide or a quick jump. From sensory organs in the legs, a strider detects vibrations of nearby insects. It jumps on its prey, uses its two short front legs to grab the insect, then injects a

Water striders are common insects that scull on the surface of many streams in the park.

liquid that stuns and dissolves it. Water striders themselves are seldom eaten; apparently they taste horrible.

Caddisflies, stoneflies, mayflies, and other aquatic animals play specialized roles in the stream ecosystem. Some are shredders, cutting up leaves and other organic material in the stream with their mandibles. Others are collectors, including some mayfly nymphs that sweep in debris with hairs on their legs, caddisfly larvae that spin webs underwater, and clams that pump water and food through their bodies with a siphon system. Scrapers, of which snails are the best example, scoop up microscopic algae from rock. Piercers, most notably certain caddisfly larvae, have mouthparts that allow them to suck fluids from algae.

Moving up the stream food chain we encounter salamanders, animals with which the Smokies are particularly blessed. The formidable hellbender, a completely aquatic salamander that can grow to 20 inches in length, has been found in most of the larger streams in the park below 2,500 feet. Another salamander that is entirely stream-dwelling (and found only in streams in the southern Appalachians) is the shovelnose salamander. Park biologist Willis King collected the first shovelnose specimen in Abrams Creek in 1937. A wide-ranging species, shovelnose salamanders have since been found in nearly all watersheds at all elevations in the park.

The shovelnose *(Leurognathus marmoratus)* is a shy, sluggish, lungless salamander, about 3 $\frac{1}{2}$ to 5 $\frac{1}{2}$ inches long. It bears a resemblance to dusky and blackbelly salamanders, with a dark brown back with light blotches. Its flat skull gives it its common name. These salamanders lay their eggs in May and June, and the female stays with the eggs until they hatch in September and October. Shovelnose salamanders spend a minimum of 23 months as larvae. When they are about an inch long, they metamorphose. It may be five or six years before the females can reproduce.

To indicate just how complex — and unpredictable — food webs can be, consider this. Normally, shovelnose salamanders prey on stonefly nymphs, positioning themselves where currents cause insects to drift within their grasp. In an aquarium experiment, however, the reverse occurred. Stonefly nymphs killed immature shovelnose salamanders captured from Smokies streams, then ate their legs. Perhaps the aquarium provided better opportunity for the reversal of roles, but some insects do normally prey on vertebrates in streams. These include fisher spiders, which feed on fish, and water tigers, predaceous diving beetles, that eat tadpoles and small fish.

Crayfish often are the meat and potatoes of the stream. This freshwater relative of the lobster has received attention from naturalists for a long time. A recent Smithsonian Institution bibliography of the crayfish "from Socrates until 1985" numbered more than 400 pages. In it was listed one of the greatest classics on crayfish, Thomas Henry Huxley's *The Crayfish: An Introduction to the Study of Zoology,* first published in 1880. Anyone wading in a stream in the Smokies, barefoot and with crayfish nibbling on his toes, might, with Huxley in hand, become a novice zoologist.

The "river lobster" walks on the bottom of shallow waters on four pairs of legs. When mature, crayfish are about three or four inches long, dull greenish or brownish in color, with a hard exoskeleton. They breathe by means of feathery gills. To accommodate growth, the external skeleton, made of the same material as insect exoskeletons, is molted periodically in a fascinating process: the crayfish lies on its back and, over the course of

Though found at all elevations, raccoons are most common along streams at low elevations, where they eat salamanders and other aquatic creatures. Hickory and beech nuts and grapes are also favorite foods of these omnivores.

Tennessee Wildlife Resources Agency

a few hours, vigorously wriggles its body free of its cast, leaving the animal defenseless for a few days until a new exoskeleton grows back.

For most of the day, crayfish remain under cover in burrows excavated into streambanks. Toward evening they come out to feed along the streambed, darting under rocks at any sign of threat. Seated at the entryway to its burrow, the crayfish captures insect larvae, water snails, tadpoles, frogs, and even other crayfish as they pass near. Crayfish take in many times their weight in food, but after an early growth spurt, they grow very little.

During mating, males deposit sperm (Huxley ever so delicately called it "fecundating material") onto the female's thorax. The eggs she deposits become attached to the swimmerets beneath her tail. All winter, her movements aerate and wash the eggs in the water. In spring, females emerge from burrows carrying up to 200 of the berrylike eggs, which hatch in May or June. The mother's tail serves as a kind of nursery, where the young crayfish remain attached for a few days.

The dominant genus of crayfish in the southern Appalachians is *Cambarus.* This entire genus, in fact, has its center of origin in east Tennessee, possibly in the region's swift-flowing, highly oxygenated streams. Some crayfish have kept to the mountain brooks and riffles while others have adapted to the quieter waters of larger streams.

In the streams, the crayfish's major predators are fish. Beside the streams, frogs, raccoons, and otters seek them. Crayfish do have a defensive weapon: a pair of powerful pincers. Also, as salamanders and lizards can give up their tails to escape predators, the crayfish can readily sacrifice a limb and grow another.

Of course, fish are the aquatic creatures most people expect to find in streams. And Smokies streams are teeming with fish — 79 species, both native and non-native, have been collected from park waters. These include many species of minnows, chubs, daces, darters, shiners, sculpins, and suckers.

By far the most widespread and abundant native fish in the park is a minnow called the central stoneroller *(Campostoma anomalum).* Stonerollers are widely distributed over about two-thirds of the United States, from the Saint Lawrence River south to Alabama and as far west as Wyoming and Texas. Stonerollers are found in all streams in the park, up to about 3,000 feet in elevation. The very steep streams above that elevation are not their preferred habitat. In some streams, they outnumber and outweigh all other fish species combined.

These big minnows sometimes reach almost a foot in length. They are locally called hornyheads, for their highly developed nuptial tubercles, which are the most extreme of any of the minnows.

Stonerollers like to make nests in clean rubble and gravel stream bottoms. Schools of nest-building stonerollers will destroy the existing redds (nests) of rainbow trout. This competition for spawning beds means that where stonerollers are abundant, trout reproduction is severely reduced.

A large stream mammal, the beaver, suddenly reoccupied Great Smokies in 1966, after one or two centuries of absence. In the 1700s, they were found all over Tennessee, and in 1762 were reported common in the Little Tennessee River. But in the 1800s, heavy trapping for their pelts (beaver skin hats were then the height of fashion) wiped out the beaver in this area. By 1896, one observer said it was likely that none remained in east Tennessee. The beavers that suddenly reoccupied the park in 1966 came from western North Carolina, though the exact source is unknown. They expanded their range to the Tennessee side of the park, and signs of their activity and dam building have been found at several places in the park.

Beaver, however, cannot settle in the fast, steep streams found in most of the park. The streams they have reoccupied are the slower-moving streams at lower elevations. Even in these places they still cannot build dams very successfully, and instead they live in the streambanks. Only nine potential beaver dam sites have been identified in the park, along Abrams Creek in Cades Cove. Though reoccupation of original habitat by a native species is always encouraging, the total number of beavers is likely to remain low. Thus, the effects of beaver dams — warmer water and silting — are expected to be minimal, and the beavers will have little detrimental effect on woody plants, especially their favorites, flowering dogwood, tuliptree, and black birch. Benefits are likely, especially for river otters, which often reuse beaver dens.

River otters were also present in the past, but by 1936, the year the park was created, they were gone. Endangered in Tennessee, otters were reintroduced into the park in 1986 and in 1988 on Abrams Creek and the Little River. Bass, hogsuckers, and especially crayfish are important otter foods that are abundant in park streams.

Along most lower elevation streams in the park, belted kingfishers can easily be spotted perching watchfully on an overhanging sycamore branch. The kingfisher's scientific name, *Ceryle alcyon*, comes from Greek mythology. Alcyone (or Halcyon) was the daughter of Aeolus, god of the wind. Legend has it that Alcyone, in grief over the death of her husband Ceyx, threw herself into the sea and was transformed into a kingfisher.

These are fish-eating birds, with small fish such as stonerollers making up most of their diet. A pair of adults with six to eight young need to catch about 90 fish a day to sustain the family. Riffles well-stocked with fish are "prime real estate" for kingfishers, says one ornithologist. Kingfishers will also take crayfish, especially if a stream is silted from heavy rains and fish cannot easily be seen. Tadpoles, lizards, frogs, toads, newts, grasshoppers, butterflies, beetles, and, occasionally, berries also are eaten.

When a kingfisher spots food, it dives with deadly aim headfirst into the water, grabs the fish in its long, straight bill, and returns to its perch to bludgeon the fish to death on the branch. If the fish is not then fed to a young nestling, the adult will toss it into the air and gulp it down.

Belted kingfishers tend to be solitary except during nesting, when a monogamous pair excavates a tunnel in a sandy streambank. They may spend three weeks digging with their bills and feet until the nest burrow is up to seven feet long; it is usually more than four feet above the water, so the eggs and nestlings are well protected against flooding. The nest, lined with the scales and bones of fish, is placed at the end of the burrow. Anytime from April to July the female will lay six or seven white eggs, which are incubated for 23 days. The chicks, born naked and helpless, stay in the nest another 23 days.

Unlike most North American birds, the female belted kingfisher is more brightly colored than the male, with her reddish breastband. Both sexes have the dapper white collar and ragged blue-gray crest that make these large birds unmistakable. There are other signs of sex-role reversals in kingfishers as well —

White-barked sycamore trees grace streamsides in the Smokies.

females more aggressively defend feeding territories and nest sites, and they spend less time than the males tending to duties like building the nest, incubating the eggs, and feeding the young.

The sycamores in which kingfishers often perch are among the most beautiful trees in the Smokies. These trees spread their branches widely and gracefully over the streams, and their gnarled roots are often bared by constant water action. The sycamore's thin outer bark sloughs off in layers, giving the tree a mottled gray, green, and white color that makes the trunk look "patterned with sunshine," in Donald Culross Peattie's words. The flowers are not especially noteworthy on the sycamore, but the fruits are. They are large balls that hang on the tree all winter, accounting for the common name of buttonball. The minute seeds within the fruits are carried downstream and deposited on wet mud, where they germinate. Like other riverine trees in the park, such as common alder, box-elder, winged elm, sweetgum, and black willow, sycamores grow rapidly and are well adapted to survive the inherently unstable riverine environment.

A shrub called spicebush *(Lindera benzoin)*, a relative of sassafras, is also fairly common along streamsides. The large red berries produced by the plant in late summer and fall are rich in fat and are eagerly taken by birds such as the robins and other thrushes. For migrating birds, the fat-rich berries are a valuable source of food that will sustain them through their long-distance travels.

Spicebush takes its name from the spicy aroma released by the crushed leaves and twigs. That strong aroma comes from phenols, compounds that make the plant hard to digest. One caterpillar, however, the spicebush swallowtail, eats primarily spicebush leaves. These insects have developed a couple of sneaky ways to confound predators. The spicebush caterpillar has large "eyespots" on its head, which seem to confuse or startle potential predators. When it becomes an adult butterfly, the female spicebush swallowtail, a palatable species, mimics the unpalatable pipevine swallowtail and thus avoids being eaten by birds.

The streams of the Smokies draw me. I love nothing more than to sit with my back against a sycamore and watch the water dance around and past the huge boulders, to study the miniature plant world that sprouts among the sycamore's roots, to turn over rocks and find an insect living in its own world. I begin to understand why the Cherokees went to the water to pray.

Part Two
The Animals

6
Saving the "Spec"
Decline and Restoration of Brook Trout

In the swift, clear waters of a stream high in the Smoky Mountains, an annual autumn rite takes place. The surrounding hillsides are aflame with the reds, yellows, and oranges of maples, tuliptrees, and birches. Days are deliciously warm, nights frosty. Sensing the shortening days and colder water, brook trout know it is time to mate. The male has reached sexual maturity, and the female, now two years old, prepares to lay her eggs.

In the polished pebbles of the streambed she vigorously digs a small depression called a redd. She has sensed the best place to locate the redd, in gravel of just the right size and where there is an upwelling of water. Perhaps detecting a chemical signal from the female, the male begins courting, making passes over, under, and around her while fighting off other interested contenders.

When the pair is ready to spawn, the female stays in the redd, her fins spread against the stones. The male darts to her side and arches his body to hold her. Their mouths gape, and both visibly vibrate for a few seconds during spawning. In a perfectly timed meeting, he discharges milt, she her eggs.

For the next hour, the female methodically covers the eggs with an armor of gravel that will protect them against winter floods and ice. In spring, normally in early March, those eggs will hatch, and a new generation of brook trout will swim in the waters. The act of reproduction has fulfilled the highest mission of these animals — continuation of their kind. As the egg and sperm joined, the genetic information that says "brook trout" was passed on.

How much longer this autumn ritual will continue is uncertain for brook trout in the Smoky Mountains. The species has encountered a number of threats, so that now its survival in the streams of the southern Appalachians is precarious. What has happened to brook trout is a litany that can be read for other species as well. It concerns human acts, both reckless and well-meaning, sometimes undertaken in the absence of information about the highly tuned adaptations and needs of the fish.

The brook trout is a colorful fish, with distinct mottled or wormlike green markings on its back, bright red spots splashed on its sides, and black and white stripes on its lower fins and tail. Among mountain people, the red spots have earned the fish the common name of speckled trout, or "spec" for short.

A less visible characteristic, but one important in telling brook from brown trout, is what are called vomerine teeth. In brook trout these teeth are in a small patch at the front of a bone in the roof of the mouth, while in brown trout they are fully developed along the length of the bone.

The salmonids — trout, salmon, and char — probably originated 100 million years ago, though the oldest known fossil is a British Columbia specimen that lived 45 to 50 million years ago. Brook trout, *Salvelinus fontinalis*, are chars.

The brook trout is a truly North American species. Its range extends from Hudson Bay to New England and south along the Appalachian Mountains to northern Georgia. That range has been expanded by successful introductions into states west of the Mississippi River and as far away as South America, Africa, and New Zealand. Brook trout are the only members of the salmon family native to the eastern United States.

In the Smoky Mountains, brook trout were doing well at the beginning of the 20th century. They inhabited some 425 miles of streams at both higher and lower elevations, to as low as 1,600 feet. From 1903 through 1935, loggers ripped through nearly two-thirds of the watersheds

Great Smoky Mountains N. P.

in what is now the national park. Brookies suffered from logging activities in several ways.

The critical shade provided by trees over the streams was gone, allowing water temperatures to rise above what is optimum for brookies. The clearing of the forest, skidding operations, and ensuing fires let soil pour off the denuded hills, contributing loads of sediment that clogged the fishes' spawning grounds. Temporary splash dams were built on the streams to hold logs in a reservoir. Then the dams were blown up, and the mass of logs roared downstream, dislodging rocks and taking out prime trout habitat along the way.

Park streams were stocked with great numbers of non-native rainbow trout and a northern strain of brook trout during the 1930s. Fingerlings were raised in hatcheries in the park and carried to the streams in milk cans.

Early mountaineers didn't let the "spec" go unnoticed. They caught brook trout by the hundreds, using everything from simple cane poles to nets and dynamite. A dentist, it is said, once accepted payment of 200 brook trout, a day's catch, for services rendered.

In the face of logging and overfishing, the brookies retreated into the headwaters of the park, generally above 3,000 feet elevation, where logging activities had stopped or had never occurred. To keep the fishery

A park service employee electrofishes for brook trout in a Smokies stream. Electrofishing, which stuns fish but does not kill them, is used to capture and tag trout as part of the park's ongoing restoration work and genetics studies.

Rose Houk

alive, the logging companies and citizens started stocking the streams with trout. As early as 1910, rainbow trout were being placed in nearly every stream in the park. Milk cans full of fingerlings were dumped into the streams from railroad trestles and any other accessible point. After the park was established, the Park Service continued stocking trout, both rainbows and later a northern strain of brookies. Until 1947, a hatchery on Kephart Prong, with rearing stations at Cades Cove and the Chimneys area, furnished the fish.

The rainbows proved incredibly popular as a game fish and were successful at taking over former brookie streams. But the fish played a couple of tricks on the biologists. They had assumed that introduced rainbows would not be able to reproduce, but they did. Second, they thought brookies would move downstream and reoccupy former territory as the forest regrew after logging. But the brook trout did not.

The decline of brook trout in the Great Smokies has been steady since the early 20th century: in 1937 a park biologist showed a 55 percent decline in their range. An additional 15 percent shrinkage was documented by the mid-1950s. A survey of all the park streams from 1972 to 1977 found brook trout in only 123 miles of streams, while rainbow trout occupied nearly 80 percent of the thousand miles of trout waters in the park. To complicate the situation, another non-native trout, the brown, began to invade park waters from surrounding states by the mid-1950s and was reproducing in 50 miles of stream occupied by rainbows by the 1970s.

Some of the complex, intertwined reasons offered for the decline of the brook trout involve the biology of the fish. Brook trout grow slowly and generally are small (a trophy fish from mountain streams is seven inches long). Their life span is short; and none older than three years has been found in the park recently. Brook trout are also susceptible to many diseases.

Environmental conditions are another factor. In summer, the water temperature of streams in the Smokies ranges from 55 to 65 degrees Fahrenheit, which is optimum for brook trout. In winter, however, ice can build up in streams in the highest elevations, which may affect the survival of incubating trout eggs buried in sediment. Where brook trout and rainbows are present in the same area, brook trout may lay only 100 eggs per redd, compared to 800 by rainbows. Thus, any factor that may diminish egg supply could decrease brook trout numbers.

In spring, floods can roar down Smokies streams, muddying the water, scouring the channels, and affecting survival of young trout. Park streams are also slightly acidic. Brook trout can tolerate more acidity than other species, but their tolerance has limits. If acidity increases, dropping below a pH of 6.0, the fish may experience an imbalance of ions in their bodies, and eggs and embryos may die. Parasites such as flukes, various worms, and lice also kill fish. The combination of all these factors, rather than a single one, is likely helping to limit brook trout recovery.

The Major Suspect: Rainbow Trout

The major suspect in the brook trout decline is the introduced rainbow trout. These two species share similar food and habitat requirements. Are

Electrofishing for Brook Trout

It was not exactly a wilderness experience I was having this June morning. The generator drowned out the natural sounds of Rock Creek, a small stream near Cosby, Tennessee, and a blue cloud of diesel fumes wafted through the air. I slogged through pools and clambered over big boulders in the creek, following a crew of Park Service biologists who were electrofishing for brook trout.

One of the crew carried the generator on his back and probed the stream pools with two long-handled wands. Fish are attracted to the electrical charge at the end of the wands and are then stunned and netted. In a short time, 10 brook trout had been captured and dumped into a white plastic bucket. These fish would not be going back into the stream.

Back at the vehicles in the parking area, we began work. Stan Guffey, red bandana tied on his head, directed the process, writing notes on a clipboard. A piece of muscle tissue, an eye, and the liver of each trout were cut out and placed in individual test tubes and dropped in a cooler of liquid nitrogen.

Guffey, a doctoral student at the University of Tennessee at Knoxville, would take

they competing, and if so, for what? And does one have an advantage over the other?

The two often live in the same pools in a stream, but they use different parts of the pool. Brookies stay along the sides, sometimes facing downstream in quieter water with cover overhead. Rainbows, on the other hand, swim in the turbulent water near the heads of the pools.

Eggs of the fall-spawning brookies hatch in February or March. The young grow quickly, reaching about one and a half inches in length by mid-June. Rainbows spawn and hatch in the spring, and by September they have caught up with the brookies. By the following spring, rainbows have surpassed brookies in size. Any size advantage the brook trout may have enjoyed is quickly lost, and by adulthood the average rainbow is two to three inches longer and weighs 1.8 times more than the brookie.

Soon after they hatch, both species try to defend their territories. When rainbow and brook trout are the same size, brook trout can compete successfully in defensive encounters. But as the size difference increases, rainbows gain an advantage over brookies — that higher body weight may affect reproductive ability, social position in pools, or territory rights in riffles and runs.

The two species may also compete for food, because both eat many of the same things, mainly insects such as stoneflies, mayflies, and caddisflies. Brook trout, especially larger ones, also often feed on crayfish, which live on the bottom of streams.

the trout parts back to his lab. There he would look at certain enzymes in their DNA to determine the genetic makeup of the fish. Like many other researchers, Guffey maintains that southern brook trout are clearly different from the northern strain. What he wants to know, he says, is how different.

Watching the dissection of the brook trout made me uneasy, not because I'm especially squeamish but because I had a nagging feeling that I might be watching the last of a species sacrificed for science.

But in talking with Stan Guffey on the drive out to Rock Creek, I came to understand that he is working for the brook trout, not against it. The fish, the streams, and these mountains are too important to him. When he hikes, Guffey refuses to treat water from the creeks and springs in the Smokies. It is important to his soul, he says, to know that the water is still pure enough to drink untreated.

Perhaps the knowledge of what has happened to other species in the past gave rise to my uneasiness. It is no secret that brook trout in the southern mountains are in trouble. But recent park studies have found more pure southern brookies than were expected; perhaps the "spec" will make it.

Given the rainbow's competitive edge over brookies, park biologists decided to see what would happen if they removed rainbows from brook trout habitat and kept the two from mingling. One glimmering promise was the concept of barriers. Good-sized waterfalls along streams are believed to block the upstream movements of rainbows. Hence, the plan was to keep brookies upstream, rainbows downstream.

In 1976 the Park Service began brook trout restoration efforts on several park streams, most of which had waterfalls or cascades that were hoped-for barriers. The trout were removed by "electrofishing": A generator and motor are attached to two wands, one a negative electrode, the other positive. When electrical current flows to the electrodes in the water, the fish are stunned and can be easily netted.

Carrying backpacks loaded with 40 pounds of electrofishing equipment, biologists and volunteers went to streams where both brook and rainbow trout were present, on Road Prong and Taywa, Silers, Beetree, Sams, Starkey, and Desolation creeks. Both species were captured and tagged with fin clips. Rainbows were carried downstream of the barriers, and brookies were returned to the place of capture.

Ten years later, no rainbows were left on Taywa and Silers creeks. Even more encouraging was the finding that there were more and bigger brook trout in the streams. Electrofishing appears to work best on smaller streams 15 to 18 feet wide, but depending on the number of rainbows initially present, three to five years of continuous effort are needed to remove all of them. Results on the other streams were not as promising, possibly because the rainbows managed to negotiate the waterfalls after all. Or perhaps too few rainbows were removed from the brookies' sections.

Later research in the park showed that vertical falls of six and a half feet or higher seem to block upstream movement of the rainbows. Cascades are more complex. These sloped falls with jumbled boulders along their length may actually provide springboards for high-jumping rainbows. The barrier concept is especially significant because attempting to restore brook trout in streams with passable barriers is simply not worthwhile.

There is one more wrinkle in this complicated story, involving the strain of brook trout from New England that the Park Service stocked in Smokies streams in the late 1930s. Old-timers have long insisted that the "spec," the southern brook trout, is a different animal from its Yankee cousin. The southern brookies, they say, look different — bigger eyes, brighter red spots, longer fins and snout — and taste better. After doing genetic tests that involved grinding up trout organs in blenders, biologists concluded that the old-timers were right. Physical differences don't make a subspecies, but genetic differences do. The southern and northern brook trout are indeed distinct subspecies, possibly even different species.

For the brook trout, the question of its pedigree is more than a technicality. The Park Service is legally obliged to protect or reintroduce native species. If the southern brook trout is classified as a subspecies, it may also qualify for nomination as an endangered or threatened species under the federal Endangered Species Act. If the brook trout is "listed," its critical habitat would have to be protected and a plan devised to recover its populations.

Interest in brook trout is keen throughout the Southeast, where similar declines have been seen. State wildlife agencies in North Carolina, Georgia, and Tennessee are sharing in efforts to restore the fish, as are private groups, especially Trout Unlimited.

Only about 40 miles of Smokies streams are protected by functional barriers now. Park officials, pinning their hopes for the brook trout on identifying more true barriers, hope someday soon to be able to lift the moratorium on brook trout fishing in the park — in place since 1975 — and to restore a viable brook trout fishery in at least 100 miles of stream in the park.

7
Of Bears, Boars, and Chestnuts

"All words about the American Chestnut are now but
an elegy for it."
                              —Donald Culross Peattie

F olks in the Smokies used to say that if it was a good mast year, it
would be a cold winter. They noticed such things in fall, because
they fattened their hogs on "hard" mast, the nuts produced by chestnut,
oak, hickory, and beech trees. They would put bells on their sows and
let them run wild in the woods to eat their fill of the calorie-rich nuts.
"The acorns hit in the fall, and the chestnuts hit, and law, it wasn't no
trouble to drive in a big herd of fat hogs," recalls former Cades Cove
resident John McCaulley.

Happy hogs and weather forecasters are not the only ones who depend
on a good mast crop. Blue jays, squirrels, chipmunks, wild turkeys, and
black bears also pack away the nuts to build fat reserves to carry them
through the winter. One important constituent of the mast crop—
chestnuts—is now gone. All that is left of the American chestnut are
saplings and determined sprouts rising from old stumps.

The American chestnut, *Castanea dentata*, was one of the most important trees in the eastern deciduous forest. It grew from southern Maine across the upper Midwest as far as Wisconsin and Michigan, down through Indiana and Illinois and south to Alabama and Mississippi. In the Smokies, the chestnut was the monarch in cove hardwood, closed oak, and open oak-pine forests, growing at elevations up to 5,000 feet.

Creamy blossoms adorned the trees in June, and bur-covered seed pods held rich brown nuts. In some places, chestnuts accounted for more than a third of the forest cover and were equaled in size only by tuliptrees. One monster chestnut tree on the west slope of the Smokies measured 33 feet in circumference in 1859; another, just slightly larger, lived in 1915 on Big Creek in North Carolina.

For southern Appalachian people, the chestnut tree was more than a marvelous sight. Its straight-grained wood was ideal for cabin logs, furniture, split-rail fences, and even caskets. The nuts that fell to the ground were an important cash crop; families raked up chestnuts by the bushelful and took wagonloads of them to sell in nearby towns. They cooked chestnuts for themselves too, sometimes using a Cherokee recipe for cornmeal-wrapped chestnut dumplings.

A fungus rang the death knell for the American chestnut. First noticed by a forester in the Bronx Zoo in 1904, the fungus was unintentionally introduced, likely on Asian chestnut trees imported as nursery stock. Scientists call the fungus *Cryphonectria* (formerly *Endothia*) *parasitica*. Insects, birds, and the wind carry the sticky spores of this parasite long distances. The spores insinuate their way into cracks and wounds in the bark of the trees, forming orange-colored cankers. The fungus spreads into the inner bark and girdles the tree. Leaves above that point die, followed by limbs, and in two to ten years the entire tree is killed.

Though their Asian counterparts evolved with immunity, American chestnuts as yet display no resistance to the blight. Millions, some say billions, of American chestnut trees covering more than nine million acres have been killed by the blight since it was introduced.

The blight hit the Smokies around the mid-1920s, and by 1935 most of the chestnut trees were gone, except for a chestnut-silverbell stand on a few hundred acres on the ridge between Gregory Mountain and Ekaneetlee Gap in the western section of the park. Trees on Welch Bald were still producing a good crop of nuts in the fall of 1938, but by the early 1940s, no one harvested chestnuts in the Smoky Mountains. Fearing the dead trees would serve as lightning rods, the Civilian Conservation Corps cut them down in the park.

The big gap left in the forest by the death of this major species was filled primarily by chestnut oaks, red oaks, and red maples. By the late 1950s, there were no healthy chestnut trees in the Smokies, no signs that the species had acquired any immunity to the blight, and little hope that the source of the fungus could be removed.

Still, people have refused to give up on the American chestnut. As if to echo that human hope, the trees themselves seem unwilling to succumb to the blight. Though they may be dead above ground, many chestnut trees maintain living roots from which green sprouts grow. Healthy chestnut sprouts and seedlings can be seen in many places in the Smokies, but eventually they are killed by the blight. Though not immune to the blight, the sprouts nevertheless contain genetic information necessary for experiments aimed at breeding resistant trees.

Today, the Great Smoky Mountains National Park is working with several other organizations and agencies to develop such a breeding program. Flowering American chestnut sprouts from the park are grafted onto resistant Chinese chestnuts and hybrid trees. The offspring of this union are then backcrossed with the Chinese chestnut.

A potentially more promising development has been the discovery of a weak (hypovirulent) strain of the blight — essentially a "blight of the blight" that spreads through trees in the wild, weakens the original blight, and lets the trees survive. This hypovirulent strain was first found in the European chestnut species, but tests in Connecticut and Michigan have shown that it also appears to be spreading in American chestnuts.

What made the chestnut so valuable as a mast tree was that it yielded prolific crops every year, while oaks produce acorns only sporadically. In some years, acorns literally rain down from the trees, while in other years the crop is a failure. In lean mast years, especially, competition for food among wildlife may be fierce. Not only do native animals such as black bears find less mast available, when it is available they must compete with an introduced species, the wild boar, which consumes huge amounts of acorns in the fall.

Wild Boars

Thirteen proved a very unlucky number for Great Smoky Mountains National Park in 1912. That was how many European wild boars were shipped to Murphy, North Carolina, in that year. The boars were imported for a private game preserve on Hooper Bald, about 15 miles south of the present boundary of Great Smoky Mountains National Park. Brought in along with the boars by ox-drawn wagon was a Noah's ark of other animals: 8 buffalo, 14 elk, 6 mule deer, 34 bears, 200 wild turkeys, and 10,000 ring-necked pheasant eggs.

In 1920, more than a hundred boars escaped from a 500-acre enclosure and went forth and multiplied. A convicted poacher who hunted in the park for 27 years has said the first boars were seen on the North Carolina side of the park in Bone Valley around 1946 to 1948. In 1958, he went on, hunters on the Tennessee side of the park became interested in hunting "hogs," as they are known locally.

In 1958, Herrick Brown, president of the Smoky Mountains Hiking Club, reported that he and his wife had seen a baffling sight on a hike in the Blockhouse Mountain area. At Haw Gap, Herrick wrote, the ground had been torn up "by some sort of grubbing operation." He thought it may have been bears, but then noticed that the sod had been removed. Two years earlier the area had been a beautiful meadow, but on this visit they could barely find a "patch of grass large enough to camp on." A year later, efforts to control wild boars began in the park and have continued at varying levels for more than 30 years.

The wild boar, though the same species as the domestic pig, *Sus scrofa*, differs physically. The wild boar has bristly, pronged fur, a wedge-shaped head, and small, pointed, hairy ears. Its hooves are narrower and its legs longer. Boars are successful animals on all fronts — they are omnivorous feeders, fast breeders, quick learners, and evasive prey.

They have invaded from west to east in the park, advancing on average a mile and a half each year. And they've made quite a mess along the way. In their quest for food, wild boars plow through the park like rototillers, greatly disrupting plants and soil. Signs of these mobile, wide-ranging animals have been found at all elevations and forest types in the Smokies.

An average-sized, 125-pound boar can eat 1,300 pounds of mast in six months. From September through February, boars pretty much depend on hard mast, primarily oak and hickory nuts. When mast is available, it makes up 60 to 85 percent of their diet. When it is not available, wild pigs turn to other foods. In their stomachs have been found beetles, snails, fly larvae, and a host of other insects, seven species of salamanders (including Jordan's salamander, found only in the Smokies), two species of reptiles, and two species of mammals. They will also eat the eggs of wild turkey and grouse, and there are a handful of reports that they have killed fawns. Favorite plant foods are wild yams and the underground corms of spring-beauties. The bulbs and roots of trilliums, violets, trout-lilies, and orchids are also boar delicacies.

Wild boars move with the seasons. In winter, they tend to stay in the lower elevations, among oak-pine and tuliptree forests. In April, they migrate up to the northern hardwoods, then move back down again in the fall as the acorns drop. Wild boars forage on grassy balds both summer and

Non-native wild boars entered Great Smokies from a North Carolina wildlife preserve in the early 1900s. They have been the target of a control program ever since, because of the damage their rooting causes to native plant and wildlife species.

Great Smoky Mountains N.P.

winter. Their movements are tied not only to food supplies but also to temperature. Their short bristly hairs provide little insulation against extremes of heat and cold.

Boars are fecund animals. They can breed year-round, producing an average of five piglets in a litter; occasionally a female may bear two litters a year. Thus, 100 females potentially can produce 400 piglets. Large predators are rare, and survival rate of the young is high.

Population size and reproductive success of wild boars appear to be tied directly to each year's mast crop. In one year following moderate acorn production, 60 litters were produced per 100 females; in two good mast years, 73 and 59 litters were produced. In one year in which the mast crop was a failure, however, only 13 litters per 100 females resulted. But because of their exceptional reproductive abilities, boars recover in a year or two from such declines.

Though boars are difficult to find in the Smokies because of the rough terrain and the nature of the beast, rooting damage can be used as an index for their numbers. Park biologists have estimated anywhere between 1,000 and 2,000 animals in the park.

The ill effects of boar rooting have been well documented. Up to 80 percent of the ground cover, and the understory up to four or five feet, has been disturbed on some sites. The most extensive rooting is in the northern hardwoods. Here beech grow in gaps (or passes), in communities unique to the southern Appalachians. They are the highest-elevation broad-leaf forests in the East, and damage to them is of great concern. Especially worrisome is boar rooting in wet areas that offer special habitats for animals and rare plants. Hog rooting around streams and springs causes soil erosion and silting of streams. Redback voles and shorttail shrews, which live in the leaf litter of the forest floor, have been nearly eliminated where boars intensively rooted.

Such ecologically inappropriate behavior has earned wild boars the status of Public Enemy Number One in Great Smokies. The park's first control efforts, which began in 1959, were concentrated mainly in areas accessible by roads. Some boars were trapped and removed to other areas, and others were shot ("direct reduction," in bureaucratese). In 1976, efforts were intensified and extended into the backcountry of the park.

By this time, however, the park's wild boar management activities had become entwined in what one Park Service official called "an intricate web of biopolitics." That web soon became more entangled in 1977, when the Park Service announced it had decided the best way to totally eradicate wild boars in the park was by bringing in a professional hunter and his dogs. The uproar among sport hunters and locals, for whom the boar is a popular game animal and a source of meat, was loud and hostile. Many wanted the park open to public boar hunts, while others decried the waste of meat when boars were killed and left on the ground.

The controversy led to an eight-month moratorium on killing hogs in the park. A management plan was written, the moratorium was lifted in the spring of 1978, and the park hired a local hunter who was successful in trapping a number of hogs.

A committee of outside scientists called in to review the park's boar management determined that "the European wild boar is firmly established in the Great Smoky Mountains National Park and its eradication would be highly impractical, if not impossible." The fight against the wild boar in the Smokies would go on forever.

Though scientists admitted that complete eradication did not seem feasible, they did recognize that boars are "the most biologically and politically important problem" facing the park. They favored any program that would "depopulate" the species and thus reduce the damage they cause. They recommended that park managers set priorities by considering carefully the timing, extent, and location of boar damage, and determining what type and extent of control was warranted.

Control efforts were then concentrated in summer on the high-elevation beech gaps and ridgetops, where sexually mature female hogs concentrate. North Carolina hunters were still not happy. One Graham County man declared that the wild boar should no longer be considered exotic. In his view it had become fully naturalized in the mountains and "as a result thereof has acquired full and complete rooting rights in perpetuity." In 1981 another moratorium was placed on shooting hogs, this time only on the North Carolina side of the park. Instead, a force of citizen volunteers was organized and allowed to trap and remove as many hogs as possible. Animals were transported and released in national forests in North Carolina.

Some biologists have suggested that in the battle of the boars, poor mast years might be a benefit. When acorns are scarce, hog reproduction

Bear 160's Strange Adventure

Sweat beaded on Kim DeLozier's forehead, and he threw quick glances at the clock on the wall. DeLozier and his assistants were performing a "workup" on a young male black bear. The bear had been caught at the Chimneys picnic area the night before, and had been brought into the wildlife building in a green culvert trap.

That morning DeLozier walked in carrying a black briefcase and a flashlight. He checked on the bear, huddled in the back of the trap. When anyone came near, the bear snapped his jaws and lunged. DeLozier then injected the bear with an immobilizing drug, and in less than five minutes the bear was asleep in the cage. He was laid out on an old metal stretcher and rolled into the air-conditioned room where DeLozier donned surgical gloves and proceeded with the workup.

Even tranquilized, the bear's eyes stayed open; to keep them from drying out, they were lubricated with a salve. Then a round numbered tag was clamped onto his left ear. The same number, 160, was tattooed in his lip, a number that would forever identify him. The bear's temperature was found to be normal, 101 degrees. Blood samples were drawn, and an upper premolar was pulled for later investigation of the bear's age. Finally, the bear was weighed (96.8 pounds) and measured (141 inches long). DeLozier continued

is down, the animals are not in top physical condition, and they tend to stay at lower elevations longer. Control efforts could be concentrated during this time, when removal would be easier.

To improve trapping success, the grandly named Hog Bait Enhancement Research Project has tried to find out what bait would most attract boars to traps. Corn flavored with beer, spoiled milk, strawberry, and walnut were all tried, along with whole wheat and apples. As may be appropriate for boars in the southern mountains, corn mash was their preference.

Chemical and biological substances that might attract boars to traps have also been discussed. Truffles, fungi used by hunters in Europe to attract boars, contain a substance present in the saliva of male hogs searching for mates. This may hold promise for luring estrus females to traps. Other chemical and biological controls, such as sterilizing agents or disease pathogens, have been rejected so far; such methods often are not species-specific and can spread beyond park boundaries.

Another control method being used on a limited basis is fencing out hogs. These "exclosures" have been used primarily on small, sensitive sites in the beech forest and along Abrams Creek. I came upon one that spans the Appalachian Trail between Indian Gap and Newfound Gap. It was a curious, not especially aesthetic structure to find in the middle of the to check the time. In about half an hour the tranquilizer would begin to wear off.

The technique I observed was begun in the Chimneys picnic area in 1991. It involved capturing "night-active" bears, those believed to still have a healthy fear of humans but that are nevertheless rifling garbage cans at night. The bears undergo the medical workup and are then released at the same site where they were found.

The workup gives biologists valuable data on the bears, but the main idea, says DeLozier, is that a bear will find the capture and workup such a negative experience that it will not return to the place where it encountered such unpleasantness. The biologists hope to prevent these animals from becoming hardened "day-active" bears that might have to be relocated. The lifespan of a relocated bear is usually cut nearly in half.

By 11:00, Bear 160 was on his way back up to the Chimneys picnic area. As soon as the trap door was opened, the bear bounded up the hillside, back into the forest where he belonged. DeLozier stopped and patiently explained the new procedure to a curious family standing nearby. He freely admitted that "we're just guessing what's happening" with this new procedure.

It promised to be a busy summer for Kim DeLozier and other park wildlife biologists. The next morning two more trapped bears waited to be worked up and released, perhaps to live a longer life than they might have otherwise.

trail, but it has appeared to have some positive effect. Plant recovery has been rapid when hogs are excluded. Fencing the entire park boundary has been proposed to keep out boars, but the cost would be prohibitive, and it would not solve the problem of those boars already present and reproducing in the park.

Another possible control, though its effects are still largely speculative, is introduction or reintroduction of large predators that might prey on boars. Sightings of mountain lions have been on the rise in the park in recent years, and recently reintroduced red wolves have killed a wild hog. Coyotes began to enter the Smokies in the 1980s, and hog hair has been found in coyote scat.

The total number of hogs removed each year, both by trapping and hunting, is evidence of some success. In 1986, 1,100 boars were taken; in 1987, 700; and in 1988, 375. In 1991 a low of 254 was reported. By the summer of 1992, the number was approaching 300 hogs taken. Park officials now estimate the total boar population in the park at "well under" a thousand animals. Whether the numbers indicate actual decreasing numbers of hogs or lack of success hunting and trapping them is open to question. There has also been a decline in rooting damage, however, a hopeful sign that perhaps a dent has been made in the wild boar population in Great Smokies.

Black Bears

Scientists lack firm evidence that competition occurs among animals for mast, but they say it could be happening. One hunter has supplied his observations, albeit anecdotal, that boars do compete with black bears for food. "What bears likes, hogs likes," he said. "A hog will eat almost anything," including beechnuts, acorns, hickory nuts, pine roots, grapes, even snakes. When they climb trees to get food, he said, bears inadvertently shake down food that the hogs eat. Hogs will even drive bears away from food; he witnessed a 250-pound boar drive away a bear from an oak tree.

The black bear, *Ursus americanus,* is for many people the symbol of the Smoky Mountains. The park is the center of the bears' range in the southern Appalachians, providing a sanctuary and nursery ground for them. In the Smokies, these forest-dwellers reach their highest density on the continent, a bear every one or two square miles. The total bear population in the park's 800 square miles is estimated at 400

Black bears are born in the winter den. The cubs emerge in spring with their mother, ready to eat and learn how to survive.

Great Smoky Mountains N.P.

to 600 animals. But as with wild boars, the terrain and difficulty of access make exact numbers hard to come by.

Bears have been studied extensively in the Smokies, and much has been learned about them. To gather much of this information, biologists have trapped, tranquilized, tagged, and tattooed bears. Radio transmitters have been attached to collars so bears could be tracked.

Here is some of what we know as a result of this work. Black bears in the Smokies *are* black. In other parts of their range, they can vary in color from a cinnamon phase to white. Bears are large here, about six feet tall when standing; an average-sized female bear weighs about as much as an average woman, between 120 and 130 pounds. Males weigh up to 200 or 240, though some heavier bears have certainly been found. Bears have keen senses of smell and hearing, and their eyesight may not be as bad as lore has it. They are superb climbers. In the Smokies, black bears mate in the summer and soon thereafter begin to select den sites.

Female bears in the Southeast usually den in cavities high in mature trees. In January or February, a litter of two or three cubs (sometimes one or four), is born while the mother is still in winter sleep in her den.

A newborn black bear cub weighs nine to twelve ounces, and up to four pounds when it comes out of the den. Cubs are born with their eyes closed and without teeth; their eyes open within a month or month and a half. Mother will stay close and train them through the summer and fall. The family does not break up until the following spring, when the mother once again emerges from the den. After that, the yearlings are ready to find their own dens.

Sometime between March and May the bears shiver, shake their giant heads, and emerge from their dens. The female climbs down from her den high in a tree, with her nursing cubs. She stays close to the den for several days, keeping a protective eye on her young. Males have preceded them from their own separate dens on the ground. Almost as predictably as the blooming of the trillium, each spring an orphaned cub will be brought into park offices for rearing. Finding the cub an irresistible creature, someone will bottle-feed it. Sometimes the cub lives, sometimes not.

Bears come out of their dens lean and hungry. They haven't eaten all winter and have lost a third of their body weight. Because few nutritious foods are available in spring, they live off fat stored during the fall, waiting until the serviceberries begin to ripen. They do eat green grass or squawroot, a nubby parasitic plant, but spring is a tough time for bears. If a sow is in bad straits herself, she is not able to keep up with the nutritional needs of her young. In spring, bears search for food mainly in early morning and early evening, bedding down through most of the daytime hours and keeping to a small home range.

Life for the bears takes on a new tone in summer. This is a time of fortune, and sometimes misfortune. More and more food is becoming available and plentiful, including all kinds of berries, which may make up 40 percent of the bears' diet in summer. These omnivorous mammals will also eat ants, beetles, yellow jackets, and various small mammals. In summer, bears are expanding their home ranges, males are searching for eligible females, and yearlings are separating from their mothers. And millions of people are coming to visit Great Smokies, many of whom want very badly to see, and get close to, the famous black bears.

Although most black bears are content to roam in the thick forest, a small percentage of them are more opportunistic. They learn quickly to associate food with people. Bears that beg, steal food, and tear open backpacks are called panhandlers. Their behavior is influenced directly by the activities of people, who want to feed them, pet them, and take their pictures. Though no one has yet been killed by a bear in the Smokies, more than 100 injuries were reported in the park between 1964 and 1976. Seventy-one percent of those occurred along the Newfound Gap and Clingmans Dome roads, the two most heavily traveled highways in the park. A sizable number of those injuries resulted when people tried to feed or pet bears. People, it seems, do not learn as fast as bears.

Of the more than 700 incidents of property damage during the same period, a third occurred when food and coolers were left visible at campgrounds and picnic areas, in tents, trailers, unguarded backpacks, or in vehicles. Some of the stories are humorous (but only if someone else's vehicle was attacked). One animal became known as "Old Volkswagen." This particular bear once feasted on some fried chicken he found on the seat of a VW. After that, he habitually broke into cars of that make.

Backcountry use in the park rose exponentially between 1964 and 1976. And bears have quickly come to equate backpacks with gorp and granola bars. Many bear incidents were noted at the large, heavily used trail shelters along the extremely popular Appalachian Trail. Now, hikers and backpackers are fenced inside the shelters, to lessen the temptation for the bears.

Crowding by people is most likely to stimulate aggressive behavior on the part of panhandling bears. The bears practice an approach-avoidance technique toward people — charging, then retreating. Apparently parents transmit the panhandling penchant to their young. Once ingrained, the habit is difficult to break, and some bears become "habitual criminals."

The sad result of some of these confrontations has been the "disposal" of problem bears — 18 were destroyed between 1964 and 1973. Only one, however, was killed between 1978 and 1989. The incident occurred one evening at the Chimneys picnic area. A bear simply rose up beside a woman walking by the creek, grabbed her when she started to run, and swung her around. The woman, who survived with broken bones, said the attack was unprovoked. Bear 79, as it was called, was killed following the incident. It had been captured and relocated twice from the Ramsay Cascades Trail area and transported a good distance from the place where the final attack occurred. Since then, another extremely aggressive bear and an orphaned cub have also been put to death.

More than 300 bears were captured and relocated in the park between 1964 and 1976, the majority of which came from Cades Cove and the Newfound Gap-Clingmans Dome areas. Because of their uncanny navigational skills, bears must be moved at least 10 to 18 miles away to prevent them from returning to familiar ranges.

To reduce the likelihood of bear encounters, park officials have installed bearproof garbage cans, permanently closed some areas, and issued more citations to people caught feeding bears. Backpackers are advised how to suspend their packs between trees at backcountry campsites.

The other major event going on in bears' lives in summer is breeding. A three- or four-year-old female bear is ready to reproduce. She will go into estrus around mid-June. Younger males will vie with older, bigger males for mates, but the more venerable bears usually win. That battle often involves head-to-head combat, with wounds inflicted in the process.

Only after mating has occurred does the female ovulate. Then an interesting physiological response occurs. The fertilized egg does not immediately implant on the wall of her uterus, but instead remains unattached for nearly five months, until she is safely inside her winter den. Delayed implantation, as this is called, is an adaptation that has evolved in a number of mammals. It allows them to put off the rigors of pregnancy so that other matters, such as tending to young and obtaining food, can be attended to during the fruitful days of summer. The female black bear produces a litter every two years, making for a relatively low reproductive rate.

Fresh bites and claw marks about six feet up on tree trunks are a sign that the breeding season is in full swing. Why bears leave these marks on trees is not clear, although it may be a way to delineate territory. Such markings, along with scat, tracks, and diggings in yellow jacket nests at the base of trees are signs that bears have been in the area.

As the muggy summer days ease into fall, the forest light begins to change. Days grow shorter, nights cooler. It is in autumn, that the passing of the chestnut takes on great significance. As in summer, the bears are spending most of their time out looking for food. But now, the search intensifies as they ready themselves for winter. Without the reliable supply of chestnuts, bears, like other native animals and the non-native wild boar, turn to the produce of the oaks.

In good acorn years, all the animals have enough. Unlike boars, bears have an edge in being able to climb trees to get to the acorns first. They will gorge on the acorns, gaining three to five pounds a day, perhaps increasing their weight 50 percent, most of it in fat. In bad years (oaks produce a good acorn crop only once every three to five years), all the animals must compete for a scant supply. Without the acorns, black bears will not gain enough fat to see them through the winter, and the females' eggs may not implant. Fewer cubs will be born, and many more young bears will die.

Bears are forced to expand their home ranges to find acorns in autumn, in some cases roaming 100 square miles rather than the 20 to 50 square miles they cover in summer. Great distances can be crossed in a day, but the travel exposes the bears to accidents and poachers. An estimated 45 to 80 black bears are killed illegally in the park each year, though these figures may be low because poachers often work at night, with dogs, guns, traps, and CB radios.

Most of these bears are killed for little more than their claws, teeth, or gall bladders. Dried bear gall bladders are considered an aphrodisiac in Asia, one for which people will pay considerable money. An undercover

Great Smoky Mountains N. P.

In the past, Smokies visitors have encouraged "panhandling" bears by feeding them. Feeding bears in the park is prohibited and now carries a hefty fine.

operation called Operation Smoky showed the extent of bear poaching in the southern mountains, including the park. At the end of the operation in August 1988, 266 bear gall bladders, 385 claws, 77 feet, four heads, nine hides, and one cub had been confiscated.

By mid-November, most Smokies bears are ready to turn in for the winter. Something—probably lower temperatures, precipitation, dwindling food supplies, or their own body fat levels—tells them when it's time. By mid-December they have chosen a den site, most commonly in an old birch, red oak, red maple, or hemlock tree. Bears in the Smokies den either in a dry, well-protected cavity high in a tree or in a hollow stump on the ground. Sometimes they select dense thickets of berry bushes. The bears gather rhododendron and hemlock boughs and shred the woody pulp inside the tree cavity to make a warm, comfortable bed.

Then the bears retire, not for true hibernation but for long periods of inactivity and sleep. Their digestive system begins to change as winter comes on, tightening into a knot of tissue. During the bear's winter sleep, its metabolism may slow by half, but its body temperature does not drop as drastically as in other hibernating mammals. They do not eat or drink, and bodily wastes are processed internally and sent back into the bloodstream in the form of protein.

The bears will live through the four months of winter sleep on the extra fat they added during the fall feeding frenzy. Then young will be born and the annual cycle starts again.

8
A Smokies Specialty
Salamanders

The Smoky Mountains have been famous for a long time for one particular group of animals, the salamanders. Here salamanders reach their highest abundance and diversity outside the tropics.

People here have long recognized this richness. In the late 1920s, the American Museum of Natural History sent a representative to the Smokies to do some "salamanderin'." With Wiley Oakley, the "roaming Man of the Mountains," to assist in the search, the museum's William G. Hassler set out with knapsacks, cloth collecting bags, and mattocks. The two men thrashed through tangled rhododendron thickets, turning over stones along the streams. As they reached higher elevations, their search was rewarded. They found the unusual redcheek salamander under rotten, moss-covered logs. The redcheek is a variation of Jordan's salamander, which elsewhere is a dark gray or black. Only in the Smokies do these sleek salamanders have bright red blotches on their cheeks.

Though salamanders are found throughout the Appalachians, the unglaciated southern reaches of the range are a veritable paradise for salamander aficionados. The mountains' isolated peaks, cool, moist climate, and multiple microhabitats have allowed a complex array of these amphibians to evolve, including an entire large group, the lungless salamanders.

Warm evenings after a rain are the best times to go salamanderin'. Even then, you do have to look. These are furtive, almost totally nocturnal animals. They live mostly in the silent, dark world under rocks, logs, and leaves. Sometimes they will surprise you — one morning I nearly stepped on a blackchin red in the parking lot at the Ramsay Cascades trailhead. But that is the exception rather than the rule. Salamanders often are cryptically colored and when uncovered will scurry in a flash back under a rock or log.

Representatives from five of the world's nine families of salamanders are found in the Great Smokies. Twenty-five species have been recognized in the park (though the total number may vary from 23 to 28, depending upon whose records and taxonomy are consulted.)

Smokies salamanders come in all colors and all sizes, from the inch-and-a-half-long pigmy to the foot-and-a-half long hellbender. Salamanders live at all elevations and in all habitats in the park — in sinkholes, near seeps and springs, in and beside streams, and on land, both in the deciduous and spruce-fir forests. There's the marbled and spotted, zigzag and dusky, Santeetlah and slimy, seal and Blue Ridge spring, the longtail, three-lined, and four-toed. One of the more common is the beautiful blackchin red, unusual for its bright coral-colored, black-spotted body.

The population of stream-dwelling salamanders in the Smokies is probably the greatest in the world. Among them, the totally aquatic shovelnose is a cosmopolitan species, found at all elevations and in all watersheds. The blackbelly, seal, mountain, and Blue Ridge two-lined are also widely distributed. The Santeetlah, imitator, and Jordan's are found only at high elevations. Two are found only at low elevations — the longtail and three-lined — the longtail only on the Tennessee side of the park, the three-lined only on the North Carolina side.

The hellbender is the granddaddy of them all. These are whoppers, with a record 29½-inch female captured in the 1940s by a boy fishing in the Little Pigeon River. A naturalist who saw this singular specimen declared that this "thick-bodied, flabby" creature "is surely one of the world's ugliest."

Because of their formidable size and bad looks, and because they were believed to be poisonous predators, hellbenders were classed as "varmints" during the Depression. Local residents were rewarded for those they killed. Hellbenders are not poisonous, but, as do many salamanders, they emit noxious skin secretions to deter their enemies.

Hellbenders spend most of their time burrowed into the clay bottoms of the larger, lower-elevation streams, well concealed by their dull brown to olive green coloring. At night they come out to forage for crayfish, insect larvae, worms, suckers, and minnows. Hellbenders breed in early autumn. Males compete for nesting sites and then make nests under rocks or submerged logs in the stream bottom. Females will often share a nest site, and the males guard the nests and eggs. Up to 500 eggs are laid in a row, like a string of beads. Hellbenders are a primitive form, retaining the trait of external fertilization of their eggs. Most salamander eggs are fertilized internally.

In folklore, salamanders were creatures of the flame. Seeing them crawl from the logs in their fireplaces onto the hearths, European peasants thought the salamanders had actually emerged from the flames. Other fables speak of the salamander as a sort of lizard that lives in fire, overcoming the heat by the chill of its own body. Salamanders do superficially resemble lizards, and some live in chilly mountain streams. Unlike lizards, though, salamanders lack claws or scales and have soft, moist skin (which they shed fairly frequently and then consume). However, salamanders are not reptiles but amphibians, cousins to the frogs and toads.

Salamanders make almost no sound, and they lack eardrums and middle ears; they sense vibrations through their forelegs, chins, and a row of sensory pits along the head and body called lateral line organs. Their sense of smell, aided by cells in the nasal passage called Jacobson's organ, provides their chief means of detecting what is happening in their environment. They also have good vision, which is most important in finding food.

Salamanders possess a bony skeleton, four limbs, two nostrils, and a three-chambered heart, all key characteristics of amphibians. And like all amphibians they are ectothermic, or "cold-blooded," meaning their body temperature fluctuates with the surrounding environment. To control their body temperature, they must move from one place to another. Generally, amphibians cannot tolerate temperatures above 100 degrees

Fahrenheit. They must also keep their skin moist. If it becomes very hot (or cold) and dry they must go underground.

Although they are amphibians, not all salamanders lead amphibious lives. So varied are the life histories of different species of salamanders that it is difficult to make generalizations about them. Some metamorphose from aquatic larvae into terrestrial adults. Others are entirely aquatic, some even retaining the larval form into adulthood. More than half of all salamander species are purely terrestrial, lacking any aquatic stage but never straying far from the cool moisture of a rotting log.

Many species breed in the spring (though some breed in fall, winter, or summer). Most salamanders spend a good deal of time and energy in elaborate courtship affairs, which assures they are mating with the right species and the right sex. Most courtship involves the male working hard to persuade the female and to transfer his sperm.

Males of some species develop teeth during courtship. With these teeth, they abrade the skin of the female and rub a special gland against the wound, injecting a hormonal substance into the female to increase her receptivity. The male dusky salamander similarly secretes a substance from his snout and cheeks that he rubs against the female in a sort of irresistible "kiss." She then follows him and picks up sperm that he has just deposited in a jellylike sac called the spermatophore.

The male slimy salamander, a lungless salamander named for its gluey skin secretions, does a little courtship dance. He raises and lowers his limbs while nudging the female with his chin. The male slimy grasps the female with his mouth, then maneuvers his tail beneath her chin. The female then straddles his vibrating tail and the pair moves away together. This tail-straddling walk is unique to members of the lungless group.

Timing of breeding is especially important to species like the marbled and spotted salamanders, both in the genus *Ambystoma*. These stout-limbed, robust-bodied animals are called mole salamanders for their burrowing habit. They leave their burrows and return to ponds each year in large numbers to breed. Because ponds are extremely rare in the Smokies, here the marbled and spotted must seek out limestone sinkholes. Most pond salamanders, like the spotted, migrate to the sinkholes to breed and lay eggs in early spring. The larvae hatch in mid-March or early April.

But the marbled salamander tries to beat the odds by breeding early. The female migrates to the sinkholes in autumn and lays her eggs on land just before the rains. The eggs are then covered by water as the pond fills. Larvae hatch in late November, giving them a head start in growth and allowing them first choice of the small aquatic animals. The following spring, the marbled larvae are larger than the spotted larvae and can eat them too.

Female salamanders lay gelatinous clusters of eggs, on a stream boulder or plant stem if an aquatic species, or under a log if terrestrial. The egg masses of some species like the mole salamanders are as big as a softball. But as some salamanders evolved toward reproduction on land, the number of eggs laid has decreased, and females stay with the eggs to protect them.

In aquatic salamanders, the larva that hatches from an egg looks something like a tadpole. Unlike tadpoles, the young of frogs and toads, salamander larvae have external gills, teeth, and fully formed limbs. Most will metamorphose into full adults, sometimes as long as

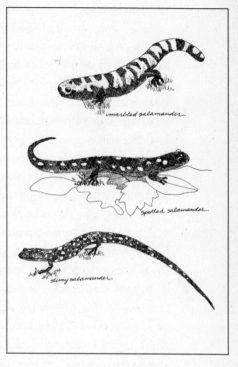

four years hence. In terrestrial salamanders, the larval stage is completed within the egg, and the young hatch fully developed. They look like miniature versions of the parents.

For those salamanders that metamorphose from larvae into adults, that change is profound and stressful. During metamorphosis, the animal undergoes a total reorganization of its body tissues as it loses external gills and forms lungs and eyelids. The major advantage of metamorphosis is that it allows a species to colonize an entirely different environment — land rather than water. But during metamorphosis the animal is especially vulnerable to predation.

Some salamanders, like the mudpuppy, avoid these pitfalls entirely by permanently remaining larvae. Sexually mature mudpuppies are simply larger versions of the larvae; even adults retain flamboyant red gills. This rather mysterious process, called neoteny, appears to be genetically ordained in some species, while in others environmental conditions appear to determine whether they metamorphose or not. Thyroxin, the thyroid hormone essential to metamorphosis, simply doesn't work in neotenic species.

Salamanders are the tailed amphibians, and this feature of their anatomy plays an important role in their survival. Should a predator nab a salamander's tail (or other body part), the salamander simply dispenses with the tail and escapes. The process is called autotomy. The sacrificed body parts can be regenerated.

Along with autotomy, salamanders have evolved other strategies that give them an edge against predators. One of the most important is their noxious and toxic skin secretions. Immobility, in which the salamander feigns death, is another technique. A bird predator, for example, will simply ignore immobile salamanders, while those that move are attacked. Salamanders can also bite. While usually voiceless, some can make noises that startle or confuse a predator. Many engage in elaborate defensive postures, curling their bodies and contorting their tails in positions worthy of the greatest yoga master.

Usually salamanders combine a number of these antipredator strategies — wild side-to-side tail flipping will be followed by immobility or a body position that aims skin secretions directly at a predator. Two-lined and longtail salamanders coil their bodies and elevate their tails when attacked by shrews and blue jays. A shrew biting the tail of one of these salamanders will back off and wipe its mouth, giving the salamander time to escape. A garter snake trying to eat a slimy salamander might have its mouth glued shut. In some cases, skin secretions have caused predators to regurgitate salamanders unharmed!

Another defensive strategy practiced by salamanders is mimicry. In one style, known as Batesian mimicry, a palatable species mimics a noxious model. For example, the red-spotted newt passes through an "adolescent" terrestrial stage called the red eft. The eft emits a neurotoxin so powerful that even minute amounts can kill a mouse in 20 minutes. The redback salamander has a red form that resembles the eft. Though the redback is actually palatable, predators are apparently fooled by the mimicry and avoid both species. Another Smokies species, the imitator salamander, is named for its mimicry of the cherry red blotches of the redcheek salamander. The imitator is palatable, while the redcheek is noxious. But predators stay away from both.

Salamanders are voracious carnivores that swallow their prey whole. They eat mostly insects, frog tadpoles, and other salamander larvae, in some cases those of their own species. Aquatic salamanders open their mouth and throat and suck in the prey with a mouthful of water. Terrestrial salamanders have evolved dexterous tongues that they swiftly extend to great lengths to snatch fast-moving prey. Their tongues have small, sticky pads on the end to secure the prey. These salamanders employ an "ambush" feeding strategy: they simply sit and wait for an insect to come within tongue's reach.

Salamanders make up the greatest biomass of any vertebrate in the eastern deciduous forest. In the Smokies, total salamander biomass is believed to exceed that of all birds and mammals combined. Though salamanders may in turn become little "protein packets" for predators, as one biologist described them, for the most part salamanders are extremely long-lived. (The hellbender, along with a related Japanese species, holds the longevity record — 55 years in captivity.) Such longevity and slow turnover mean that salamanders tie up a great amount of energy in the food web. Ecologists thus consider them a stabilizing factor in the ecosystems in which they live.

Research on larval stages is reinforcing this long-lived, slow-growing aspect of salamanders. For some species, the time spent as larvae is longer than first believed. The larval stage of shovelnose salamanders, for example, has been found to last nearly three years, instead of ten months as previously estimated. The larval stage, then, is not just a flash in the pan for salamanders, as it is for other amphibians.

All salamanders hatch with gills of one kind or another. Those that live in streams with plentiful dissolved oxygen have reduced gills; terrestrials have large gills without filaments; and in most adult amphibians, lungs replace larval gills upon metamorphosis. That is the norm. But again, salamanders resist attempts at generalization. One of the largest and most successful groups, the lungless salamanders, defies the norm. Members of this family, the Plethodontidae, are the only vertebrates that have neither lungs nor gills as adults. Instead, they breathe through their mouths and through thin skin rich in capillaries.

Another distinguishing characteristic of the lungless salamander is the grooves along each side of its nose that act as smell receptors, helping it pick up prey and identify mates.

Lungless salamanders probably got their start in the cold, swift mountain streams of the Appalachian Mountains. Here the most primitive forms of the family are found, and the most primitive species still occupy the original habitat niche — mountain streams. Because this specialized habitat has been available since the end of the Paleozoic Era, these forms have been able to persist.

Lunglessness makes sense for aquatic species because air-filled lungs would cause them to float and be carried away in the swift current. Curiously, though, a number of lungless species are terrestrial. While breathing might be a problem for a lungless animal on land, these species have found suitable habitat — with high humidity, available underground retreats, and acceptable temperature ranges — in the mountains. The terrestrial lungless salamanders probably descended from the mountain stream group.

Among the terrestrial lungless salamanders is a genus called *Plethodon*, the object of some pioneering ecological experiments in the Smokies and nearby Balsam Mountains. Two fairly abundant species in the Smokies, the redcheek *(Plethodon jordani)* and the slimy *(Plethodon glutinosus)*, were the subjects of a five-year project testing the assumption that "equivalent" species in contact deal with competition by diversifying their niches. When either species was removed from the area, the other gained in population, demonstrating that the two were competing. The competition was far more intense in the Smokies.

Were they competing for food? The redcheek and slimy eat much the same things, mainly insects and other small invertebrates. Or perhaps they were competing for burrows, where these nocturnal species seek refuge during the daytime. Food and foraging habitats turned out not to be the limiting factors for these species, but nesting sites might be. Unfortunately, it will take more knowledge about the nesting habits of redcheek and slimy salamanders before the question can be answered.

Lungless salamanders in the Smokies exemplify the development of various species and races in isolation. Over evolutionary time, millions and millions of years, the mountains have served as laboratories for the development of interesting new species and races.

Each mountaintop has produced endemic species or races — ones found nowhere else. Salamanders of the high-elevation spruce-fir forests of the Smokies, such as the redcheek and pigmy, have essentially evolved in these forests as if on islands. When the spruce-fir forests were more widespread during glacial times, salamanders ranged more freely and could interbreed. But as the climate warmed and the spruce-fir forests retreated to higher elevations, the salamanders adapted to that forest also retreated. They could not negotiate the unsuitable habitats of the intervening valleys. Hence the redcheek and others became what are known as relict populations.

Such specialization can render a species especially vulnerable. Thirteen species of salamanders occur in the spruce-fir forest; three in particular, the imitator, redcheek, and pigmy, are characteristic of this forest. The extensive die-off of Fraser fir in the last 30 years, caused by infestation of an introduced insect, the balsam woolly adelgid, is likely to seriously affect these salamanders — but exactly how is still unknown.

Amphibians in general, and salamanders in particular, are sensitive indicators of environmental deterioration or habitat losses. Silting of streams, either by the rootings of wild boar or other activities, can be detrimental to Smokies salamanders. Silting affects the stream substrate, which in turn affects populations of aquatic insects that salamanders eat. In addition, wild boars are known to eat salamanders.

Acid deposition has also harmed salamanders in the Smokies. During heavy rains, soils are leached and the acid levels in streams rise dramatically in sudden pulses. When water leaches through acidic rock like the Anakeesta Formation, found at high elevations in the Smokies, such pulses can be deadly. Runoff from a roadcut operation in the Anakeesta raised the acidity of streams and killed salamanders and brook trout downstream.

Thus salamanders, the Smokies specialty, may serve as the proverbial canary in the coal mine. The presence of such incredible diversity of species is a sign of healthy environment. On the other hand, a decline in salamander populations may tell of a deteriorating environment. They still have much to teach us.

Tennessee Wildlife Resources Agency

Small mammals such as woodchucks and chipmunks are favored foods of the bobcat.
These carnivorous felines are fairly common residents throughout the park.

Where to Find Wildlife

Mammals

Bear jams are an unusual phenomenon peculiar to Great Smoky Mountains National Park. Whenever and wherever a **black bear** is sighted, traffic halts, videocameras appear, and you are likely in for a long wait if you are on a narrow, one-way road.

Black bears usually begin to appear in the park in the spring, after they have emerged from their winter dens. They are seen fairly frequently along the Roaring Fork Motor Nature Trail, the Cades Cove loop road in the western part of the park, and the Newfound Gap Road (Transmountain Highway)

between Sugarlands and Oconaluftee. Bears also commonly roam the Cosby Campground on the east side of the park. Along nearly any of the 900 miles of trails through the park, bears can be seen during spring, summer, and fall. Hikers should take precautions with their packs and food. Should a bear turn up, take all your food and leave the area.

In spring, sows and cubs are often out together. Under no circumstances should you come between a mother and her young. Never approach any bear too closely to get a photograph. Likewise, do not attempt to feed bears. These animals are wild and are fully capable of feeding themselves with food offered by the forest.

Evidence of the presence of bears can be found throughout the park. Look for claw marks on tree trunks, diggings at the base of trees where they have pursued yellow jackets, and tracks in wet mud along trails.

Another large mammal that creates a stir is the **whitetail deer**. Deer, scarce when the park was first established, have become far more common. Though they inhabit the deciduous woods, deer can assuredly be seen nearly any time of year in the grassy meadows in Cades Cove. Early in the morning or at dusk, herds of them are out in great numbers in the fields.

Cades Cove is one area in the Great Smokies not maintained in its natural state. Instead, the cove is a historic district intended to recreate pioneer times of the 1800s, when nearly 700 people lived and farmed in the valley. Agricultural activities such as mowing and grazing are permitted, to keep the fields open. Deer find the hayfields especially to their liking; they also browse the leaves, buds, and juicy stems of hemlocks, maples, oaks, dogwoods, and redbuds. The forest surrounding the cove provides good bedding areas for them. In fact, the deer herd has become so large and concentrated in Cades Cove that park managers are concerned about disease and parasite outbreaks, as well as the harm done to native and rare plants by their heavy browsing.

Other mammals likely to be seen in and around Cades Cove include **raccoons** and foxes. Both **red foxes** and gray foxes are found in the park, but gray foxes are more abundant. The red foxe can be distinguished by its white-tipped tail and its black legs and feet. **Woodchucks**, also known as groundhogs, have made their homes in Cades Cove. On a bicycle or on foot, a person can easily find their burrows. If you sit patiently, one of these rotund rodents may soon become curious enough to poke its nose out.

Campers are familiar with the nighttime raidings of **striped skunks** and **spotted skunks**. The occasional **opossum**, also mainly nocturnal, may be seen. Near streams, look for furbearers, including **muskrats, beaver**, which suddenly returned to the park in the 1960s, and **river otters**, reintroduced in recent years along Abrams Creek and Little River.

Birds

More than 200 species of birds, including residents and migrants, live in the diverse habitats provided by the Smokies. Only a small sample can be given here. The pocket-sized guide *Birds of the Smokies* lists accounts of a hundred species and good places to see them. Birdwatchers need to be good listeners, too, for the woods are thick. You usually have a much better chance hearing than seeing birds.

Wild turkeys, once uncommon, are occasionally seen in Cades Cove. Along streams, **belted kingfishers** and **Louisiana waterthrushes** (in summer) are common. In the lower, deciduous forests, listen for the **red-eyed vireo, ovenbird**, and the **black-throated green warbler**. The **ruby-throated humming-bird**, the only hummingbird species in the East, appears in the Smokies in summer, dipping into tubular flowers such as purple rhododendron on the heath balds or lobelia (cardinal-flower) along the streams.

The hammering of **pileated wood-peckers** echoes throughout the woods, especially the low-elevation hardwood forests they favor. If you see one of these large birds, you will know it by its out-landish red topknot.

With their *who cooks for you, who cooks for you all* call, **barred owls** are clearly identifiable. These owls are heard by nearly anyone who spends a night or two camped out in the Smokies. Once in a while, they are heard calling in mid-day. **Eastern screech-owls** are also common; **great horned owls** are present, but not so common.

At higher elevations, into the spruce-fir forests, are birds of northern affinities. Among them are the **raven, black-capped chickadee, golden-crowned kinglet, red-breasted nuthatch, red crossbill, saw-whet owl, Blackburnian** and **Canada warblers, veery**, and **winter wren**. Some of these birds remain in the high forests through the winter, but most move to lower elevations in the park or to Central and South America. Migrating songbirds begin returning to

Tennessee Wildlife Resources Agency

At dusk or dawn, the great horned owl may be heard calling, usually in lower elevations of the park and most often in December and January.

the park by the middle or end of March. Almost as if they refuse to be outdone by the beautiful spring wildflowers, the birds are dressed in their brightest breed-ing plumage and are singing for all they're worth.

Amphibians and Reptiles

With 25 species of salamanders, the Great Smokies is nearly unmatched in the temperate world in representatives of this group. Various salamanders occupy all habitats at all elevations in the park. Among the more common are the **blackchin red, seal, northern two-lined,** and **slimy**. The **redcheek**, found only in the Smokies, is sometimes seen in abundance in the spruce-fir forest. Usually in streams and wet places throughout the park, members of the toad and frog world are abundant. **Spring peepers**, **wood frogs**, and **green frogs** fill the forests with their croakings and chirpings. **American toads**, found from the lowest to highest elevations, attain impressive sizes in the mountains.

A variety of reptiles — turtles, lizards, and snakes — are found in the Smokies, though turtles are not as diverse because of the lack of ponds and pools. The **eastern box turtle** is the most common, but it is found only below 4,000 feet elevation. Box turtles build nests in soft mud, often along newly built trails, and hibernate in depressions under brush. Lizards are found most often in the drier, pine-oak forests, the most common being the **fence lizard**. **Five-lined skinks** are most prevalent at low elevations.

With nearly 2,000 miles of streams in the park, the **northern water snake** finds much available habitat. Locally this dark brown snake is called a "water moccasin." The water snake, however, is not poisonous, as is the true water moccasin, the cottonmouth, unknown in the Smokies.

The only two species of poisonous snakes in the park are the **copperhead** and **timber rattlesnake**. Copperheads prefer rocky hillsides, old stone fences, and abandoned buildings, and are found

mostly below 2,500 feet elevations. Timber rattlers are found at all elevations in the park, especially in thickly vegetated and rocky areas, and have been encountered on the grassy balds.

Sleek **black rat snakes**, good climbers, are not infrequently seen slithering along trees and boulders beside trails. Their relatives, the **corn snakes** and **garter snakes**, are among other common Smokies species.

Whitetail deer, common in deciduous woods, have increased in numbers since the park was established. This one was on the Chestnut Top Trail.

WILDLIFE CHECKLISTS

MAMMALS

Opossum	*Didelphis marsupialis*
Masked Shrew	*Sorex cinereus*
Southeastern Shrew	*Sorex longirostris*
Northern Water Shrew	*Sorex palustris*
Smoky Shrew	*Sorex fumeus*
Longtail Shrew	*Sorex dispar*
Pygmy Shrew	*Microsorex hoyi*
Shorttail Shrew	*Blarina brevicauda*
Least Shrew	*Cryptotis parva*
Hairytail Mole	*Parascalops breweri*
Eastern Mole	*Scalopus aquaticus*
Starnose Mole	*Condylura cristata*
Little Brown Myotis	*Myotis lucifugus*
Keen Myotis	*Myotis keeni*
Indiana Myotis	*Myotis sodalis*
Small-footed Myotis	*Myotis leibii*
Silver-haired Bat	*Lasionycteris noctivagans*
Eastern Pipistrel	*Pipistrellus subflavus*
Big Brown Bat	*Eptesicus fuscus*
Red Bat	*Lasiurus borealis*
Eastern Big-eared Bat	*Plecotus rafinesquei*
Eastern Cottontail	*Sylvilagus floridanus*
New England Cottontail	*Sylvilagus transitionalis*
Eastern Chipmunk	*Tamias striatus*
Woodchuck	*Marmota monax*
Eastern Gray Squirrel	*Sciurus carolinensis*
Eastern Fox Squirrel	*Sciurus niger*
Red Squirrel	*Tamiasciurus hudsonicus*
Southern Flying Squirrel	*Glaucomys volans*
Northern Flying Squirrel	*Glaucomys sabrinus*
Beaver	*Castor canadensis*
Rice Rat	*Oryzomys palustris*
Eastern Harvest Mouse	*Reithrodontomys humulis*
Deer Mouse	*Peromyscus maniculatus*
White-footed Mouse	*Peromyscus leucopus*
Cotton Mouse	*Peromyscus gossypinus*
Golden Mouse	*Ochrotomys nuttalli*
Hispid Cotton Rat	*Sigmodon hispidus*
Eastern Woodrat	*Neotoma floridana*
Boreal Redback Vole	*Clethrionomys gapperi*

Cottontails are found from the lowest to the highest elevations in the Smokies, in woods, fields, and brier patches.

Meadow Vole	*Microtus pennsylvanicus*
Yellownose Rock Vole	*Microtus chrotorrhinus*
Woodland Vole	*Microtus pinetorum*
Muskrat	*Ondatra zibethica*
Southern Bog Lemming	*Synaptomys cooperi*
Meadow Jumping Mouse	*Zapus hudsonius*
Woodland Jumping Mouse	*Napaeozapus insignis*
Coyote	*Canis latrans*
Gray Wolf	*Canis lupus* (extirpated)
Red Wolf	*Canis rufus* (reintroduced)
Red Fox	*Vulpes vulpes*
Gray Fox	*Urocyon cinereoargenteus*
Black Bear	*Ursus americanus*
Raccoon	*Procyon lotor*
Fisher	*Martes pennanti* (extirpated)
Long-tailed Weasel	*Mustela frenata*
Mink	*Mustela vison*
Spotted Skunk	*Spilogale putorius*
Striped Skunk	*Mephitis mephitis*
River Otter	*Lutra canadensis* (reintroduced)
Mountain Lion	*Felis concolor* (extirpated)
Bobcat	*Lynx rufus*

Wild Boar	*Sus scrofa* (non-native)
Wapiti or Elk	*Cervus canadensis* (extirpated)
Whitetail Deer	*Odocoileus virginianus*
Bison	*Bison bison* (extirpated)

A wary woodchuck sticks its nose out of its burrow in Cades Cove. "Whistle-pigs" are common in meadows and along mowed roadsides.

AMPHIBIANS AND REPTILES

Frogs and Toads:

Northern Cricket Frog	*Acris crepitans*
American Toad	*Bufo americanus*
Common (Woodhouse's) Toad	*Bufo woodhousii*
Eastern Narrowmouth Toad	*Gastrophryne carolinensis*
Peeper Treefrog, Spring Peeper	*Hyla crucifer*
Gray Treefrog	*Pseudacris chrysocelis*
Chorus Frog	*Pseudacris triseriata*
Bullfrog	*Rana catesbeiana*
Green Frog	*Rana clamitans*
Pickerel Frog	*Rana palustris*
Southern Leopard Frog	*Rana sphenocephala*
Wood Frog	*Rana sylvatica*

Salamanders:

Spotted Salamander	*Ambystoma maculatum*
Marbled Salamander	*Ambystoma opacum*
Green Salamander	*Aneides aeneus*
Hellbender	*Cryptobranchus alleganiensis*
Northern Dusky Salamander	*Desmognathus fuscus*
Imitator Salamander	*Desmognathus imitator*
Seal Salamander	*Desmognathus monticola*
Mountain Dusky Salamander	*Desmognathus ochrophaeus*
Blackbelly Salamander	*Desmognathus quadramaculatus*
Santeetlah Dusky Salamander	*Desmognathus santeetlah*
Pigmy Salamander	*Desmognathus wrighti*
Northern Two-lined Salamander	*Eurycea bislineata*
Junaluska Salamander	*Eurycea junaluska*
Three-lined Salamander	*Eurycea longicauda guttolineata*
Longtail Salamander	*Eurycea longicauda longicauda*
Spring Salamander	*Gyrinophilus porphyriticus*
Four-toed Salamander	*Hemidactylium scutatum*
Shovelnose Salamander	*Leurognathus marmoratus*
Redback Salamander	*Plethodon cinereus*
Zigzag Salamander	*Plethodon dorsalis*
Slimy Salamander	*Plethodon glutinosus*
Jordan's (Redcheek) Salamander	*Plethodon jordani*
Mud Salamander	*Pseudotriton montanus*
Blackchin Red Salamander	*Pseudotriton ruber*
Mudpuppy	*Necturus maculosus*
Red-spotted (Eastern) Newt	*Notophthalmus viridescens*

Turtles:

Common Snapping Turtle	*Chelydra serpentina*
Painted Turtle	*Chrysemys picta*
Common Map Turtle	*Graptemys geographica*
Loggerhead Musk Turtle	*Sternotherus minor*
Eastern Box Turtle	*Terrapene carolina*
Spiny Softshell	*Trionys spiniferus*

Lizards and Snakes:

Copperhead	*Agkistrodon contortrix*
Green Anole	*Anolis carolinensis*
Worm Snake	*Carphophis amoenus*
Scarlet Snake	*Cemophora coccinea*
Six-lined Racerunner	*Cnemidophorus sexlineatus*
Racer	*Coluber constrictor*

Timber Rattlesnake	*Crotalus horridus*
Ringneck Snake	*Diadophis punctatus*
Corn Snake	*Elaphe guttata*
Rat Snake	*Elaphe obsoleta*
Five-lined Skink	*Eumeces fasciatus*
Southeastern Five-lined Skink	*Eumeces inexpectatus*
Broadhead Skink	*Eumeces laticeps*
Eastern Hognose Snake	*Heterodon platirhinos*
Prairie Kingsnake	*Lampropeltis calligaster*
Common Kingsnake	*Lampropeltis getula*
Milk Snake	*Lampropeltis triangulum*
Northern Water Snake	*Nerodia sipedon*
Rough Green Snake	*Opheodrys aestivus*
Slender Glass Lizard	*Ophisaurus attenuatus*
Bullsnake	*Pituophis melanoleucus*
Queen Snake	*Regina septemvittata*
Eastern Fence Lizard	*Sceloporus undulatus*
Ground Skink	*Scincella lateralis*
Brown Snake	*Storeria dekayi*
Redbelly Snake	*Storeria occipitomaculata*
Southeastern Crowned Snake	*Tantilla coronata*
Common Garter Snake	*Thamnophis sirtalis*
Smooth Earth Snake	*Virginia valeriae*

Tennessee Wildlife Resources Agency

The copperhead is one of two species of poisonous snakes in the park. They gather in group dens in autumn to hibernate, sometimes with other kinds of snakes.

FISHES

Rock Bass	*Ambloplites rupestris*
Central Stoneroller	*Campostoma anomalum*
Rosyside Dace	*Clinostomus funduloides*
Mottled Sculpin	*Cottus bairdi*
Banded Sculpin	*Cottus carolinae*
Fantail Darter	*Etheostoma flabellare*
Redline Darter	*Etheostoma rufilineatum*
Bigeye Chub	*Hybopsis amblops*
Northern Hog Sucker	*Hypentelium nigricans*
River Chub	*Nocomis micropogon*
Tennessee Shiner	*Notropis leuciodus*
Smoky Madtom	*Noturus baileyi*
Yellowfin Madtom	*Noturus flavipinnis*
Rainbow Trout	*Oncorhynchus mykiss* (introduced)
Blacknose Dace	*Rhinichthys atratulus*
Brown Trout	*Salmo trutta* (introduced)
Brook Trout	*Salvelinus fontinalis*
Creek Chub	*Semotilus atromaculatus*

BIRDS

Common Loon	Green-winged Teal
Horned Grebe	American Black Duck
Pied-billed Grebe	Mallard
Band-rumped Storm Petrel	Northern Pintail
American White Pelican	Blue-winged Teal
Double-crested Cormorant	Northern Shoveler
American Bittern	American Wigeon
Least Bittern	Ring-necked Duck
Great Blue Heron	Lesser Scaup
Great Egret	White-winged Scoter
Little Blue Heron	Common Goldeneye
Green-backed Heron	Bufflehead
Black-crowned Night-Heron	Hooded Merganser
Yellow-crowned Night-Heron	Common Merganser
Snow Goose	Red-breasted Merganser
Brant	Ruddy Duck
Canada Goose	Black Vulture
Wood Duck	Turkey Vulture

Osprey
Swallow-tailed Kite
Mississippi Kite
Bald Eagle
Northern Harrier
Sharp-shinned Hawk
Cooper's Hawk
Northern Goshawk
Red-shouldered Hawk
Broad-winged Hawk
Red-tailed Hawk
Golden Eagle
American Kestrel
Merlin
Peregrine Falcon
Ruffed Grouse
Wild Turkey
Northern Bobwhite
King Rail
Virginia Rail
Sora
Common Moorhen
American Coot
Sandhill Crane
Lesser Golden Plover
Semipalmated Plover
Killdeer
Greater Yellowlegs
Lesser Yellowlegs
Solitary Sandpiper
Willet
Spotted Sandpiper
Semipalmated Sandpiper
Least Sandpiper
Ruff
Common Snipe
American Woodcock
Red-necked Phalarope
Red Phalarope
Laughing Gull
Bonaparte's Gull
Ring-billed Gull
Herring Gull

Sooty Tern
Rock Dove
Mourning Dove
Black-billed Cuckoo
Yellow-billed Cuckoo
Barn Owl
Eastern Screech-Owl
Great Horned Owl
Barred Owl
Northern Saw-whet Owl
Common Nighthawk
Chuck-will's-widow
Whip-poor-will
Chimney Swift
Ruby-throated Hummingbird
Belted Kingfisher
Red-headed Woodpecker
Red-bellied Woodpecker
Yellow-bellied Sapsucker
Downy Woodpecker
Hairy Woodpecker
Red-cockaded Woodpecker
Northern Flicker
Pileated Woodpecker
Olive-sided Flycatcher
Eastern Wood-Pewee
Yellow-bellied Flycatcher
Acadian Flycatcher
Alder Flycatcher
Willow Flycatcher
Least Flycatcher
Eastern Phoebe
Great Crested Flycatcher
Western Kingbird
Eastern Kingbird
Scissor-tailed Flycatcher
Horned Lark
Purple Martin
Tree Swallow
Northern Rough-winged
Swallow
Bank Swallow
Cliff Swallow

Wild turkeys prefer clearings and edges of the forest and have been seen around the cemeteries in Cades Cove.

Barn Swallow
Blue Jay
American Crow
Common Raven
Black-capped Chickadee
Carolina Chickadee
Tufted Titmouse
Red-breasted Nuthatch
White-breasted Nuthatch
Brown Creeper
Carolina Wren
Bewick's Wren
House Wren
Winter Wren
Sedge Wren
Marsh Wren
Golden-crowned Kinglet
Ruby-crowned Kinglet
Blue-gray Gnatcatcher
Eastern Bluebird
Veery

Gray-cheeked Thrush
Swainson's Thrush
Hermit Thrush
Wood Thrush
American Robin
Gray Catbird
Northern Mockingbird
Brown Thrasher
Water Pipit
Cedar Waxwing
Loggerhead Shrike
European Starling
White-eyed Vireo
Solitary Vireo
Yellow-throated Vireo
Warbling Vireo
Philadelphia Vireo
Red-eyed Vireo
Blue-winged Warbler
Golden-winged Warbler
Brewster's Warbler

Lawrence's Warbler
Tennessee Warbler
Orange-crowned Warbler
Nashville Warbler
Northern Parula Warbler
Yellow Warbler
Chestnut-sided Warbler
Magnolia Warbler
Cape May Warbler
Black-throated Blue Warbler
Yellow-rumped Warbler
Black-throated Green Warbler
Blackburnian Warbler
Yellow-throated Warbler
Pine Warbler
Prairie Warbler
Palm Warbler
Bay-breasted Warbler
Blackpoll Warbler
Cerulean Warbler
Black-and-white Warbler
American Redstart
Prothonotary Warbler
Worm-eating Warbler
Swainson's Warbler
Ovenbird
Northern Waterthrush
Louisiana Waterthrush
Kentucky Warbler
Connecticut Warbler
Common Yellowthroat
Hooded Warbler
Wilson's Warbler
Canada Warbler
Yellow-breasted Chat
Summer Tanager
Scarlet Tanager
Northern Cardinal
Rose-breasted Grosbeak

Blue Grosbeak
Indigo Bunting
Dickcissel
Rufous-sided Towhee
Bachman's Sparrow
Chipping Sparrow
Field Sparrow
Vesper Sparrow
Lark Sparrow
Savannah Sparrow
Grasshopper Sparrow
Henslow's Sparrow
LeConte's Sparrow
Fox Sparrow
Song Sparrow
Lincoln's Sparrow
Swamp Sparrow
White-throated Sparrow
White-crowned Sparrow
Dark-eyed Junco
Snow Bunting
Bobolink
Red-winged Blackbird
Eastern Meadowlark
Rusty Blackbird
Common Grackle
Brown-headed Cowbird
Orchard Oriole
Northern Oriole
Purple Finch
House Finch
Red Crossbill
White-winged Crossbill
Common Redpoll
Pine Siskin
American Goldfinch
Evening Grosbeak
House Sparrow

Part Three
The Threats and the Promise

9

The Harvest
Logging, Fire, and Clearing in the Great Smokies

When she was 80 years old, Ethel Huskey recalled a verse of the "Daddy Bryson" song:

> *Still Daddy stood bravely at his post of duty*
> *'Til his soul was called*
> *To meet his God,*
> *The logs they fell upon him*
> *Poor Daddy breathed his last.*

The song tells the story of a train wreck. The brakeman couldn't stop the train as it careened down Jakes Creek near Elkmont, and "Daddy" Bryson and a fireman were killed in the wreck. The year was 1909. Both men were working for the Little River Lumber Company, one of the biggest landowners and timber operators in the Smoky Mountains in the early part of this century.

Besides the human toll that logging took, the forest lost much of its life too. But in time a forest can recover from disturbance, even disturbance as severe as the massive cutting that took place in the Smoky

Mountains in the first 30 years of the 20th century. Nearly two-thirds of the land within the present park boundaries was cut during this intensive corporate logging era. It has been estimated that two billion board feet of lumber were taken out.

The Smokies were logged in the 19th century too, but on a limited basis by local people who selectively cut only the best hardwoods — walnut, cherry, ash, and tuliptree. With oxen or mules they pulled out the huge trees and took them to small, nearby sawmills. They cut mainly along the streams and lowlands, for the inaccessibility of the mountains and lack of mechanization prevented incursions into the higher, steeper land.

But as the 20th century opened, demand for hardwoods increased, along with prices. Corporations based in New York and elsewhere entered the Smokies, and the era of large-scale, mechanized logging began in earnest.

The Montvale, Ritter, Kitchin, and Suncrest companies operated on Hazel, Eagle, Bunches, and Big creeks on the North Carolina side. Daddy Bryson's employer, the Little River Lumber Company, concentrated on the Little River watershed in Tennessee. In 1901, the company purchased 85,000 acres of timberland in the watershed for three dollars an acre. It set up a band saw mill in Townsend, Tennessee, a town named for Colonel W.B. Townsend, president of the company. A railroad was built along Little River to connect the mill to Elkmont, 15 miles upstream. Elkmont became a bustling mill village where workers were housed and fed.

Along with many other Smokies visitors, I have camped at Elkmont, now a village of tents and RVs. I've walked along the Little River and listened to the frogs sing at night. It is a peaceful, inviting place, one that has always felt good to call a temporary home. But each time I walk up the nature trail along Mids Branch, the era of logging comes to mind. The trees are small, the forest open. Dark cinders stain the ground, and rusted spikes protrude from logs, reminders of a time when Elkmont must have been anything but peaceful.

Spurs of the Little River Railroad extended beyond Elkmont, up Mids Branch and Jakes Creek and almost to Clingmans Dome in the highest part of the Smokies. When one area was cleared, the rails were pulled up and moved to cutting sites deeper in the mountains. Where rails

Sawyers use a crosscut saw to take out a red spruce. Loggers worked their way into the highest elevations of the park to cut spruce when it was in demand for building airplanes during World War I.

Great Smoky Mountains N.P.

could not penetrate, other means of getting out the timber were used. Splash dams, such as those built below the mouths of Blanket and Meigs creeks, formed lakes that were jammed with timber. When the dam was broken, sometimes by dynamiting, the logs could be rafted miles downstream. This method worked especially well for tuliptree, a buoyant wood that floats much better than denser hardwoods.

Sometimes logs were "skidded" down hillsides along oiled wooden troughs. Logs were also loaded into cars attached to an incline machine called the "Sarah Parker," powered by steam and run up and down on a cable. Skidding operations were at least as detrimental to the land as the removal of so many trees. Huge areas were laid bare to accommodate the equipment, hastening erosion and hindering tree reproduction.

A key part of logging during this era remained unmechanized — the actual tree-cutting. Trees were felled with a crosscut saw, the loggers'

Great Smoky Mountains N.P.

A Clyde overhead skidder loads up a huge log for transport. Skidders made it possible to quickly clear an area of even the biggest trees.

"misery whip." A sawyer on either end of the saw cut along the notch marked by a third man, the lead chipper. Each three-man crew worked feverishly to meet a daily quota of 10,000 board feet. So big were some of the trees in the Smokies that three 16-foot lengths of tuliptree could fill a day's quota.

Tuliptree, or yellow poplar, was the most commercially valuable tree in the southern Appalachians, according to natural historian Donald Culross Peattie. When the great hardwood resources of the mountains were first tapped, "Poplar was the prize of extensive selective logging," he wrote. Actually not a poplar but a member of the magnolia family, this fast-growing tree has clear, light wood used for boxes, siding, furniture, and musical instruments. Tuliptrees grow straight and true, attaining heights of nearly 200 feet in the southern Appalachians.

Early on, tuliptrees less than 30 inches in diameter at the stump were shunned by the timber cutters. But by 1905, according to Peattie, mills were happy to get 14-inch trees. Some monstrous, unreachable virgin tuliptrees — specimens exceeding five feet in diameter — managed to

Great Smoky Mountains N. P.

escape the rapacious logging in the Smokies. A record tree in the park measures almost 24 feet in circumference.

But the hardwoods were not all the timber barons wanted. They also sold trees to be made into pulp, for which they cut softwoods like spruce and hemlock. The use of spruce for airplanes during World War I fanned greater demand for that species. Other trees, like chestnut oak, were taken for their bark. The tannins in the bark were leached out and used to process hides.

Logging companies cut over the woods to lay rail for hauling logs. The Little River Lumber Company put in track along the Little River from Elkmont to the mill in Townsend, just outside the present-day park.

The Little River Company cut hard and heavy for about two decades. From 1901 to 1920, the company consistently cut 40,000 board feet an acre on its holdings. Ultimately, more than 70 percent of the watershed of the East Prong of the Little River was logged. The company also cut on the Middle Prong of Little River from 1926 to 1939, the last logging in the park.

Equally intense were the operations of Champion Fibre Company, which concentrated on the North Carolina side of the park. Champion owned 92,000 acres, a good share of it along the crest of the Smokies and in the Oconaluftee and neighboring Deep Creek drainages. Smokemont,

Elkmont's counterpart, was the location of a mill that cut spruce into logs and pulp, to be fed to Champion's huge pulp plant in Canton, North Carolina, just east of the park.

It was the disappearance of much of this area's last great stand of forest that finally led to protection of the Great Smoky Mountains as a national park. Various proposals and individual efforts for some kind of protective designation had been offered and argued since the 1890s. But in the 1920s, in the wake of the destruction of corporate logging, the debate took on great urgency. By this time, the United States had a National Park Service, which was managing large parks carved from the vast public domain in the western United States. Potential sites in the East were being sought, too, but creation of a national park east of the Mississippi would require purchase of private lands.

In 1924, the federal government's Southern Appalachian National Park Committee evaluated a number of places in the mountains to determine suitability for a park. At the urging of a group of Knoxvillians, including Mr. and Mrs. Willis Davis and Colonel David Chapman, members of the committee went to the tops of the "Big Smokies." The committee found that "the Great Smoky Mountains easily stand first," but because the Smokies had certain "handicaps" — excessive rainfall and ruggedness that might hamper development — the Blue Ridge of Virginia was recommended instead as the first national park in the southern Appalachians.

Thus battle lines were drawn, and a flurry of lobbying, debating, and legislating ensued. The logging industry in North Carolina expressed adamant opposition to the idea of a park. In July 1925, during an especially significant hearing in Asheville, the Carolina Lumber & Timber Association resolved "That the Lumber and Timber industries of this section are opposed to the segregation of enormous areas of forest lands and lands suitable for growing forests into dead hands, where it cannot be used, no matter how vital its use may be to the industries of this State, or to the material needs of the nation."

Horace Kephart, a midwesterner who at age 42 adopted the Smokies as his home, stood firmly on the other side. He had witnessed firsthand what logging had done to his beloved mountains and feared for the remaining virgin forest. In an emotional plea Kephart asked, "Why should this last stand of splendid, irreplaceable trees be sacrificed to the greedy maw of the sawmill? Why should future generations be robbed

Timber was sometimes skidded out on wooden troughs or chutes such as this one in Sugarlands.

Great Smoky Mountains N.P.

of all chance to see with their own eyes what a real forest, a real wild-wood, a real unimproved work of God, is like?"

In 1926, Congress passed, and President Calvin Coolidge signed, an act establishing Great Smoky Mountains National Park — not immediately but sometime in the undetermined future. Establishing the park, however, entailed one big catch: money. (When all purchases were finalized, the total sum would amount to nearly $12 million.) Initially, the money was to come not from the federal government, but from private donors and the states of Tennessee and North Carolina. The land acquisition was one of the most complex ever undertaken. Along with the timber companies' huge holdings, more than 6,000 smaller parcels in the hands of farmers and other owners had to be acquired.

Colonel W.B. Townsend had for some time been negotiating to sell a sizable chunk of the Little River Lumber Company's land. He did so in

November 1926, making it the first large parcel to be bought for the park. The tract consisted of 76,507 acres of land, bought at $3.57 an acre, only 50 cents more an acre than the company originally paid. Townsend drove a hard bargain, though. The terms of the purchase included an ironic provision — the company could continue to log virgin trees for 15 more years.

The other large land owners, notably the North Carolina timber companies and specifically Champion Fibre, were not nearly so acquiescent. Champion owned much of the virgin timber, including some of Clingmans Dome and Mount Guyot, all of Mount LeConte, the Chimneys, and the Greenbrier area, and was of no mind to sell. After a round of litigation and mediation, however, in 1931 Champion finally sold its 92,000 acres for $3 million.

By 1934 nearly all the land for the park had been bought. The states came up with $4 million, the Laura Spelman Rockefeller Memorial with $5 million, and finally the federal government with $3 million. The government then faced the task of managing more than 400,000 acres of land, much of it in bad shape from the abuses of the logging era.

Fire

> "Fire is a good servant but a poor master."
> — Finnish proverb

Fire was one of the most damaging byproducts of corporate logging, with its high degree of mechanization. The use of powerful machinery, especially the skidders, led to rapid denuding of large areas and a tremendous buildup of uprooted and unused trees. The huge piles awaited only a wayward spark from a coal-fired locomotive to ignite them.

During and after this logging, a third of the watershed of the East Prong of Little River burned, more than half of Big Creek, 18 percent of Oconaluftee, and 11 percent of Cataloochee Creek. The drought year of 1925 aggravated the situation. Intense fires swept through the logged-over areas, resulting in an extensive burn on Charlies Bunion on the crest of the Smokies and in other places.

Though the fires of the corporate logging years were the most intense in the park area, human-caused fires were an instrument of disturbance

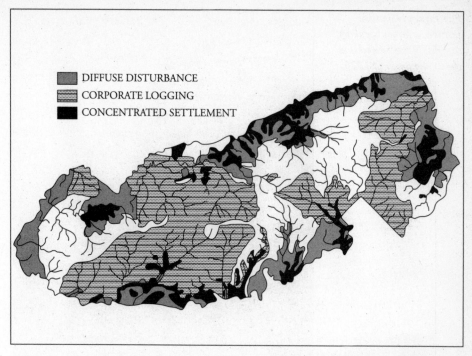

DIFFUSE DISTURBANCE
CORPORATE LOGGING
CONCENTRATED SETTLEMENT

in the southern Appalachians for a long time before logging began. For native Americans, who arrived in the
region about 12,000 years ago, fire was a tool in their arsenal of forest management almost from the beginning.

*Corporate logging, set-
tlement, and other
disturbance before
establishment of Great
Smoky Mountains
National Park in
1934.*

The Cherokees were an active part of the ecosystem of
the southern Appalachians. The Cherokees called them-
selves the People of Fire, and the element of fire was as important to them
as water. With controlled fires, they removed trees and cleared vegetation
to obtain farmland and to improve hunting. The Cherokees also noted
other benefits bestowed by fire. It allowed propagation of fire-adapted
species such as the pines and good nut- and acorn-bearing trees, exposed
soils to germinating seeds, added organic matter to the soil, and killed
plant pathogens and harmful insects.

The Cherokees probably burned the areas around their villages to prevent the indiscriminate and more destructive results of uncontrolled natural
fires. Those burnings were usually light because the Cherokees used fire-
rings, in which fires burned inward in a circle. Charcoal found in ponds
near the Smokies and in Cades Cove indicates the deliberate use of fire.

Fire ravaged Charlies Bunion, a famous peak on the crest of the Smokies, in the drought year of 1925.

Great Smoky Mountains N.P.

(The actual causes and extent of landscape and ecological changes in the pre-European Southeast, either because of climate change or human modifications, remains a matter of debate among paleoecologists and others.)

White settlers in the mountains also had a strong tradition of burning, perhaps for many of the same reasons as the Indians: to clear the "rough," or understory plants, to promote grass and woody sprouts for livestock, to kill insect pests, and to aid berry reproduction.

One-time Smokies farmer and logger Roy Myers recalls that in the fall the mountaineers would "burn the leaves so they could see chestnuts." Sometimes, though, such fires could be unselective. As Myers says, "You set the mountains afire, it didn't just burn where the chestnuts was. It burnt the whole durn thing." In the spring too, when the forest was dry, fires would burn out of control. "Some man set a match to it, couldn't put it out . . . . That March wind a-blowin' sent it from one ridge to another, under your feet. You'd better be runnin'." Myers remembers helping fight a large fire in the Gregory Ridge area in 1936 that "burnt over the whole mountains."

More information on historic fire in the Smokies comes from a survey of 10,000 square miles of the southern Appalachians in 1901 and 1902 by H.B. Ayres and W.W. Ashe. "The three agencies that have wrought changes in the forests of the Southern Appalachians" they reported, "are fires, lumbering, and clearing of lands for farming." Though severe burning had destroyed timber in some portions, light fires had caused greater damage by destroying seedlings, litter, and humus. The two found evidence of such fires over about 80 percent of the land area.

Though they did not assign cause, natural or human, to fires, Ayres and Ashe did find that burning was not uncommon on the northwest side of the Smokies. Along the East Fork of the Little Pigeon above Webb Creek, they observed that "most of the ridges have been burned over, and much of the timber on them has been killed and replaced by brush." At Alum Cave Creek: "Some scalds on ridges. About 500 acres severely burned." At Jakes Creek: "Fires have run over most of the ridges." On 24 square miles of the Little River Basin: "At least half of this tract is burned over annually." In Cades Cove: "Fires are set whenever they will run, and the forest shows the effect of this practice." And on Abrams Creek: "Fires are very frequent. Many trees have been injured or killed, but no large areas are entirely deadened."

The frequency of fire in the Smoky Mountains has changed drastically. From 1856 until the time the Smokies became a park, the interval between fires was 10 to 40 years. After 1940, when the National Park Sevice policy of total fire suppression was in effect, that interval grew to probably thousands of years, which for all practical purposes removed fire as a force in shaping the natural ecosystem.

In some Smokies plant communities, however, fire has an important role. In the western part of the park, for example, a pine-oak forest grows on the drier, rockier south- and west-facing slopes and ridges. Table Mountain, shortleaf, pitch, Virginia, and white pines share the canopy with scarlet, chestnut, white, and black oaks. Black gum, sourwood, and red maple may also be present, with serviceberry, mountain laurel, trailing arbutus, and galax making up the shrub and herb layer. The pine-oak forest is home to gray squirrels, whitetail deer, wild turkey, ruffed grouse, box turtles, and fence lizards, among others. This forest, the pines in particular, requires the open, sunny conditions and mineral seedbed that fire produces. Even a few, small, scattered burned areas allow these species to reproduce and grow. Grassy and heath balds also may have originated from fire, and fire helps maintain their open aspect.

Recognizing fire's role in the Smokies, the park is formulating a new policy. The change is part of an evolution in the philosophy of fire ecology over at least two centuries. That philosophy has swung from Indian and pioneer ideas about the beneficial effects of fire, to a view of fire as an "enemy" of the forest that must be totally suppressed, back to an appreciation of fire's role in the ecology of natural systems.

The reorientation of fire policy in the national parks came about in the 1960s and 1970s. Though prevention and suppression were not abandoned, "prescribed" fire became part of fire management. Suppression is still a first response, especially to minimize impacts of very hot, destructive wildfires in areas like the Smokies, where 60 years' worth of fuel had built up. Now, some natural fires are allowed to burn, or fires are intentionally set under a prescribed set of conditions that include humidity, wind, and moisture content of the fuel.

In the Smokies fire management plan, in draft stage in 1992, all unplanned, human-caused fires would be suppressed. Naturally ignited fires would be allowed to resume a role as a force of nature (within the constraints of air quality and other park values). In the plan, the park is divided into three units. Below 4,500 feet elevation, prescribed fire would be used to perpetuate rare species and to control exotic (introduced) species. Above 4,500 feet, prescribed fire would be employed to maintain balds, control exotics, and for other purposes. In the historic, special use, and developed areas, all lightning and unplanned human fires would be suppressed. Prescribed fire could be used to reduce fuels around buildings, control exotics, enhance habitat for rare species, or contribute to a more authentic historical scene.

Two interesting cases of a dependence on fire involve two Smokies species, one a pine, the other a woodpecker. Table Mountain pine (*Pinus pungens*) grows on dry tablelands, ridges, and slopes only in the central and southern Appalachians. "Its place," writes Donald Culross Peattie, "is high on mountain ridges, where it looks down on the soaring buzzards, where the wildcat lives and the rattler suns his coils."

Great Smoky Mountains N. P.

The aftermath of logging and burning on Clingmans Dome in the 1920s.

This medium-sized tree, also called bur pine, poverty pine, and prickly pine, does not reach great heights, usually only 40 to 60 feet. In the Smokies it grows best between 3,000 and 4,500 feet elevation. Settlers used Table Mountain pine for charcoal and rough lumber, and they found its turpentine good wound dressing. The knotty, brittle wood, though, has kept the species from being in big demand among timber operators.

In the forest, Table Mountain pine is important for its seeds, which are food for nuthatches, chickadees, woodpeckers, and red crossbills. Deer, turkey, and grouse nest and browse in the understory. And a moth larva, the mountain pine coneworm, feeds only on the cones of Table Mountain pine.

Fire is central to the Table Mountain pine's regeneration. Its large, egg-shaped, prickly cones often stay closed for several years after ripening, remaining on the trees for as long as 20 years. The cones are serotinous, meaning they require high heat to open and release their seeds. Sometimes the cones will open with hot summer temperatures, but fire also releases them. Fire destroys competing oaks as well, and clears the way for the pine, a quick colonizer of burned land. Without fire, invading oaks become dominant and Table Mountain pines decline.

In the Smokies, Table Mountain pine is an object of interest, largely because of its relationship with fire. Fire apparently prepares a mineral-rich seedbed in which Table Mountain pine seeds can sprout. The seeds do not seem to germinate in hardwood duff.

Perpetuation of other pine species in the Smokies may help save an endangered bird, the red-cockaded woodpecker. Listed as a federally endangered species in 1970, only 30 isolated populations of this woodpecker, about 7,400 birds, remain in its original range. That range included eastern Oklahoma, southeast Missouri, and eastern Kentucky south to the Gulf of Mexico and Florida.

Red-cockaded woodpeckers have been brought to the verge of extinction by agricultural and logging practices, fire suppression, predation, pine bark beetles, and competition for nest sites by red-headed woodpeckers and flying squirrels. A single natural disaster, Hurricane Hugo, wiped out the nesting trees of nearly one-fourth of the entire population when it hit the Francis Marion National Forest in South Carolina in the 1980s. Fire is important to the red-cockaded woodpecker because its absence allows hardwoods to thrive, but the birds prefer nearly pure stands of mature pines. Also, red-cockaded woodpeckers avoid nesting sites where the understory has started to grow up around the pines.

In the Great Smokies, red-cockaded woodpeckers are at the edge of their range. First reported in the park in 1936, the species has never been common. Only one colony was observed in the southwest section of the park in 1979, and a year later *Picoides borealis* was reported as "extremely rare, perhaps nearing extinction" in the Smokies.

Red-cockaded woodpeckers build their nests in pine trees, favoring shortleaf and Virginia pines in the park. Unlike other woodpeckers, they select live, not dead, trees more than 50 years old. To save effort in what can be a year-long process to carve a nest cavity, they often choose trees infected with red-heart fungus.

The rat snake is one of the red-cockaded woodpecker's main predators. Perhaps to deter snakes from entering, the birds actively maintain the resin coating around the nest cavity. The birds also scale the bark off the trunk, making it smoother. Rat snakes trying to climb the trees cannot get any purchase on the smooth tree, and the resin sticks to their scales. That glow of reddish resin has inspired people to call the pines "candle" trees; one observer has called them a "beacon" that indicates the presence of red-cockaded woodpeckers.

The social organization of red-cockaded woodpeckers is complex and fascinating. They form clans of two to nine birds that includes one breeding pair, their young, and other adults, usually males, called helpers. The helpers assist in incubating and feeding the young birds, making new nests, and defending territory. Each clan lives in a colony of cavity trees. In addition to cavity trees, a clan also needs 100 to 250 acres of surrounding trees for foraging territory, where they can obtain the spiders, centipedes, ants, and cockroaches they eat.

To manage forests for this endangered species, clearings in which pines can regenerate must be created. Where an active colony has been found, the hardwoods can be mechanically removed within an area of about 50 feet. Another possibility, perhaps the best for long-term perpetuation of the pines, is fire. Its use will be tricky, however, and has not yet been tried. Initially, fire would be needed to get rid of hardwoods so that pines could become established. Virginia and shortleaf pines, especially, will grow quickly on the thin soils in old fields and clearings. But once established, these pines are especially susceptible to intense wildfire until they reach a certain size. Then the area could be maintained with cool, controlled burns to prevent a potentially catastrophic buildup of forest duff and encroachment of hardwoods.

Park Service managers have an uphill battle, however, in promoting the use of fire. People do not come the Smokies, or to any national park for that matter, to see blackened forests and smoke-filled skies. They come for the greenery, the wildflowers, the autumn colors, and the grand mountain scenery. The fate of a rare bird they may never see, or a less-than-mighty species of pine tree, will likely not sway public opinion much.

In the wake of the extensive forest fires in Yellowstone National Park in 1988, prescribed-burn policies of federal agencies have experienced a setback, to put it mildly. Because ecosystems are so complex, the role of fire is necessarily complex too.

Clearing

"At present trees of choicest timber are killed to make fields on which corn cost $1 a bushel, or to be grazed until worn out and gullied by rapid erosion. On these clearings the mountaineers make only a miserable living."

This was the scene in the southern Appalachians in the early part of this century. The picture was one of incredible waste of the forests by the earliest settlers. It is difficult, however, for those of us living in the late 20th century to imagine the vast forests these people encountered. At one time the entire eastern United States was cloaked in trees. So continuous was the canopy that a squirrel, it was said, could hop from branch to branch for many miles without ever touching ground.

When white settlers entered the Smoky Mountains they soon cleared land for planting. Here a young man plows a field on a typical homestead.

The Great Smoky Mountains were among the last frontiers to settlers, but enter them they finally did, at the end of the 18th century. After the Revolutionary War, veterans received 50-acre land grants for 75 cents. One settler, Dr. Joseph Dobson, chose a piece of land in the fertile valley of the Oconaluftee River in 1790. His claim

Great Smoky Mountains N.P.

Great Smoky Mountains N. P.

marked the arrival of pioneers to the Smokies. Others followed: John Jacob Mingus, Ralph Hughes, and Abraham
Enloe, with faraway neighbors in Cataloochee by the
1830s. On the Tennessee side, the Reagans and Ogles settled Gatlinburg in the early 1800s, the Whaleys in
Greenbrier, the Olivers in Cades Cove in 1818. The
choicest spots for homesteads were the flat river bottoms,
but as the population grew the settlers worked their way

*Tanbark stripped from
white oak or chestnut
trees was used by tan-
neries to cure hides.
The hides were soaked
in a mixture of the pul-
verized bark, which is
high in tannin, and
water.*

higher into the mountains. To gain any level land to plow and plant, the
trees first had to be cleared. An ax would do for the smaller trees, but the
mountaineers killed the largest trees by simply girdling them, cutting a
circle into the bark to stop the flow of life-giving sap. Areas of girdled
trees were called "deadenings."

The uses of wood for a pioneer family were legion. Some of the trees
would become cabins, smokehouses, and corn cribs, others fences, fuel,
furniture, tools, buckets, wagon wheels, and looms, all of which were
needed to maintain self-sufficiency on a small farm up this cove or that
holler. The settlers sheltered and fed themselves from the forest.

For a hundred years before the Smokies became a national park, pastures were cleared and fields plowed. In 1934, when the National Park Service took over the land, the settlers had to leave their homes. (Some did so willingly, others did not.) The old homesites can still be seen, if you look closely. Mosses and greenbrier vines often hide the stone foundations of a cabin or a rock wall. The forest is reclaiming the land.

      ઢ   ઢ   ઢ

In 1961, the U.S. Department of the Interior appointed a board to look at management of wildlife and natural processes in the national parks. The chairman of that board was ecologist A. Starker Leopold, and the result of the board's investigation, issued in 1963, is now called the Leopold Report. The Leopold Report became a central document in managing national parks. Its most significant guiding recommendation was that national parks should preserve or re-create "the ecologic scene as viewed by the first European visitors." Parks, essentially, would be "vignettes of primitive America."

Knowing the history of disturbances in the Great Smokies is important in attempting to restore the scene to the way it looked when Europeans first arrived. Such knowledge can also help answer ecological questions about how succession takes place; it provides what scientists call "baseline" data with which they can compare the past to the present. And it is crucial in making day-to-day, on-the-ground resource management decisions; for example, should fire be used to protect the habitat of the endangered red-cockaded woodpecker?

Yet the question inevitably arises, is the re-creation of primitive America possible? Though they may be protected, ecosystems in national parks, like ecosystems in all landscapes, are constantly changing. They change both in response to the natural processes of birth, growth, and death and to human disturbances that accelerate, interrupt, or set back those processes.

Management of national parks, then, is necessarily paradoxical: systems that must change are preserved, and human influence is introduced to try to correct past human-related damage. How policy guides and accommodates the inevitability of change and uncertainty is a matter of continuing dialogue.

10
The Rare and Endangered Ones

For the first time in nearly a century, the howls of wolves are being heard at night in the coves and forests of the Smoky Mountains. In November 1991, a family of red wolves was reintroduced into the Cades Cove area of Great Smoky Mountains National Park. The last red wolf was taken from the woods of east Tennessee in 1905, but some still roamed in isolated places in the Southeast.

Many eyes are watching the progress of this reintroduction in the Smokies, the first national park in the United States in which a large carnivore has been reintroduced. The success or failure of the project will heavily influence attempts at reintroductions of wolves and other top predators elsewhere.

The red wolf is one of the most endangered mammals in North America. There are only about 200 of them left in the world, and most of those are in captivity. At one time, red wolves were much more abundant. When first described in the 18th century, they ranged from the Atlantic seaboard to as far west as central Texas and Oklahoma and north to the Ohio River Valley.

In only another 50 years, however, *Canis rufus* was nearly gone from its original range. The red wolf had been driven to the far edges of its woodland, swamp, and river bottom habitat in the Southeast by too many people, too little land, and unmerciful predator control programs.

By the 1970s, shreds of a red wolf population — about a hundred animals — remained in the wild only on the coast of Louisiana and Texas. Their numbers had reached such a low point that the wolves could not find mates of their own species. They began interbreeding with coyotes, creating hybrid offspring.

This hybridization created the possibility of the red wolf becoming extinct. Biologists decided to place all the remaining wild red wolves in captivity to breed. In 1975, the red wolf was declared extinct in the wild in this country. Paradoxically, this was the first step toward salvation of the species; the goal of the captive breeding program was always to reestablish wild populations.

Removing the wolves from their habitat was risky, because of the loss of wildness that can occur in captive animals. Opponents voice strong concern that breeding in a zoo will rob a species of its ability to adapt and survive in the wild — the animals will associate people with food and will no longer be able to respond to the vagaries of natural selection. That is, they may no longer be able to be wolves.

But the captive breeding program for red wolves proceeded. Fourteen "pure" red wolves became the progenitors of the recovery program. In 1987, their offspring had increased to the point that it was time to release eight pioneers back into the wild. The Alligator River National Wildlife Refuge on the coast of North Carolina was the chosen site, and the wild population there has now grown to more than 20.

Though red wolves have so far fared well in the swamps of North Carolina, the southern Appalachian Mountains provide a different challenge. The decision to release wolves in the Great Smokies was made because the park has a large land area, it is protected by the National Park Service, and prey animals for the wolves are plentiful. Such secure areas are the wolf's only hope of surviving as a wild animal.

The concerns over reintroducing the wolf, however, are much more than biological. Public acceptance is key to any endangered species program, and is particularly critical in wolf reintroductions because people have such strong opinions, both favorable and unfavorable, toward the animal.

With some nine million visits a year, Great Smoky Mountains National Park offers a chance to see how wolves would fare in the presence of humans. In addition, houses and farms with livestock border the park, and 250 head of cattle are pastured in Cades Cove, where the first release, which was experimental, occurred. It provided another test — a big one — of whether wolves would prey on domestic cows, calves, sheep, and other livestock.

The opposition from farmers was tempered by the establishment of an indemnity fund to reimburse them for any livestock lost to wolves. And the wolves were fitted with tranquilizer collars that could be activated remotely; any animal causing trouble would be recaptured.

Red wolves are one of three large members of the canid, or dog, family in North America. The relationship among red wolves, coyotes, and gray wolves is complex and central to the reintroduction program. Both red wolves and their larger counterparts, gray wolves, are believed to be native to the Smoky Mountains, though early observers made no distinctions between the two. Red wolves are lankier than gray wolves and longer legged (some say they are built for running through the swampy bottomlands). An adult male red wolf weighs between 60 and 80 pounds, while a female is 50 to 60 pounds. Red wolves range in color from reddish or cinnamon to brown, gray, yellow, and black. As wolves disappeared from the Southeast, coyotes, smallest of the three canids, quickly expanded their range. Coyotes have been present in the Smokies since the early 1980s and are treated as native animals in the park.

To determine the interactions between wolves and coyotes, coyotes were tracked to map out their home ranges. The apparently small numbers of coyotes and their more opportunistic eating habits made it likely that the wolves and the coyotes could share the park successfully, though the wolves have shown some aggression toward the coyotes when they encounter one another.

In January 1991, two pairs of adult red wolves were brought in from a national wildlife refuge in Florida. To acclimate them to their new habitat, they were held in enclosures in Cades Cove. Four months later, in April, five pups were born to one pair, an eight-year-old male and a four-year-old female.

The experimental release of the animals into the park, scheduled for the summer, was delayed while a special regulation was enacted that effectively drew boundary lines the wolves would not be allowed to cross. Within the park, the wolves would be fully protected. But if they moved outside park boundaries and were found preying on livestock, a property owner could take measures — even shooting the wolves — without threat of prosecution.

Finally, on November 12, 1991, with a fanfare of media attention, the pens were opened and four wolves — the two parents and two of their female pups — were released into the Smoky Mountains. Every movement of the radio-collared animals was followed closely by biologists, to determine the animals' home ranges, diet, and those critical interactions with coyotes, livestock, and people.

The shy wolves, generally night hunters, were actually most active in early morning and evening. As the Cades Cove road opened to traffic each day, they retreated into the woods. The mated pair usually stayed together, and the pups were nearby. One wolf traveled up to two miles from the release site, and the female wandered out of the park, apparently lured by three cow carcasses. Though such easy pickings were undoubtedly attractive, the wolves hunted and ate mostly natural prey — raccoons, rabbits, grouse, and deer.

One of the earliest stories to make its way through the local grapevine was that a wolf had approached a cow and been chased away by the bovine. Then there was the Christmas Eve killing of a chicken by the male wolf, which left the indemnity fund three dollars poorer. The news worsened during the spring calving season in Cades Cove, when six calves were killed. Biologists kept constant vigil to determine if it was coyotes or wolves doing the killing. The male wolf was found guilty of killing one calf, costing the fund $250. After another incident with turkeys on private property just outside the park, the male was deemed too old and too accustomed to people to be a good candidate for reintroduction. He was recaptured and brought back in permanently.

Despite that setback, the year-long experiment was considered a success. The real test, though, is whether the first generation, the pups born in the acclimation pens, will reproduce in the wild. For the Smokies wolves, there is no answer to that question yet. It will take another two to three years to find out, after the females and males have sexually matured. Another big question is whether the wolves will move to the higher elevations, or go lower, where the human and livestock populations are greater.

In October 1992, an adult male, his mate, and their four pups were released in Cades Cove. There are no plans to recapture them, and others will be released in other parts of the park as the gradual permanent reintroduction continues. The park eventually could be home to 50 to 75 wolves. And the Smokies program could be the core of more wolf reintroductions into other parts of the southern Appalachians, perhaps into national forests bordering the park.

A pall was cast over the entire red wolf program in the summer of 1991, just as the release of the wolves in the Smokies was imminent. The question centers on whether the red wolf is a true species. Two researchers engaged in genetic studies of red wolves published results showing that the red wolf's DNA is identical to that of coyotes and other wolf species. They looked at DNA found in cellular structures called mitochondria. That DNA is inherited only through the mother and has little effect on how an animal looks or behaves. The researchers will also look at DNA in the nuclei of cells to determine if the red wolf has any unique genetic material that qualifies it as a species.

> ### Saving the Wolf
> "The uniqueness of [the red wolf] is that it was deliberately extirpated from the wild. Only through . . . reintroduction . . . into secured areas . . . such as Great Smoky Mountains National Park can the species have any chance of surviving as a truly wild animal."
>
> —Warren Parker, U.S. Fish & Wildlife Service Proposal to Reintroduce the Red Wolf into Great Smoky Mountains National Park

The results are undeniably significant, because legally an animal cannot be listed and protected under the Endangered Species Act unless it is a bona fide species. Some use the studies to question the expenditure of funds for an animal that is not a species but a hybrid. Even before the genetics studies were done, at least one member of the red wolf recovery team had held that the red wolf is a cross between the gray wolf and coyote.

Others say the genetics studies, though convincing, are only one tool. Other evidence, including an exhaustive survey of wolf and coyote skulls by taxonomists, shows the red wolf is a distinct species. Fossil evidence, too, indicates that the red wolf was around 750,000 years ago, perhaps even before gray wolves.

The results of genetic studies have not swayed me from the strong, even thrilling, hope that the red wolf will continue to roam free in the

Smoky Mountains. On a Saturday morning about a month after the wolves were first released, I went to Cades Cove. My plan was to hike the trail to Abrams Falls, but a hard, cold rain fell constantly all morning. Instead, I drove slowly around the loop road, stopping at the pullouts, searching the gray, misted fields and the dark, forested edges with binoculars. It was a long shot, I knew, but I strained to catch a glimpse of a wolf. Though I never saw one that day, I was content with the knowledge that the wolves were there. Perhaps one day I will be privileged to hear their haunting wild howls fill the cove.

The Hope of Abrams Creek

A walk along Abrams Creek provides a chance to see another reintroduced animal. In the past several years, people have reported seeing young river otters along the creek, where the first otter reintroduction was undertaken in the park in 1986.

Abrams Creek was chosen for the initial reintroduction because it is the longest stretch of slow water in the park, with deep pools that contain plenty of fish. The pools' silty bottoms also mean good habitat for crayfish, one of the otters' main foods.

Otters are made for the water, with their dense, insulating fur, long, muscular bodies, webbed toes, short legs, and tapered, rudderlike tail. They close their small ears and nostrils when they are in the water, and their hind feet have rough pads for traction on slippery streambanks and rocks. Otters swim gracefully underwater and dog-paddle on the surface. If food becomes scarce along the waterways, otters will move overland, but only at a slow lope.

Like wolves, otters became extinct in the Smokies because of the acts of humans. Trappers sought otters for their sleek, brown fur, which was in high demand. Although the pelts of *Lutra canadensis* in the southern mountains were not considered as good as those from animals in the Northwest, this did not help save the animals. A traveling fur merchant told Smokies explorer Samuel Buckley in 1858 that the otter skins he bought among the mountains "equal in fineness and goodness those of the north." But to get the highest price for the furs, the merchant said, he was obliged to send his skins to New

Abrams Creek and Cades Cove

Great Smoky Mountains N. P.

River otters have traveled impressive distances since they were reintroduced into park streams in the 1980s.

York through Ohio and the Erie Railroad to convince purchasers that they had come from the Northwest.

Overtrapping and logging, which destroyed their habitat, eliminated otters from East Tennessee. The last reliable sighting of "orters," as they are called in the mountains, was in Cataloochee in 1936, just two years after the Smokies became a national park.

Fifty years later, this beautiful aquatic mammal, cousin to weasels and skunks, is once again swimming in the clear streams of the Smokies. In 1986, 11 otters were brought to Tennessee from North Carolina. Before their release, radio transmitters were implanted in their stomachs so the otters could be tracked.

Two weeks after the March release on Abrams Creek, two otters were dead. One was old and died of unknown, but possibly natural, causes. The other had been entangled in a fishing net in Chilhowee Lake and drowned. The remaining otters, however, built dens and began reproducing. A few even moved into the Little River watershed.

The six otters that stayed in Abrams Creek paired off and distributed themselves throughout the drainage, with little overlap in their ranges. The average home range of each pair was about nine miles of stream, less than half the size of the ranges of otters reintroduced in other places. Otters form strong attachments to certain sites that are determined by available food and shelter and social interactions with other otters. Those sites then become the focus of a home range. Within a home range, otters seem to frequent some areas more than others. On Abrams Creek, those "activity centers" were always near long, deep pools close to the dens. The otters built their dens among rock crevices and caves above the water line, sometimes in thick vegetation.

Otters tend to leave their feces, or scat, at well-used "latrine sites." Along Abrams Creek, the latrine sites are often moss-covered stream-banks and sometimes prominent boulders. These sites are scent markers important in otter communication.

The female otter and her young form the social group. Males and females interact, but rarely do two animals of the same sex associate.

Female otters can breed at age two, but males are not sexually mature until they are five to seven years of age. Otters mate between December and March, but as with black bears, the embryo does not implant in the female's uterus until later — another 10 months in the otter's case. Once implantation occurs, gestation lasts about two months. One to four, usually two, young are born, blind and toothless but fully furred. The young stay with the mother for eight or nine months while she teaches them how to swim. Sometimes they seem so reluctant she must drag them bodily into the water; but perhaps they are only playing, a trait for which otters are well known.

A long-standing myth about otters is that they will eat great numbers of desirable game fish such as trout. Though these carnivorous mammals will occasionally take trout, Smokies otters eat mostly crayfish and "rough" fish such as stonerollers and suckers. In Abrams Creek, in fact, 95 percent of all otter scats contained crayfish. In winter they may eat more fish, because crayfish are in burrows then. In spring, when frogs, toads, and salamanders are breeding and more plentiful, amphibians may make up more of the otters' diet.

Because some of the Abrams Creek otters migrated naturally to the Little River, it was chosen as the site of a second reintroduction. A few days after Christmas in 1988, two adult otters were released on the upper Little River, and at least a dozen more have been released since. Four have been found dead; one was shot outside the park. Some of the Little River otters, along with their counterparts on Abrams Creek, have traveled to the North Carolina side of the park. Such long-distance journeys are not unknown among these animals. So far, otter reintroductions are a happy success story for the Smokies.

Again we go to Abrams Creek, to follow the progress of two reintroduced fish species that are possible otter prey, smoky and yellowfin madtoms. Madtoms, small members of the catfish family, got their colorful common name for the poisonous fluid at the base of their spines that feels like a bee sting to anyone who gets a dose of it. Until they were reintroduced, neither species had been found in Abrams Creek since 1957, the year that federal and state biologists undertook a "reclamation" project. This reclamation involved treating 15 miles of Abrams Creek with a toxic chemical called rotenone to kill all the native fish. The gates were about to close on the dam on the Little Tennessee River that would form Chilhowee Reservoir on the southern boundary of the park. In the wisdom of those days, it was believed that ridding the Little Tennessee and its tributary, Abrams Creek, of "trash" fish would create pristine waters for rainbow trout — non-native game fish that would be stocked in Chilhowee once it began to fill.

In June 1957, rotenone was dumped into Abrams Creek. Thirty-one fish species were eliminated, including the madtoms. At the time, no one cared much about these small, secretive fish. No one even knew what the smoky madtom was. The fish that went belly up during the reclamation project were simply put in jars and sent off to the Smithsonian Institution. The smoky madtom was first described by science in the 1960s. Thus, what was then the world's only known population of smoky madtoms assumed the dubious distinction of becoming extinct even as it was discovered.

In 1980, smoky madtoms were found in Citico Creek in the Cherokee National Forest, downstream from Chilhowee Reservoir. The species was immediately placed on the federal endangered species list and a recovery plan for them was drawn up.

The recovery effort, which began in 1986, involves collecting madtom eggs or larvae from Citico Creek. The eggs are then hatched and the young fish are reared in an aquarium in Knoxville. Thousands of smoky and yellowfin eggs or larvae have been collected, and hundreds of the fish have been released into Abrams Creek.

Madtoms are so secretive in their habits that biologists have at times resorted to nighttime snorkeling to search for them. Only a handful of smoky madtoms has been seen since the reintroduction began, but some were males guarding nest cavities, a sign that the fish may have begun reproducing.

The lack of any great numbers of madtom observations could be due to some habitat difficulties. Madtoms prefer to forage on gravel bottoms in clear streams. They are especially sensitive to silt, and Abrams Creek may be having some silting problems.

From Abrams Creek, we turn to the skies over the Smokies to find the other major wildlife species to be reintroduced in recent years. It is a remarkable raptor, the peregrine falcon. These birds of prey are renowned for stupendous flight speeds, and have been clocked at 180 miles an hour in a dive for prey. Handsome slate-gray birds, peregrines were once found everywhere in the world except Antarctica.

The saga of the demise of peregrines is now widely known. They became endangered when they ingested the pesticide DDT in their foods. Peregrines proved especially sensitive to DDE, a byproduct of the breakdown of DDT. DDE prevents calcium from forming in the developing egg; when eggs were laid, the shells were so thin they were crushed during incubation. Other reproductive problems showed up as well — reduced sexual drive, weakened pair bonds, and a tendency to eat rather than incubate the eggs. Other chemicals such as PCBs and dieldrin, an insecticide that lowers the birds' hormone levels, may be more responsible for these problems.

Peregrines were year-round, breeding residents in the Smokies in the early decades of this century. A birder reported in April 1929 that he had discovered a peregrine nest in a cliff on the slope of Mount LeConte. The nest contained three eggs, which he collected with the aid of a rope ladder tied to rhododendron bushes.

In 1932, members of the Great Smoky Hiking Club saw the nest of a "duckhawk," as peregrines were then called, near Alum Cave. The group hiked to the nest, or eyrie, on the north side of a narrow pinnacle of blue shale. That nest, which had been inhabited the previous year, was

Tennessee Wildlife Resources Agency

Fledgling peregrine falcons have been released on Greenbrier Pinnacle. It is hoped that the falcons will return to nest in the places where they learned to fly.

vacant, but a new one was found on a ledge about 50 feet away. The nest, a "mere depression" hollowed out in the soil, contained three newly hatched peregrines: "The three small downy white youngsters," wrote one of the hikers, "huddled together so that it was difficult to tell if there was one or three." The parents of the nestlings dove at the intruders and tried to drive them away.

In 1936, peregrines were reported numerous times on Mount LeConte, where they tried to carry off chickens kept at the backcountry lodge there. Those who saw the peregrines were awed by their legendary flight abilities. One observer wrote in 1938 that "all ornithologists who visit the Park hope to see" this rare and spectacular bird. On June 13 at Clingmans Dome, the unknown author and group were not disappointed. From the observation tower they "suddenly caught sight of one of the falcons sweeping across the landscape with the speed of an arrow. As we looked, it was joined by another and then a third one. For twenty minutes they gave us a demonstration of meteoric aerial prowess . . . diving downward from far above, then rapidly soaring

Tennessee Wildlife Resources Agency

Mountain lions, also called panthers and cougars, are native to the Smokies, and reports of mountain lion sightings in the park persist. Until their reestablishment in the wild can be confirmed, lions are officially considered extirpated.

across or wheeling about the mountain spurs with the aid of the stiff breezes."

By 1940, however, peregrine falcons had become rare in the park. In 1944 there was no evidence of peregrines nesting at the traditional Alum Cave site. By this time, the once cosmopolitan, wide-ranging peregrines were beginning to decline not only in the Southeast but all over the country. By the mid-1960s, peregrines had disappeared as a breeding bird in the eastern United States, largely because of the effects of DDT. DDT was banned from most uses in the United States in 1972.

In August 1984, peregrine falcons were reintroduced in the park on Greenbrier Pinnacle, a high remote peak in the northern part of the Smokies. It was one of two spots selected for reintroduction of peregrines in the South. The other was Grandfather Mountain in North Carolina. Others have since been added in the southern Appalachians.

The Smokies peregrine project uses a technique called hacking, a term from ancient falconry that referred to young falcons feeding at a tree stump or post called a hack board. In modern hacking, captive-bred birds are kept and fed at hack sites until they are old enough to fly and hunt on their own.

Four month-old peregrines were brought to the Smokies and kept in cages, or "hack boxes," for six weeks on a high, isolated cliff on Greenbrier Pinnacle. Each was fed one dead chicken a day through a tube above the hack box, so the peregrines would not imprint on their feeders and associate people with food.

The young peregrines were kept at high elevation (above 4,500 feet) until they learned to fly, hunt on their own, and defend themselves. For the first three to five days after release, the young peregrines practiced on smaller prey — they chased their siblings, hunted butterflies, and took some practice dives at vultures, hawks, and ravens. In six to eight weeks, however, they were catching small birds on the wing, especially swifts. And by that time, they were likely able to avoid one of their major predators, the great horned owl.

Because peregrines consider home the place where they learned to fly rather than where they were born, the hope is that the birds fledged on Greenbrier Pinnacle will return to the park to nest. Peregrines have been seen in the park, and adult pairs have been documented elsewhere in the southern Appalachians.

There have been unconfirmed reports of peregrines nesting in the park, but no nesting sites have been located. Still, hopes are high, for peregrines have made stunning comebacks. They nest not only in the wild but also on skyscrapers in cities, where one of their favorite foods, domestic pigeons, is abundant.

Other species of wildlife, notably some large mammals, became extinct in the Smokies in the 18th century. One, the bison, or buffalo, once roamed in small herds in eastern Tennessee, but became extinct in the mid-1700s. A proposal to reintroduce bison in the park was put forth briefly in the late 1980s, but it never gained much ground.

A big predator, the mountain lion, was last seen in the Smokies in 1920. This animal reportedly was killed near Fontana Village in the southwest corner of the park. The demise of this great predatory cat is a story not unlike that of the wolf — it was hated for its alleged killing of livestock, and white settlers and bounty hunters saw to its extirpation in the mountains.

Nevertheless, sightings of lions and their signs in the park are reported periodically. Usually the reports have been of a single cat, though an adult with kittens has been reported in two different areas of the park. Many reports come from the Cataloochee area, some from the Greenbrier and Cosby areas, and a few from Cades Cove and other places scattered throughout the park. Not surprisingly, most sightings are near areas with high deer densities. Whitetail deer are a mainstay of the mountain lion diet, and deer have become more common since the park was established. While mountain lion sightings and their signs are never disregarded, park wildlife officials maintain that most sightings are of pet lions that have escaped from nearby homes.

The Little, Live Things

Undeniably, the greatest attention to endangered species is lavished on the "charismatic megafauna" such as mountain lions, wolves, and bison. Small fish, insects, and plants receive far less fanfare. Few people get very excited about a liverwort that doesn't even have a common name. Nevertheless, these species can be important indicators of environmental health. The Smokies serve as an important refuge for rare native plants, many of which are sensitive barometers of unnatural interference.

Keeping track of rare and endangered plants in the Smokies is a big job. The park contains almost 1,300 native vascular plant species, more than any other national park. The diversity of nonvascular plants, including about 430 species of mosses and lichens, is also among the highest in North America. In all, 327 vascular and 192 nonvascular plants are considered rare within the park, with five or fewer populations known.

Work has just begun on the enormous task of finding out, first, what is out there, second, whether it is in danger, and third, how the species can best be protected. Plant conservation took a big step forward in 1988 when Great Smoky Mountains became the first national park to have a Natural Heritage Program. This program is a network of a private nonprofit conservation organization, The Nature Conservancy. It includes a computerized inventory and location of all uncommon plants of special concern and establishes criteria for ranking rarity.

One of the highest-priority species in the park, because of its endangered status at the global, national, state, and park levels, is the Appalachian avens. This member of the rose family, whose yellow flowers bloom in July, is known to science as *Geum radiatum*. Avens is endangered both botanically and legally. It was listed as endangered on the federal list in 1990, which means it is in danger of extinction throughout all or a significant portion of its range.

In the Smokies, Appalachian avens has been pushed to the brink (literally and figuratively) by the trampling of human feet. It also appears to be threatened by air pollution and low reproduction. Only one population of the plant is known in the Smokies, on vertical cliffs high on Mount LeConte, one of the most popular hiking destinations in the park. (The avens was collected on top of Gregory Bald in 1935, but that population is probably extinct.) So inaccessible are some of the remaining plants that botanists must rappel over the cliffs to study them.

Like many rare plants, Appalachian avens is endemic here, restricted to a few high peaks in the southern Appalachians. An estimated 30 percent of the rare plant species in the Smokies are southern Appalachian endemics, which usually grow in specialized habitats. Because there are so few populations, each lost population means great genetic loss. This puts endemics at greater risk of extinction in the long term.

Another 20 percent of rare species in the park are disjunct populations separated from their main range. Forty percent are peripherals, at the limits of their ranges. In these isolated and fringe populations, genetic exchange is greatly restricted, ranges cannot be expanded, and environmental factors that drive natural selection are different, all making them more vulnerable.

Other plants of special concern in the Smokies include the heart-leaved paper birch *(Betula cordifolia)*. Though only about 100 of these trees have been found, they appear to be healthy and the population stable. As an insurance policy for the future, botanists have climbed some of the trees and collected seed for germination at a native plant nursery.

Another monitored species is Rugel's ragwort, whose entire range is in the Great Smokies. Rugel's ragwort *(Cacalia rugelia)* grows in the high-elevation spruce-fir forest. Its habitat is changing because of the death of most of the Fraser firs from infestation of the balsam woolly adelgid. The changes caused by the fir die-off will affect Rugel's ragwort, though what those effects will be over the short and long term are still unknown.

Other species, like the wahoo, or burningbush *(Euonymus atropurpurea)*, a gentian called American columbo *(Frasera caroliniensis)*, and the Virginia chain fern *(Woodwardia virginica)*, are being heavily browsed by a native animal, the whitetail deer. Fencing may be necessary to exclude the deer and protect the plants. The rootings of the non-native wild boar are also threatening some plants, including a lovely orchid, the rose pogonia *(Pogonia ophioglossoides)*. Because they are coveted by plant collectors, orchids are also especially vulnerable to poaching in the park. A few rare species may be threatened by operations of the Park Service, including roadside mowing, ditching of wet areas, and building and maintaining trails.

Once threats to the plants have been identified, the question is whether to remove the threat or to move the plant, the least desirable option. Meanwhile, seed banks are being established for many of the plants so they can be propagated for future revegetation efforts.

Why all the effort spent on these few "hothouse" specialties of the plant world? What is the value of a Rugel's ragwort, or even a red wolf or a river otter? Why do they matter, and what do they represent? An even larger question is what is the value of their home, the Great Smoky Mountains? And how can the values of the Smokies be assured when threats are coming from far outside the boundaries of the park? These are complex questions with no easy answers, but we will explore them in the next chapters.

11
Clouds over the Mountains
Threats to the Smokies

My husband and I hiked to Mount LeConte on a perfect April day, the air as clear as I had ever seen it in the Smoky Mountains. The views from the Alum Cave Trail were spectacular. At the top of LeConte the path passed through a remarkable stand of trees. They were remarkable because they were Fraser firs, still alive, one of the last stands of this species in the southern Appalachians.

Five backpackers had arrived before us and laid out their sleeping bags on the row of wooden bunks in the shelter. Packs were hung on nails in the wall to guard against the depredations of the resident mice. The hikers were from South Bend, Indiana, on the final day of a week-long trek along the Appalachian Trail. As the men related their experiences along the trail, it was obvious they had been deeply affected by the trip — the people they had met along the way, the camaraderie they had felt with one another. Ben, who seemed especially introspective that evening, commented on a disturbing sight — all the dead fir trees they had seen in the forest, "killed by acid rain," he'd heard.

He and his friends had walked through the worst of the dying grounds, in the northeast section of the Smoky Mountains from Cosby westward. The gray skeletons of dead firs were all too frequent companions, made more ghostly by the fog that so often engulfs this high-elevation forest. The dead firs reminded me of the word used by early settlers to describe the groves of trees they girdled: "deadenings," they were called. We were witness to the drastic changes in the greatest remnant of old-growth spruce-fir forest in the southern Appalachians. And with good reason, we were all disturbed by that sight.

Though acid rain may have played a part in the Fraser firs' demise, the primary cause of death is an insect, the balsam woolly adelgid.

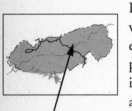

Mount LeConte

Like the blight that killed the noble chestnut trees, the balsam woolly adelgid was an import, entering Canada and the northern United States from Europe on contaminated nursery stock, probably before the turn of the century. The adelgid was first identified in Maine in 1908. It took the chestnut blight only about 30 years to wipe out one of the dominant trees of the eastern hardwood forest. The adelgid's host trees are not as widely distributed as the chestnut was, and the insect took a little longer to arrive in the southern Appalachians. Once present, however, the balsam woolly adelgid wreaked destruction with frightening rapidity.

Balsam woolly adelgids feed on true firs. From their balsam fir hosts in the Northeast, they spread south to Fraser fir, the balsam's southern Appalachian counterpart. Fraser fir proved the species most susceptible to the insect's attacks. The balsam woolly adelgid was identified on Mount Mitchell in the North Carolina mountains in 1957. By that time, the entire mountain was infested, indicating the insect might have been established as early as 1940.

That the location was Mount Mitchell was significant. Mount Mitchell is the tallest peak in the eastern United States and is centrally located to all the Fraser fir stands in the southern Appalachians. It is located in a part of the Appalachian chain that trends north-south, providing a ready corridor for the insect's dispersal.

By 1963, the balsam woolly adelgid had made it to the Smokies. It was first observed on Mount Sterling, on the northeast boundary of the park. All the infested trees were cut down, but the following year an adjoining area was under attack. By 1969, 2,700 acres of Fraser fir were reported infested. Ten years later, all the fir stands in the park had become infested. All the firs on Mount Sterling had been killed by the adelgid, and half of those on the southern end of the Balsam Mountains were gone. Adelgid activity had become highly visible from Newfound Gap to Clingmans Dome, near the southern limits of the tree's range in North America.

The tiny balsam woolly adelgid *(Adelges piceae)* was at one time called an aphid. It is not a true aphid, but a member of the jumping plant lice family. Though they may appear to jump, the wingless adelgids actually are dispersed largely by wind. As air is forced up over a mountain, it picks up speed as it passes the summit. On the leeward side of the mountain, the air slows and falls in eddies. In June and September, when such wind eddies are loaded with adelgid larvae and sometimes eggs, tall firs on the leeward side of the mountains are easy hosts. Gravity also acts as an agent of dispersion, as adelgids fall from the crowns of trees onto understory fir saplings and seedlings. People and other animals can also unknowingly carry the insect's eggs or larvae from one area to another.

Adelgids feed exclusively on plant sap, using specialized mouth parts. When they land on a fir, they attach themselves to the bark and insert a long, slender, rod-shaped stylet. Through the stylet they suck sap from the bark and inject a poison that disrupts the flow of water and nutrients from the roots to the crown of the tree.

All adelgids that feed on North American firs are females — they reproduce asexually and do quite well without males. Their fecundity, in fact, is spectacular: one female can lay 100 to 250 eggs. In the relatively salubrious climate of the southern Appalachians, she can potentially produce four generations of offspring a year.

The adelgid's complex life cycle consists of an egg, three larval stages, and metamorphosis to an adult. Females lay purplish brown or orangish eggs on the bark of a tree, attaching the eggs with silken thread. The first generation of larvae hatch in about 12 days and are called crawlers, because this is the only stage when the insect is mobile. Crawlers then insert their stylets into the bark and begin feeding. At this stage, called the first-instar nymph, they become stationary and overwinter. The next stage of development begins the following spring, when the host tree renews its growth cycle and the larvae start to feed.

During this stage their bodies become covered with a waxy secretion that keeps them from drying out. The secretion, like silken white threads, is the "wool" that gives the woolly adelgid its common name. They become even woollier as adults, which occurs in only a month or so. In two or three days, they begin reproducing.

Secretions in the adelgid's saliva cause the growth of abnormal, large, thick wood cells called redwood, essentially premature heartwood. For reasons still unclear, the Fraser fir's normal defense mechanisms are unable to seal off the feeding site and contain the adelgid secretions. On Fraser firs, adelgids attack the crowns and trunks, and the most common and most severe attacks are on the boles of trees that have reached cone-bearing age, about 20 years old.

As the water and nutrient supply is cut off, the tree cannot photosynthesize and begins to lose vigor. The outward manifestation of adelgid attack is a change in the color of the tree's foliage — from healthy blue-green to yellow-green and finally red-brown. Medium-sized and mature firs are susceptible to infestation and die in only a few years. Firs in advanced stages of reproduction respond variously; some die but some recover when the adelgid attacks stop. The adelgids do not seem successful in building and maintaining infestations on healthy young trees or seedlings.

The diagnosis for the future of Fraser fir in the Smokies is not optimistic. Seed-bearing trees will soon be gone, with mature trees left only in scattered areas. The accumulation of standing dead trees represents a great deal of fuel buildup in the forest. Should a fire occur, viable fir seeds in the soil could be destroyed, and a seedbed more suited to pioneer species like pin cherry and mountain ash would be created.

Planting fir seeds or seedlings will succeed only if the balsam woolly adelgid is gone and cannot be reintroduced, — and if the winds don't blow the wrong way and reintroduce the aphid into the Great Smokies.

The only treatment for adelgid infestations for some time was pesticides, especially lindane, which is unacceptable because it persists in the environment. For several years, trees in the Clingmans Dome and Balsam Mountain areas have been sprayed with an insecticidal soap developed in Canada that is less toxic and less persistent. The soap (potassium oleate) kills adelgids by removing their protective waxy covering. But the spraying effort cannot save the current generation of Fraser firs. The only hope, though it may be a false one, is that the next generation of trees might be saved.

More than 90 percent of all the Fraser firs in the Smokies are dead from an infestation of an alien insect, the balsam woolly adelgid.

In North America, balsam woolly adelgids have no known parasites or diseases that could reduce or damage their populations. Insect predators have had little effect on them either. In a biological catch-22, a tree's carrying capacity is the only check on adelgid population growth. Once that carrying capacity is exceeded, the adelgid population crashes. But by that time the tree is beyond help and will die shortly. It can be only five to ten years from the time of infestation until tree death.

Looking back to Mount Sterling, where the first infestation of adelgids was found in the park, the understory Fraser firs that survived the first infestation and ones that have grown from seed since have reached the age at which they could support adelgid populations. Firs around Clingmans Dome have become infested. Prevailing winds blow eastward from Clingmans Dome to Mount Sterling, sending adelgids on a return trip, creating a 35- to 60-year cycle of initial infestation, limited recovery, and regeneration and reinfestation of the adelgids.

In the early 1990s, Keith Langdon, resource management specialist for the Smokies, described Fraser fir as only "a faint echo of what it was." In Shenandoah National Park in Virginia, the firs have almost been wiped out, Langdon noted. The story, he said, is likely to be the same for the Great Smokies: though a few remnant trees will survive and some will sporadically produce seeds, like an echo it comes back more and more faintly.

What Happens Now?

A more pressing question now is, what happens in a forest community of two dominant tree species when one of those trees is eliminated? It seems obvious that something will happen to those plants and animals that thrived in the shady, cool, moist conditions of the spruce-fir forest. With a good portion of the canopy gone, plants such as blackberries that favor sunny openings take immediate advantage of the holes left by dying Fraser firs. Yellow birch and mountain ash also increase. With no protection from another large tree growing nearby, the shallow-rooted red spruces are more subject to windthrow. Where they are not blown over by the wind, red spruces spread their crowns to close the canopy, and spruce seedlings increase. Fraser fir seedlings are also prolific, but many will not reach reproductive age before another adelgid attack.

Mosses, lichens dependent on fir bark, and certain birds, mammals, amphibians, and insects tied to the spruce-fir habitat are likely to be affected by changes in the forest's dynamics. More subtle and probably not detectable for some time will be changes in decomposition and mineralization rates, disruptions of the chemical cycles between geology, plants, and animals, and a possible net loss of nutrients from the ecosystem.

Birds of the spruce-fir forest have proven to be one of the earliest barometers of the changes. Breeding bird censuses taken on Mount Collins before and after invasion by the balsam woolly adelgid reveal that densities for all species together had declined 37 percent. Birds such as black-capped chickadees, golden-crowned kinglets, vireos, and red-breasted nuthatches that lived in the canopy were most affected. Some species densities are so low that local extinctions are possible. Yet even in the face of extreme changes in the habitat, no species has been lost on Mount Collins, indicating a surprising stability in this relatively simple bird community.

A bird census in the spruce-fir forest on Mount Guyot showed a strikingly similar drop in bird populations — 36 percent — before and after the adelgid arrived. Two species, the robin and Blackburnian warbler, had disappeared from the study area on Mount Guyot. Robins were once fairly common on Mount Guyot. The absence of the Blackburnian warbler, a beautiful songbird, from the treetops is especially disturbing.

Though birds of drier, open areas would be expected to increase where edges are created by canopy openings, only a few — Canada and chestnut-sided warblers and rufous-sided towhees — have done so on Mount Guyot. This indicates that new openings in the spruce-fir have themselves become islands. There are no adjoining disturbed areas to supply large numbers of new recruits such as catbirds, towhees, thrashers, and Canada or chestnut-sided warblers. Despite their mobility, these birds cannot negotiate the barriers of the hardwood trees that still border the spruce-fir.

Most breeding bird species in the park's spruce-fir forests are at the southernmost limits of their ranges and exist in small, scattered populations. There is no pool of individuals that could come into the forest to rebuild bird populations. Fortunately, however, a "seed crop" of breeding birds appears to be hanging on in the spruce-fir forest, even in the highly altered open canopy. If the firs should ever regenerate and survive, new generations of birds might once again recolonize the forest.

Has air pollution played a role in the death of the Fraser fir? No one knows for certain. What is known is that balsam woolly adelgids on firs in the northeastern and northwestern United States have not spread beyond a hundred miles inland from the coasts. Cold winters may be prohibiting their survival, but in those regions there is also a mixing of ocean and land air, which dilutes pollution. In the inland mountains of the Southeast, such mixing does not occur.

Fraser fir is the only fir infested by balsam woolly adelgids that grows in an area with potentially harmful levels of air pollution. The fir and other high-elevation conifers may be more vulnerable to pollution carried in precipitation because of the higher rainfall they receive, nearly twice the amount that falls on the lower elevations in the Smokies. The high surface area of the needles on conifers, with their ability to comb moisture from clouds, means another moisture gain. Despite the fact that greater precipitation dilutes pollutants, if that moisture carries pollutants, the spruce-fir forests may be receiving added doses simply by virtue of their existence at high elevations.

Air Pollution

Maloney Point on the Little River Road offers one of the most scenic vistas in the Smokies. But one day late in June, as I stood looking out on the Sugarlands Valley, I noted a murky, almost yellowish tinge to the air that obscured the wave of mountain ridges normally seen from the point.

The yellowish haze, I discovered later, was due to a high concentration of ozone — one of the highest, in fact, that had been measured in the park since air quality monitoring began. A high-pressure system of stagnant air had been sitting over the Southeast most of the week, creating ideal conditions for high ozone concentrations. The west slope of the southern Appalachians is second only to Los Angeles in the frequency of air stagnation episodes, and summer is one of the worst times.

The bad actor is "ground-level" ozone, not the ozone higher in the atmosphere that shields us from harmful ultraviolet radiation. Ground-level ozone forms when sunlight reacts with hydrocarbons and nitrogen oxides emitted from vehicle exhaust and by burning fossil fuels.

Good visibility is one of the major assets of the Smokies; and because the park is a Class I area under the federal Clean Air Act, the government must assure that the air here is not degraded. The situation is ironic, given that the Smokies were named for the haze that so often swirls around the mountains. But the natural haze, created by moisture and plant transpiration, is bluish. Ozone haze is yellowish.

The Great Smokies were named for the bluish natural fogs and clouds that often appear in the mountains. A yellowish haze, however, is a result of pollutants.

For years, comparison photographs have been taken several times a day, every day, from a station on Look Rock on the western edge of the Smokies. The photos show worsening visibility over the years. In the region encompassing the Smokies, visibility has declined nearly 30 percent.

The mountains seem especially vulnerable to ozone. At lower elevations, ozone levels are low at night, peaking in late day as sunlight reacts with nitrous oxides and hydrocarbons. At higher elevations, ozone levels peak in the middle of the night. But at higher elevations, they also maintain a sustained, chronic level.

That bad air I saw does more than obscure the view. The toxins in ozone also damage plants. The damage can be seen on the leaves, in the form of dark stippling and premature aging. Ninety-five plant species in the park are potentially sensitive to ozone. The leaves on black cherry, sassafras, tuliptree, and milkweeds, in particular, show the classic symptoms of brown and purple flecking on the top surface that results when leaf cells are damaged by ozone. Leaves also may just curl up and die prematurely. The leaves in the canopy layer, the part of the forest that bears the brunt of air pollution, are especially subject to ozone damage.

Acid rain is the other big pollution concern in the park. In 1852, English chemist Robert Angus Smith analyzed the chemistry of rain near Manchester, England, and noted air with sulfuric acid that faded textiles and corroded metals. Twenty years later he coined the term "acid rain."

By the mid-20th century, a link was made between what falls from the sky and what is in lakes and other bodies of water. The widespread death of trees, first conifers and then broad-leaf species, in Europe and Scandinavia in the 1970s and 1980s raised the public's consciousness of the detrimental effects of acid rain.

Because acid pollution can actually be both wet (rain and snow) and dry (gases and particulates), the term *acid deposition* is more precise. In the Smokies, in fact, dryfall and cloudwater account for more acidity than rainwater does.

Acidity level is a function of the number of hydrogen ions in a substance. It is measured on a 14-point pH scale, with 7.0 being neutral, above 7.0 basic, and below 7.0 acidic. Distilled water has a pH of 5.7, and vinegar is 3.0. Rainfall pH in the Smokies now ranges between 4.3 to 4.4, and cloudwater pH is 3.6 to 3.8.

Throughout the world, acid deposition has been tied to an increase in fossil fuel burning, specifically sulfur dioxide and nitrogen oxides released into the atmosphere. These chemicals travel long distances through the atmosphere, and along the way they interact with sunlight, moisture, and other chemicals in the air to produce sulfuric and nitric acids. The acids eventually return to the ground via rain, snow, or clouds, or in particles and gases.

Two high-elevation stations in the Smokies, one on Noland Divide and another at Indian Gap, are part of a network of sites in the United States, Canada, and Norway where the effects of acid deposition on forests are being monitored. Trends show nitrogen and sulfur levels in the Smokies nearly double those at any of the other sites.

Acid deposition interacts with plants and soils in several ways. For example, hydrogen ions can leach nutrients from soils. Soils in the Smokies are already acidic, with little if any buffer against additional acid. Indeed, soils where spruces grow are so acidic that further acidification by acid rain may be impossible. Aluminum is an element of special concern, for if mobilized by acid rain it can reduce the uptake of water or nutrients through a plant's roots.

Acid deposition is a suspect in a dramatic decline in red spruce growth in some parts of the country, including New England, the Adirondacks, and the Smokies and other parts of the southern Appalachians. On Mount Mitchell in North Carolina, spruce growth rates began to decline after the 1950s, with the declines becoming drastic in recent years.

An abrupt reduction in growth of spruce in the Smokies and Black Mountains occurred in the early 1970s. The amount of new wood the trees produced each year declined in trees above 6,000 feet elevation. Crown thinning, flecking on the needles, and dieback at the growing tips of the spruce have also been seen. These ill effects are not universal, however; in some parts of the park there have been no significant decreases in red spruce.

Whether acid deposition, ozone, insects, drought, or a combination have caused the damage and decline in the spruce-fir forest is a complex question without a ready answer. Cause and effect are extremely difficult to determine, and long-term monitoring will be necessary before we can know with any certainty what is going on. And as one writer observed, "there is a probability that the patient may expire while the long diagnosis is in progress."

Acidity can also affect streams and aquatic life. Effects on water quality depend upon the stream: how acidic is it naturally, and what is its chemistry, volume, buffering capacity, and geology? The water in the high-mountain streams of the Smokies is naturally somewhat acidic. Increasing acidity is known to inhibit reproduction in fish, frogs, and salamanders, and to reduce abundance of aquatic insects. And it can be lethal. Brook trout fingerlings will die if exposed to a pH of 3.6 for seven days, and high acid levels can kill salamander larvae and subadults. The Southeast is also vulnerable because it receives heavy rainstorms. Runoff from storms can cause the acid levels in streams to climb dramatically for a short time.

While scientists attempt to answer the complex questions of pollution cause and effect, politicians wrangle over laws and regulations and how much it's all going to cost—the inevitable debate over economy versus the environment. The park lost one recent battle in its opposition to issuance of a permit to build a new coal-fired boiler at Kingsport, 55 miles north of the park.

How can the values of clear air and healthy forests be quantified? I can only think back to our trip to Mount LeConte. That evening we gathered with our new-found friends at Cliff Tops to watch the sunset. As the sky turned from soft apricot to peach to indigo, we bundled up in the cool twilight. We talked softly about family and friends. Most of the time, though, we were completely content to sit in silence. At times it is impossible to assign words, much less numbers, to the value of such an experience.

The Invaders

Air pollution, though, is not the only threat to the Smokies forests. Others, perhaps more destructive and immediate, exist in the form of insect and fungus pests. Nearly 350 non-native insects and fungi have been identified in the park, many of which arrived from Europe and Asia on nursery stock. Some are of immediate concern.

At least 10 native tree species of the eastern forests are at risk of significant decline. For several of these species, severe damage has already been done. In three decades, the balsam woolly adelgid has killed nearly all the Fraser firs in the park. Chestnut blight wiped out the American chestnut in the 1930s. An imported fungus that causes Dutch elm disease killed millions of American elms in the Southeast in the 1960s. The fungus made a comeback in the Smokies in the 1980s, and nearly all the elms left in the park are infected.

Three of the biggest current threats are the gypsy moth, dogwood anthracnose, and the hemlock woolly adelgid. Since they escaped in Massachusetts in 1869, gypsy moths have spread west and south to infest a large part of the eastern United States. In the peak year of 1981, gypsy moths defoliated some 13 million acres. The Smokies are now surrounded by gypsy moths. More than a third of the park's acreage may be susceptible to defoliation. Of special concern are the forests of old-growth oak. Despite extensive releases of parasites to fight them, the only successful enemy of the gypsy moth so far has been a bacterium that unfortunately also kills all other young butterfly and moth larvae. Various insecticides and other strategies, such as disruption of mating, are still being developed and tested in the southern Appalachians.

One of the saddest losses in the park in recent years has been the death of the flowering dogwoods. These lovely understory trees grace the streamsides with starched white blossoms in early spring, and are one of the biggest attractions in the park at that time of year. A fungus called dogwood anthracnose, confirmed in the Smokies in 1988, is rapidly killing the dogwoods. In the Southeast the fungus thrives in the moist, cool places found in the mountains. It can kill a tree from the ground up in only three to five years.

Because of the devastation caused by the balsam woolly adelgid, the very word *adelgid* now evokes a bad response from anyone concerned about trees in the southern Appalachians. Another adelgid looms on the horizon, perhaps even more frightening than the killer of the Fraser firs. It is the hemlock woolly adelgid, brought in from East Asia. Since its entry into the mid-Atlantic states, the hemlock adelgid has brought swift loss of hemlocks. Hemlock woolly adelgids engage in mass feedings at the bases of a tree's needles, weakening and killing it in only one year. These adelgids infested an astounding 88 percent of hemlock stands in Shenandoah National Park in only a dozen years. In 1992 the hemlock woolly adelgid was not yet known in the Smokies, but it had reached the North Carolina border along the Blue Ridge Parkway.

There are other worrisome pests as well. In an ironic twist of fate, one destructive fungus was introduced during reforestation attempts at the end of the 19th century. Eastern white pine seeds had been sent to Germany to be reared as seedlings. When the seedlings were shipped back to the United States, alien insects and diseases hitched back with them. One was a fungus, the white pine blister rust, which can attack all five-needled conifers in North America. So far, however, the rust has done little damage to white pines in the Smokies.

A small winged insect called the pear thrips has not been found yet in the southern Appalachians, but it appears to be working its way south from New England. In one recent year, 466,000 acres of sugar maples in Vermont were damaged by thrips. Thrips eat the foliage and buds of the trees. They will likely find plenty of host species and favorable conditions in the southern Appalachians.

Introduced species may be the number one threat in the Smokies, not only to native plants but to animals as well. Pollution is of concern too, of course, but that at least is something over which we have a measure of control. The ecological effects of exotic species, however, are overpowering. The Smoky Mountains are losing pieces of their incredible natural diversity at an alarming rate.

12
The Range of Life

Someone once said that if the Sierra Nevada is the Range of Light, then the Great Smoky Mountains should be the Range of Life. The Smokies have long been recognized for the incredible biological diversity they contain, a diversity virtually unmatched in any area of similar size in the temperate world.

Biological diversity — biodiversity for short — has become a buzzword in recent years. But what does it really mean? Biologists and ecologists have been thinking and talking about biodiversity, the variety of life and its processes, for some time. The concept was clarified in the writings of forester and conservationist, Aldo Leopold, perhaps best known for his eloquent essays in *A Sand County Almanac*. In a collection of Leopold's journals called *Round River*, published in 1953, he wrote: "If the biota, in the course of eons, has built something we like but do not understand, then who but a fool would discard seemingly useless parts? To keep every cog and wheel is the first precaution of intelligent tinkering." Leopold's "cogs and wheels" are, in essence, what biodiversity is all about.

At about the same time *Round River* was published, Robert Whittaker began researching the plants of the Smoky Mountains. Whittaker, an ecologist, developed the idea of three types of diversity, which he called alpha, beta, and gamma. Alpha is diversity within a habitat, beta is across habitats, and gamma is their sum — total diversity. Each level gives rise to the next in an endless upward spiral. As Whittaker put it, "diversity begets diversity."

The Great Smoky Mountains are an excellent place to observe all the levels of biodiversity. Literally thousands of plant and animal species are interacting within a single habitat type — alpha diversity. Along with this, the elevation of the mountains gives rise to striking cross-habitat, or beta, diversity. From Sugarlands at the foot of the Smokies to Clingmans Dome, the highest point, a person can experience the equivalent of a trip from Mexico to Maine — passing from hardwood forests at the lowest elevations, through pine-oak on the drier slopes, to northern hardwoods, to the treeless balds, and finally to the spruce-fir forest. The sum of these is the total ecological diversity of the landscape.

But this is only what we see. There is also an "invisible" level of diversity, which resides in the microbial world. A good example is the mycorrhizae that live on the roots of many plants in a mutually beneficial relationship. That relationship is incredibly fragile; it cannot simply reestablish itself if disturbed. This invisible diversity is so vital, and as yet so little understood, that we cannot possibly know the full impact of any disturbances we cause in complex ecosystems such as forests.

Obviously, biodiversity is a big concept to contemplate, much less to quantify. But it can be measured, and one common yardstick is a count of the number of species present. The Smoky Mountains offer these impressive plant species totals: 125 species of native trees and an equal number of native shrubs, more than are found in all of northern Europe; 1,500 species of vascular plants (more than in all of Britain), more than 1,200 of which are flowering plants (including 9 different kinds of trillium, 25 species of violets, and 30 species of orchids); 60 ferns and allies; more than 280 mosses; and 250 lichens. That incredible diversity is controlled in the Smokies by warmth, wetness, and a climatic history that left ice age relics in the higher elevations of the mountains.

Diversity is also reflected in the wildlife that depend on the plants for food and shelter. The habitats in the forests and streams of the Smokies harbor more than 200 species of birds, 40 each of reptiles and amphibians (including 25 different kinds of salamanders), nearly 80 species of

fish, and uncounted numbers of insects and other arthropods. There are 50 species of mammals, including the lesser known but extremely important shrews, moles, bats, and squirrels.

Huge, old-growth hardwoods and hemlocks can be seen in the Albright Grove on the Maddron Bald Trail in the east end of the park.

The Great Smoky Mountains, then, give meaning to the word *biodiversity*. But biodiversity in the rest of the world is not faring as well. The Earth's natural ecosystems are losing diversity at an unprecedented rate. That loss is expressed most vividly in loss of individual species of plants and animals. Although it is true that natural extinction is a fact of life, the present rate of human-caused extinctions is alarming.

For the first time in the history of life on Earth, species are disappearing faster than they are being created by evolution. The numbers suggested for the rate of loss vary widely — from as few as one species a year to as many as 300 a day if present cutting and clearing of the tropical rain forests is taken into account. Harvard entomologist E.O. Wilson has stated, "We're easily eliminating a hundred thousand [species] a year."

In the United States, seven listed species have become extinct since the Endangered Species Act was adopted in 1973. More than 550 species

In the Albright Grove

When I asked what biodiversity really meant, the biologist told me to go to the Albright Grove. "Just sit there for a while," he said, "and you will begin to get an idea."

This collection of virgin hardwoods and eastern hemlocks stands in a cove in the northeastern part of Great Smokies National Park. I took the man's advice and hiked the three miles up the Maddron Bald Trail to Albright Grove. It was a place I had wanted to see for a long time. I walked up an old road past the Willis Baxter cabin and through a second-growth forest consisting almost entirely of tuliptrees. Dogwood blossoms were just beginning to open on this Sunday in mid-April.

Upon entering the grove, I sensed a change. It was cooler and darker, and yellow trout-lilies were blooming. Halfway through the loop, I sat beside the trail to let my senses absorb this place. Woodpeckers drummed faintly in the distance, and soft sunlight filtered into the ravine. Before me lay a giant, fallen hemlock. I mused over what it must have seen and done in its long life.

The tree was born when a tiny seed, no bigger than an eighth of an inch, fell from a cone. The seed landed on rich soil in the cool, shady, protected ravine. Its roots spread into the soil, and soft green needles began to develop above ground. Fed by the water and nutrients the fine root hairs pulled from the soil, the seedling grew into a sapling.

As the sapling continued to grow, its cells began to specialize, some becoming bark, others sapwood, others the inner core or heartwood. The tree withstood lightning strikes, bark beetles, and the browsing of whitetail deer. By age 20 it was producing its own cones and seeds.

In 50 years, the hemlock had become part of the canopy, its graceful branches casting dense shade in the forest. Only darker green rhododendron grew beneath it. Red squirrels ate its seeds, and black-throated green warblers hid nests amid its thick, limber branches. Those same soft boughs made a warm bed in a black bear's den.

As it grew and aged, the tree reached nearly 15 feet in circumference. Finally, it stopped making sapwood. Eventually, nothing was left but the dead heartwood. The hemlock crashed to the ground in a strong wind.

But as in all cases in the natural world, death gave way to life. Bacteria and fungi started to work on the log, decaying the wood and creating new ground for mosses, ferns, trout-lilies, spring-beauties — and perhaps another hemlock seedling.

remain on the list, and recovery plans have been drawn up for only about 300 of them. Some 3,700 species are "backlisted," awaiting study and decisions about their status.

And we're losing things we don't even know we have. Some 1.5 million species have been identified on the planet, but estimates of the actual number of species is astronomical. No one really knows how many there are. Estimates commonly range from 5 million to 30 million total species, but those numbers could be low by several orders of magnitude. There may be 30 million species of insects alone.

Some scientists, such as Paul Ehrlich and E.O Wilson, leading spokesmen for biodiversity, say if we had a true count of the number of bacteria, fungi, and invertebrates ("the little things that run the world," in Wilson's words), the number of species on Earth would easily be closer to 100 million.

Certainly most people want to save the beautiful furred and feathered ones — red wolves and peregrine falcons. But few people get too emotional over a microscopic fungus. Of what possible loss would it be to the world? Again, no one can say. Ecologists point out that maximum biodiversity means healthy, stable ecosystems. From a practical perspective, healthy ecosystems mean benefits to us. We need only think of a few of the plants and animals — like corn and penicillin — that have added immeasurably to our lives. Uncountable other foods, lifesaving medicines, and various other products have allowed us to survive and in some cases prosper.

One discovery involves a tree that grows in the old-growth forests in the Northwest. The needles and bark of the Pacific yew contain a compound called taxol. Taxol has turned out to be one of the most important cancer-fighting drugs now known. And there may be much more out there of potential use to *Homo sapiens*. Ehrlich and Wilson remind us that we may wish to borrow from that "precious genetic library" of biodiversity in the future.

Natural ecosystems provide other services as well. Forests make and protect soil and feed the streams, keep the gases in the atmosphere in balance and help clean the air, and store nutrients such as carbon and deliver them back to the other systems. When an ecosystem such as the Smokies spruce-fir forest loses one of its two major tree species, these services are likely disrupted and big changes will occur. Often such changes mean that biodiversity spirals down instead of up.

Beyond our debt for the practical benefits biodiversity bestows upon us, many believe we have a moral responsibility to protect other life forms with which we share the planet. This difficult-to-measure responsibility is what E.O. Wilson calls the "deep ethic" of conservation. To him, this reason for preserving biological diversity is ultimately more convincing and durable.

The major cause of the losses in biodiversity is habitat destruction and fragmentation — primarily through land-use changes brought about by the actions of people. Can anything be done about the loss of biodiversity? What are the options? Rather than waiting for a crisis and then spending large sums to save individual species near extinction, many conservation biologists propose that we concentrate instead on preserving entire habitats and everything in them.

Creating Links

A step toward protecting biodiversity exists in the United Nations' international network of biosphere reserves. This worldwide network of several hundred protected reserves is part of UNESCO's (United Nations Educational, Scientific, and Cultural Organization) Man and the Biosphere Program. Great Smoky Mountains National Park was among the first International Biosphere Reserves.

Reserves are chosen for their uniqueness and because each exemplifies one of the world's major ecosystems — forests, grasslands, deserts, islands, and others. The Great Smokies park was selected as representative of temperate broad-leaf forests or woodlands.

Great Smokies forms the core of the Southern Appalachian Biosphere Reserve Cluster. Surrounding it is a buffer zone and a fringe (or transition) area. The core is used to study the natural aspects of an ecosystem and to act as a control to compare with areas outside it. Within the reserve, long-term research is conducted on the structure, functioning, and dynamics of its ecosystems. Exotic species, air pollution, and the effects of policies such as fire suppression and logging are topics of this long-term research in the park.

Places like Great Smoky Mountains, preserved as a national park and designated a biosphere reserve, provide the greatest level of protection to biodiversity. But they are really islands in a sea of development and barriers. As in every natural area, the plants and animals of the Smokies observe no artificial political boundaries. They need to move, to disperse, in response to changes in their habitats.

Habitat fragmentation is especially significant for large predators like bears, wolves, and mountain lions that have wide ranges. One proposal for alleviating fragmentation is to connect species-rich core areas with "land bridges" so animals can move from one protected habitat to another. These corridors would help assure migrations, the animals' ability to find food and mates, and exchange of genetic material. A core natural area like the Smoky Mountains could be connected by strips of landscape to other core areas in the southern Appalachians, much as a fencerow connects small woodlots.

First, however, species need to be inventoried and suitably diverse habitats identified. Part of that information has become available through The Nature Conservancy's Natural Heritage Program, and further inventories of rare plants and invertebrates are underway in the Smokies.

Although it is unrealistic to count all the plants and animals in all habitats, the process can be helped along through what is called gap analysis. In this process, information from vegetation maps is extrapolated to highlight areas of greatest animal diversity. Land ownership and management maps are then overlaid on these, exposing gaps in the network of protected areas. Gap analysis has shown many native plants and animals presently receiving no protection.

For natural diversity to flourish, we need places like the Smoky Mountains, places where animals and plants are left alone, to do what they do in a wild environment. One of the best places in the Smokies to see true biodiversity is in the old-growth forests.

Old-Growth Forests

By now, most people have heard or read about old-growth forests, mostly because of the intense controversy swirling around those in the Pacific Northwest. This region contains some of the oldest forests in the temperate world, with 200-foot-high Douglas-firs and thousand-year-old Sitka spruces.

The controversy concerns the cutting of these forests. Many believe that logging will destroy the habitat of the threatened northern spotted owl, which nests only in old growth. Lumber companies and loggers, who speak of "liquidating" old growth, have been pitted against conservationists who believe that 800- and 1,000-year-old trees are not a

This big tuliptree and graybacks (lichen-covered boulders) are beside the Ramsay Cascades Trail.

renewable resource. They fear that once the old-growth forests are gone, not only the spotted owl will go with them, but most of the other species that live in this forest as well.

There are old-growth forests in the East too, but they have received far less attention, possibly because only small fragments remain. Great Smoky Mountains National Park boasts the largest contiguous stand of old growth in the eastern United States, grand trees that were spared the logger's saw when the rest of the land was clear-cut in the first two decades of the 20th century.

Though definitions are far from standardized, old growth generally is defined as trees 100 to 150 years old or more. A tree's age is determined by boring out small core samples and counting the annual growth rings. Old-growth forests are nature at its maximum: species diversity is rich, and trees and plants of all possible ages are present, just the opposite of the single-species, uniform-age forests cultivated strictly for their wood fiber. In the southern Appalachians, it takes 200 to 400 years for a forest to reach biological maturity.

The closest current estimate of undisturbed forest in the Smokies is some 105,000 acres, about 20 percent of the park's total 520,000 acres. That estimate is being verified by field work, in which the locations of old-growth stands are mapped, their measurements taken, and cores removed to determine their age. An individual tree's diameter, height, and crown extent are also observed. Another clue is what surrounds a tree in the forest: other species of trees, gaps in the forest canopy, the number of living and dead trees, an absence of cut stumps, and the presence of standing or downed chestnut trees. It almost becomes intuitive. Once you've spent some time with the trees, you can identify old growth without taking the measurements.

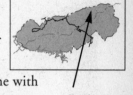

Albright Grove

Like any healthy community, old-growth forests contain not just the oldest and largest, but trees of all age classes, including dying, standing dead, and fallen dead trees. Contrary to popular opinion, dead trees — snags, stumps, and logs — are not wasted wood in a forest. In fact, they are alive with activity. Birds such as pileated woodpeckers nest in their cavities, and black bears choose them for winter dens. Voles burrow into rotted logs, and slimy salamanders favor fallen chestnut trees. In addition, dead trees are sites for nitrogen fixation, sources of energy, nutrients, and soil in the forest ecosystem, and seedbeds and nurse logs for trees and other plants. Downed trees reduce erosion on hillsides.

In streams, fallen trees create pools, riffles, and channels, and stabilize the banks. The dams they form help retain organic debris that falls in from the surrounding forest. Streams in virgin forests in the Smokies contain more than four times the volume of woody debris and ten times more material in debris dams than streams in logged forests.

Disturbances, both natural and unnatural, are also valuable in old-growth forests. Disturbances create small and large openings in the canopy through which light and water can enter so that seedlings of successional species can grow. Because of these gaps, a mosaic or patchwork of vegetation is created that is as intricate as an old Appalachian quilt.

In old-growth, cove hardwood forests, gaps are usually small. They are made by one or two trees, called "gapmakers," thrown over by wind or other natural forces. First to fill the gaps are quick-growing, sun-loving pioneer species like black locust and tuliptree. Often these pioneers are nitrogen-fixers, preparing fertile ground for the shade-tolerant species that will, over time, close the gap.

"Gapmakers" such as this fallen tree in the Albright Grove are a critical component of old-growth forests.

Old-growth forests often have been portrayed as static, unchanging systems. But studies of gap-formation rates are beginning to tell a different story. Each year openings form in about one to two percent of the total area of a deciduous forest canopy. Change, rather than stability, appears to be the norm.

Some people have suggested ways to give nature a nudge to create old-growth characteristics in younger forest. The two ingredients needed are small gaps and dead wood. To open gaps, about one percent of the land area can be cut each year. The critical element of dead wood — snags, stumps, and logs — should be left in the forest. In a young forest, though, more dead wood may be added by felling and girdling trees and even bringing in large logs. Boring cavities into trees and providing nest boxes for birds and bats can also encourage these species.

As we hiked down the Gregory Bald Trail one afternoon, my companions and I had looked at several wonderful trees and talked about old-growth forests: how you know when you're in one, what a gap looks like, what effects these trees have on the gene pool. Farther down the trail, we examined the cavity at the base of a magnificent old red oak. It was about my size, and I guessed it would be a snug place for a black bear to hole up for the winter.

As we descended, our conversation grew more philosophical, and we pondered the relationships of old growth, our planet, and our own species. We may have been hearing what E.O. Wilson calls that inner voice, murmuring that we've gone too far, disturbed the world too much. What will become of the ecosystems upon which we depend? Will we survive if their destruction continues?

Thinking beyond the lifespan of these humbling trees and this glorious forest, we considered the monumental changes the Earth, and the Smoky Mountains, have endured: floods, fires, glaciations. Perhaps because the human spirit resists despair, we voiced our hope that the Earth, Gaia, will be able to restore herself, even if we as a species do not.

Where to See Old-growth Forests and Other Plant Communities

The Albright Grove is a fine place to see undisturbed **old-growth forest**, but there are other places to recommend too:

🍃 The trail to Ramsay Cascades starts at a side road in the Greenbrier area, about 10 miles east of Gatlinburg, Tennessee. Along the four-mile trail to the falls rise huge tuliptrees, some of the biggest in the park.

🍃 The trailhead to Laurel Falls is on the Little River Road, four miles from Sugarlands Visitor Center. For the first mile and a half, the trail is paved and popular. Continue up past the paved portion a half mile or so toward Cove Mountain, where there are some majestic virgin hardwoods.

🍃 Though Smokemont, on the North Carolina side, was one of the most heavily logged areas in the Smokies in the early part of the century, a few old-growth trees remain up Bradley Fork. The trail begins from the Smokemont Campground, three miles from Oconaluftee on the Newfound Gap Road.

🍃 Near the end of the Clingmans Dome Road is a sign announcing the Noland Divide trailhead. The upper part of this trail passes through a lovely stand of virgin spruce, beech, and examples of the other conifer in this community, Fraser fir, now mainly only dead trees killed by the balsam woolly adelgid.

🍃 A grove of virgin eastern hemlocks can be seen along the three-mile hike to Grotto Falls. The trail to the falls is accessible from the Roaring Fork Motor Nature Trail. Some other inspiring hemlocks can be seen near the beginning of the Fork Ridge Trail from the Parsons Branch Road in Cades Cove.

🍃 In the magical area known as Cataloochee, on the east side of the park, are the Caldwell Fork and Boogerman trails, both of which offer outstanding specimens of old-growth trees and an off-the-beaten-path experience.

The Newfound Gap Road allows you to travel the botanical equivalent of a trip from Mexico to Maine in a driving distance of 15 miles and an elevation gain of nearly 3,600 feet. A stop at the Campbell Overlook on the Newfound Gap Road (Transmountain Highway) a few miles from Sugarlands is worthwhile for a look at the overall forest mosaic. The deciduous oak-maple-tuliptree community covers the lowest valley elevations. Slightly higher grow mixed oaks, while cove hardwoods and hemlocks inhabit the protected mountainsides and ravines. The pine-oak community takes up the drier, south-facing hillsides. The cropped thickets of heath balds can be spotted on the side of Bullhead Mountain. At the highest elevations of Mount LeConte is the boreal forest of spruce and fir.

Five miles up the road, stop at the Chimneys picnic area and hike the 3/4-mile Cove Hardwood Nature Trail. Here you will see basswood, buckeye, tuliptree, hickory, hemlock, and sugar maple, some of the constituents of the **cove hardwood forest**, a diverse, unique southern Appalachian forest type.

Because the Smokies forest is a patchy mosaic, boundaries between plant communities are not always sharp. Hikes along many trails will take you alternately through several communities as you go from wetter to drier sites. But because the western part of the Smokies is generally drier, it is the place to go for a closer look at more continuous **pine-oak forest**. Eight species of pines, including Table Mountain, Virginia, pitch, and white, and a number of oaks, including scarlet, white, and red, can be found here, with mountain laurel, teaberry, galax, and trailing arbutus often growing on the ground beneath them. The five-mile trail to Abrams Falls, which departs midway off the Cades Cove loop road, is a good introduction to this plant community.

Walking is the best way to see the curious **heath and grassy balds**, and the view is well worth the effort. One of the lowest-elevation heath balds tops Brushy Mountain. It is a three-mile hike (one way) via the Trillium Gap Trail off the Roaring Fork Motor Nature Trail. Other heath balds can be seen at close range along the Alum Cave Trail to Mount LeConte. The easiest grassy bald to reach is Andrews, two miles one way by a trail from the Clingmans Dome parking area. Both Andrews and Gregory balds are being maintained in their historic open condition by the Park Service. Gregory is famous for the wild azaleas that bloom at the end of June. It can be reached along the six-mile Gregory Ridge Trail or the four-mile Gregory Bald Trail (both distances are one way). Both trails head off from the Parsons Branch Road in Cades Cove.

To gain a view of **northern hardwoods** and **spruce-fir forest**, stop at Newfound Gap and take a short hike in either direction on the Appalachian Trail. This famous 2,000-mile footpath from Georgia to Maine reaches its highest elevations along the crest of the Smokies. Between Newfound and Indian gaps along the Appalachian Trail you pass through a beech gap. You can also see good stands of spruce-fir at Clingmans Dome and on many other peaks in the park above 5,000 feet elevation.

TREE CHECKLIST

LARGE TREES

Fraser Fir	*Abies fraseri*
Box-elder	*Acer negundo*
Red Maple	*Acer rubrum* var. *rubrum*
Trident Maple	*Acer rubrum* var. *trilobum*
Sugar Maple	*Acer saccharum*
Yellow Buckeye	*Aesculus octandra*
Heart-leaved Paper Birch	*Betula cordifolia*
Black or Sweet Birch	*Betula lenta*
Yellow Birch	*Betula alleghaniensis*
River Birch	*Betula nigra*
American Hornbeam	*Carpinus caroliniana*
Bitternut Hickory	*Carya cordiformis*
Pignut Hickory	*Carya glabra*
Sweet Pignut Hickory	*Carya ovalis*
Shagbark Hickory	*Carya ovata*
Pale (Sand) Hickory	*Carya pallida*
Mockernut Hickory	*Carya tomentosa*
American Chestnut	*Castanea dentata*
Smooth Hackberry	*Celtis laevigata*
Northern (American) Hackberry	*Celtis occidentalis*
Yellowwood	*Cladrastis kentukea*
Common Persimmon	*Diospyros virginiana*
American Beech	*Fagus grandifolia* var. *grandifolia*
American Beech	*Fagus grandifolia* var. *caroliniana*
White Ash	*Fraxinus americana* var. *americana*
Biltmore Ash	*Fraxinus americana* var. *biltmoreana*
Green Ash	*Fraxinus pennsylvanica* var. *pennsylvanica*
Green Ash	*Fraxinus pennsylvanica* var. *subintergerrima*
Honey Locust	*Gleditsia triacanthos*
Carolina Silverbell	*Halesia carolina*
Butternut	*Juglans cinerea*
Black Walnut	*Juglans nigra*
Eastern Redcedar	*Juniperus virginiana*
Sweetgum	*Liquidambar styraciflua*
Tuliptree (Yellow Poplar)	*Liriodendron tulipifera*
Cucumber Magnolia	*Magnolia acuminata*
Cucumber Magnolia	*Magnolia acuminata* f. *aurea*

Fraser Magnolia	*Magnolia fraseri*
Bigleaf Magnolia	*Magnolia macrophylla*
Umbrella Magnolia	*Magnolia tripetala*
Blackgum	*Nyssa sylvatica*
Hophornbeam	*Ostrya virginiana*
Sourwood	*Oxydendrum arboreum*
Red Spruce	*Picea rubens*
Shortleaf Pine	*Pinus echinata*
Table Mountain Pine	*Pinus pungens*
Pitch Pine	*Pinus rigida*
White Pine	*Pinus strobus*
Virginia Pine	*Pinus virginiana*
Eastern Sycamore	*Platanus occidentalis*
Pin Cherry	*Prunus pensylvanica*
Black Cherry	*Prunus serotina*
White Oak	*Quercus alba*
Scarlet Oak	*Quercus coccinea*
Southern Red Oak	*Quercus falcata*
Shingle Oak	*Quercus imbricaria*
Blackjack Oak	*Quercus marilandica*
Chinkapin Oak	*Quercus muehlenbergii*
Chinkapin Oak	*Quercus muehlenbergii* f. *alexanderi*
Chestnut Oak	*Quercus prinus*
Northern Red Oak	*Quercus rubra*
Post Oak	*Quercus stellata*
Black Oak	*Quercus velutina*
Black Locust	*Robinia pseudoacacia*
Coastal Plain Willow	*Salix caroliniana*
Black Willow	*Salix nigra*
Sassafras	*Sassafras albidum*
American Basswood	*Tilia americana*
White Basswood	*Tilia heterophylla*
Eastern Hemlock	*Tsuga canadensis*
Winged Elm	*Ulmus alata*
American Elm	*Ulmus americana*
Slippery Elm	*Ulmus rubra*

SMALL TREES

Striped Maple	*Acer pensylvanicum*
Mountain Maple	*Acer spicatum*
Smooth Alder	*Alnus serrulata*
Downy Juneberry	*Amelanchier arborea*

Smooth Shadbush	*Amelanchier laevis*
Roundleaf Juneberry	*Amelanchier sanguinea*
Hercules-club	*Aralia spinosa*
Common Pawpaw	*Asimina triloba*
Dwarf Hackberry	*Celtis tenuifolia*
Redbud	*Cercis canadensis*
Alternate-leaf Dogwood	*Cornus alternifolia*
Flowering Dogwood	*Cornus florida*
Biltmore's Hawthorn	*Crataegus biltmoreana*
Boynton's Hawthorn	*Crataegus boynotonii*
Limestone Hawthorn	*Crataegus calpodendron*
Round-leaved Hawthorn	*Crataegus collina*
Cockspur Hawthorn	*Crataegus crus-galli*
Triangle-leaved Hawthorn	*Crataegus deltoides*
Gattinger's Hawthorn	*Crataegus gattingeri*
Scarlet Hawthorn	*Crataegus macrosperma*
Palmer's Hawthorn	*Crataegus palmeri*
Hawthorn	*Crataegus pinetorum*
Common Witch-hazel	*Hamamelis virginiana*
American Holly	*Ilex opaca*
Narrowleaf Crabapple	*Malus angustifolia*
Red Mulberry	*Morus rubra*
American Plum	*Prunus americana*
Chickasaw Plum	*Prunus angustifolia*
Hortulan Plum	*Prunus hortulana*
American Mountain-ash	*Sorbus americana*

Notes to Chapters

Bibliography

Index

NOTES TO CHAPTERS

Chapter 1   The Foundation: Geology of Great Smoky Mountains
Elevation of Chimneys: Moore, *Geology of the Great Smoky Mountains.*
Stratigraphy and structure: *Geology of the Great Smoky Mountains National Park, Tennessee and North Carolina* by King, Neuman, and Hadley.
Arnold Guyot's explorations in the Smokies: from Chapter 9 in Frome, *Strangers in High Places.*
Plate tectonics and formation of the Appalachian Mountains: John McPhee, *In Suspect Terrain.*
Interpretations of seismic reflections performed by Consortium for Continental Reflection Profiling (COCORP): Frederick A. Cook, Larry D. Brown, and Jack E. Oliver, "The Southern Appalachians and the Growth of Continents," *Scientific American,* Vol. 243, no. 4, October 1980.
Pleistocene and Holocene paleoecology: from works of Paul Delcourt and Hazel Delcourt, primarily "Quaternary landscape ecology."
Fog/forest interaction: Hubert W. Vogelmann, "Rain-Making Forests," *Natural History,* March 1976.

Chapter 2   Green Mansions: The Deciduous Forest
Trees defined, and influence in forest: John R. Peckham and David J. L. Harding, *Ecology of Woodlands Processes* (London: Edward Arnold, 1982).
Evolution of deciduous forests: E. Lucy Braun, *Deciduous Forests of Eastern North America* (Philadelphia: Blakiston Co., 1950).
Cove hardwood forests: Much has been written about this famed forest community. Primary source was that portion of Robert H. Whittaker's "Vegetation of the Great Smoky Mountains," *Ecological Monographs,* Vol. 26, no. 1, 1956. Two main sources for information on specific trees: Donald Culross Peattie, *A Natural History of Trees of Eastern and Central North America,* 2nd ed. (New York: Bonanza Books, 1964); and Arthur Stupka, *Trees, Shrubs, and Woody Vines of Great Smoky Mountains National Park.*
Species diversity and forest productivity: Robert H. Whittaker, *Communities and Ecosystems.*
Trout-lily pollination: Peter Bernhardt, *Wily Violets.*
Neotropical migrants: Jennifer Ackerman, "River of Birds," *Nature Conservancy,* March/April 1992; and draft report by Kerry Rabenold, "Censusing Breeding-Bird Communities in Forests of Great Smoky Mountains to Establish Long-Term Studies," April 1992.
Forest birds: Fred J. Alsop III, *Birds of the Smokies*; and John K. Terres, *Encyclopedia of North American Birds.*
Soil types and processes of formation: Robert H. Whittaker, *Communities and Ecosystems.*
Termites: Marston Bates, *The Forest and the Sea.*

Carnivorous mushrooms: George Barron, "Jekyll-Hyde Mushrooms," *Natural History*, March 1992.

Chapter 3   Children of Boreas: The Spruce-Fir Forest
Differences between northern and southern spruce-fir: Peter S. White, "Southern Appalachian Spruce-Fir, An Introduction" in *The Southern Appalachian Spruce-Fir Ecosystem, Its Biology and Threats.*

Peter S. White, "Looking for Linnaea," article from park vertical files [source unknown], Great Smoky Mountains National Park library, Sugarlands Visitor Center.

Birds of spruce-fir: Fred J. Alsop III, *Birds of the Smokies.*

Northern flying squirrels: Donald W. Linzey, "Distribution and Status of the Northern Flying Squirrel and the Northern Water Shrew in the Southern Appalachians" in *The Southern Appalachian Spruce-Fir Ecosystem, Its Biology and Threats,* Research/Resources Management Report SER-71, Atlanta: National Park Service, Southeast Region, 1984.

Pigmy salamanders: James E. Huheey and Arthur Stupka, *Amphibians and Reptiles.*

Chapter 4   The Treeless Places: Grassy and Heath Balds
Interviews with former Smokies residents: Mary Lindsay, *History of Grassy Balds.*

Management/restoration of grassy balds: Mary M. Lindsay and Susan Power Bratton, "Grassy Balds of the Great Smoky Mountains: Their History and Flora in Relation to Potential Management," *Environmental Management,* Vol. 3, no. 5, 1979: 417-430.

Timber rattlesnakes: Arthur Stupka, interview with Mary Lindsay, 15 December 1975, in *History of Grassy Balds.*

Cooperative behavior of ravens: Bernd Heinrich, *Ravens in Winter* (New York: Summit Books, 1989).

Heath balds: Stanley A. Cain, "An Ecological Study of the Heath Balds of the Great Smoky Mountains," *Butler University Botanical Studies,* Vol. 1, Paper No. 13, December 1930; R.H. Whittaker, "Appalachian Heath Balds and other North American Heathlands" in *Heathlands and Related Shrublands,* ed. R.L. Specht, Ecosystems of the World 9A (Amsterdam: Elsevier Scientific Publishing Co., 1979).

Chapter 5   Going To The Water: Streams of the Smokies
Statistics: Charles R. Parker and David W. Pipes, *Watersheds of Great Smoky Mountains National Park: A Geographical Information System Analysis,* Research/Resources Management Report SER-91/01, Atlanta: National Park Service, Southeast Region, November 1990. Statistics in this report nearly double stream mileage and number of watersheds in the park over

what was previously known. Also see W.M. McMaster and E.F. Hubbard, "Water Resources of the Great Smoky Mountains National Park, Tennessee and North Carolina," *Hydrologic Investigations, Atlas HA-420,* U.S. Geological Survey, 1970.

Water quality: D.G. Silsbee and G.L. Larson, "Water Quality of Streams in the Great Smoky Mountains National Park," *Hydrobiologia,* Vol.89, 1982: 97-115.

Mosses: John Bland, *Forests of Lilliput.*

Aquatic insects: Peter Farb, *The Insects.*

Crayfish: T. H. Huxley, *The Crayfish;* Crayfish evolution: Perry C. Holt, ed., *The Distributional History of the Biota of the Southern Appalachians Part I: Invertebrates,* Research Monograph 1, Blacksburg: Virginia Polytechnic Institute, May 1969.

Central stonerollers: R.E. Lennon and P.S. Parker, "The stoneroller Campostoma anomalum (Rafinesque) in Great Smoky Mountains National Park," *Transactions of the American Fisheries Society,* Vol. 89, 1960: 263-70.

Beavers: Francis J. Singer, David LaBrode, and Lorrie Sprague, *Beaver Reoccupation and an Analysis of the Otter Niche in Great Smoky Mountains National Park,* NPS-SER Research/Resources Management Report No. 40, National Park Service, 1981.

Belted kingfishers: William Davis, "King of the Stream," *Natural History,* May 1988.

Chapter 6 Saving The "Spec": Decline and Restoration of Brook Trout

Brook trout reproductive behavior: Judith Stolz and Judith Schnell, *Trout.*

Brook trout decline: Several articles detail decline, but two provide excellent, succinct summaries: G. Alan Kelly, J.S. Griffith, and Ronald D. Jones, "Changes in Distribution of Trout in Great Smoky Mountains National Park, 1900-1977," *Technical Papers of the U.S. Fish and Wildlife Service.* No. 102, U.S. Fish and Wildlife Service, Washington, D.C.: 1980. Also James A. Yuskavitch, "Saved by the Barriers," *Trout,* Summer 1991.

Environmental factors in decline: John R. Robinette, "Life History Investigations of Brook Trout [Salvelinus fontinalis (Mitchill)]: Great Smoky Mountains National Park" (Master's thesis, Tennessee Technological University, August 1978).

Competition between rainbow and brook trout: Kelly, Griffith, and Jones, "Changes in Distribution."

Electrofishing and barrier studies: Yuskavitch, "Saved by the Barriers;" also, Jerry L. West, Stephen E. Moore, M. Randall Turner, *Evaluation of Electrofishing as a Management Technique for Restoring Brook Trout in Great Smoky Mountains National Park,* Research/Resources Management Report SER-90/01, Atlanta: National Park Service, Southeast Regional Office, 1990; Stephen Moore, fisheries biologist, Natural Resources Division, interview with author, Great Smoky Mountains National Park, 1 July 1992.

Brook trout genetics: Yuskavitch, "Saved by the Barriers."

Chapter 7 Of Bears, Boars and Chestnuts

History of chestnut blight: M. Ford Cochran, "Chestnuts — Back From the Brink." Also May 1937 article "Castanea dentata," in *Castanea,* Vol. 51, no. 4, December 1986: 239-244.

Replacement of chestnuts: Frank W. Woods and Royal E. Shanks, "Natural Replacement of Chestnut by Other Species in the Great Smoky Mountains National Park," *Ecology,* Vol. 40, no. 3, July 1959: 349-61.

Programs to restore chestnuts: M. Ford Cochran, "Chestnuts — Back From the Brink."

Wild boar ecology, movements, and food habits: "European Wild Hogs in Great Smoky Mountains National Park," Uplands Field Research Laboratory Volunteer-in-Parks Interpretation of Science Project, May 1985; also, briefing statement, "The Exotic Wild Hog," Great Smoky Mountains National Park public information office, 22 February 1991. Vertical files in park library contain many specific articles detailing research on wild boars.

Control of wild hogs: Jane Tate, *Controlling Wild Hogs.*

General biology and life history of black bears: The work of Dr. Michael Pelton and graduate students at the University of Tennessee Knoxville has amassed some of the most important work on black bears anywhere. Published papers and theses are too numerous to mention, but most can be found in the park library at Sugarlands Visitor Center. A highly readable book for a lay audience contains much of this information. It is *The Smoky Mountain Black Bear: Spirit of the Hills* by Jeff Rennicke (Gatlinburg: Great Smoky Mountains Natural History Association, 1991).

Bears and people: Francis J. Singer and Susan Power Bratton, "Black Bear/Human Conflicts in the Great Smoky Mountains National Park" in *Bears — Their Biology and Management,* Vertical file, "Black Bears," Great Smoky Mountains National Park library, Sugarlands Visitor Center; also, Jane Tate, "A Profile of Panhandling Black Bears in the Great Smoky Mountains National Park" (Doctoral Dissertation, University of Tennessee, Knoxville, June 1983).

Bear capture, relocation, and disposal figures: Singer and Bratton, "Black Bear/Human Conflicts."

Chapter 8 A Smokies Specialty: Salamanders

Salamander in Appalachian Mountains: Maurice Brooks, *The Appalachians.*

General accounts of various species: James E. Huheey and Arthur Stupka, *Amphibians and Reptiles.* See also Raymond Clifford Mathews, Jr., "Distributional Ecology of Stream-Dwelling Salamanders in the Great Smoky Mountains National Park" (Master's thesis, University of Tennessee,

Knoxville, August 1984).

Salamander biology and courtship behavior: Duellman and Trueb, *Biology of Amphibians;* Hairston, *Salamander Guilds.*

Antipredator strategies: E.D. Brodie, Jr., "Salamander Antipredator Postures," *Copeia,* 1977, no. 3: 523-35.

Feeding behavior: Gerhard Roth, *Visual Behavior in Salamanders* (Berlin: Springer-Verlag, 1987).

Experiments with Plethodon: Nelson G. Hairston Sr., *Salamander Guilds.*

Salmander/amphibian decline: Beth Livermore, "Amphibian alarm: Just where have all the frogs gone?" *Smithsonian,* October 1992.

Chapter 9 The Harvest: Logging, Fire, and Clearing in the Smokies

Logging history: Robert S. Lambert, "Logging in the Great Smoky Mountains National Park: A Report to the Superintendent," typescript in vertical files, Great Smoky Mountains National Park Library, Sugarlands Visitor Center; also, Wilma Dykeman and Jim Stokley, *At Home in the Smokies,* NPS Handbook 125, Washington, D. C.: National Park Service, 1984.

Establishment of national park: Michael Frome, *Strangers in High Places.*

Fire and other disturbance: Charlotte Pyle, *Vegetation Disturbance History of Great Smoky Mountains National Park: An Analysis of Archival Maps and Records,* Research/Resources Management Report SER-77, Atlanta: National Park Service, Southeast Region, October 1985.

Cherokee use of fire: Gary C. Goodwin, "Cherokees in transition: A study of changing culture and environment prior to 1775," Research Paper 181, Geography Department, University of Chicago, 1977.

History of fire in park area: H.B. Ayres and W.W. Ashe, "The Southern Appalachian Forests," Professional Paper 37, Washington, D.C.: U.S. Geological Survey, 1905.

History of fire before and after park creation: Mark E. Harmon, *Fire History of the Great Smoky Mountains National Park: 1940-1979,* Research/Resources Management Report 46, Atlanta: National Park Service, Southeast Region, March 1981; and Mark Harmon, *Fire history of the westernmost portion of Great Smoky Mountains National Park,* Bulletin of the Torrey Botanical Club, Vol. 109, no.1, Jan.-Mar. 1982: 74-79.

Park fire policy: Leon Konz, Great Smoky Mountains fire manager, interview with author, Great Smoky Mountains National Park, 16 December 1991.

Table Mountain pine: Charles E. Williams, "An Appalachian Original," *American Forests,* July-August 1992.

Red-cockaded woodpeckers: Jay Heinrichs and Dorothy Behlen Heinrichs, "The Woodpecker and the Pines," *American Forests,* March 1984; Robert G. Hooper, Andrew F. Robinson, Jr., and Jerome A. Jackson, *The Red-Cockaded Woodpecker: Notes on Life History and Management* General Report SA-GR7, Atlanta: U.S. Forest Service, Southeastern Area, September 1979.

Populations and management of red-cockaded woodpeckers in Great Smokies: Ralph W. Dimmick, Walter W. Dimmick, and Craig Watson, *Red-Cockaded Woodpeckers in the Great Smoky Mountains National Park: Their Status and Habitat,* Research/Resources Management Report 38, Atlanta: National Park Service, Southeast Regional Office, November 1980.

Forest clearing: Dykeman and Stokley, *At Home in the Smokies.*

Change and preservation: Peter S. White and Susan P. Bratton, "After Preservation: Philosophical and Practical Problems of Change," *Biological Conservation,* Vol. 18, 1980: 241-255.

Chapter 10 The Rare and Endangered Ones

Red wolf decline and recovery plan: Warren T. Parker, *A Proposal to Reintroduce the Red Wolf into the Great Smoky Mountains National Park,* Red Wolf Management Series, Technical Report No. 7, U.S. Fish and Wildlife Service, Southeast Region, October 1990.

Captive breeding and red wolf release in North Carolina: Jan DeBlieu, *Meant to Be Wild: The Struggle to Save Endangered Species Through Captive Breeding* (Golden, Colo.: Fulcrum Publishing, 1991).

Chris Lucash, interview with author, Cades Cove, Great Smoky Mountains National Park, 29 June 1992.

Current information on wolf reintroduction: "Red Wolf Update," newsletter published periodically by Public Information Office, Great Smoky Mountains National Park, Gatlinburg, TN; also, Lucash interview.

Genetic controversy: John Rennie, "Howls of Dismay," *Scientific American,* October 1991; Chris Bolgiano, "The Fall of the Wild," *Wilderness,* Spring 1992; Lucash interview.

History of otters: Francis J. Singer, David LaBrode, and Lorrie Sprague, *Beaver Reoccupation and an Analysis of the Otter Niche in Great Smoky Mountains National Park,* Research/Resources Management Report 40, Atlanta: National Park Service, Southeast Region, 1981: 9-15.

Otter reintroductions on Abrams Creek: Jane M. Griess, "River Otter Reintroduction in Great Smoky Mountains National Park" (Master's thesis, University of Tennessee, Knoxville, August 1987).

Smoky madtom reintroduction: Damien J. Simbeck, "Distribution of the Fishes of the Great Smoky Mountains National Park" (Master's thesis, University of Tennessee, Knoxville, 1990): 58-59; Morgan Simmons, "Madtoms are getting a new lease on life," *The Knoxville News-Sentinel,* 4 October 1989; Jamie Satterfield, "Park service reintroduces fish species," *The Mountain Press,* 27 September 1988; Carson Brewer, "Fish, Thought Extinct, Found in Citico," *The Knoxville News-Sentinel,* 26 September 1980.

Peregrine falcon reintroduction: from peregrine folder, vertical files, Great Smoky Mountains National Park library, Sugarlands Visitor Center.

Mountain lion reports: Nicole Culbertson, *Status and History of the Mountain*

Lion in the Great Smoky Mountains National Park, Management Report No. 15, National Park Service, Southeast Region, no date.

Endangered plants in Smokies: Susan P. Bratton, *Preliminary Status of Rare Plants in Great Smoky Mountains National Park,* Management Report 25, Gatlinburg: Uplands Field Research Laboratory, March 1979; The Flora of the Great Smoky Mountains National Park: Peter S. White, *An Annotated Checklist of the Vascular Plants and a Review of Previous Floristic Work,* Research/Resources Management Report 55, Atlanta: National Park Service, Southeast Regional Office, 1982; Janet Rock and Keith Langdon, *Rare Plant Status Report of Great Smoky Mountains National Park 1989-1990,* National Park Service, Southeast Region, April 1991; Janet Rock, Division of Resource Management and Science, interview with author, Great Smoky Mountains National Park, December 1991.

Chapter 11 Clouds Over the Mountains: Threats to the Smokies

Arrival and spread of balsam woolly adelgid through Appalachians: Christopher Eagar, "Review of the Biology and Ecology of the Balsam Woolly Aphid in Southern Appalachian Spruce-Fir Forests" in *The Southern Appalachian Spruce-Fir Ecosystem: Its Biology and Threats,* ed. Peter S. White, Research/Resources Management Report SER-71, Atlanta: National Park Service, Southeast Region, November 1984.

Feeding habitats, life cycle, and ecology of adelgids: C. Eagar in White's *The Southern Appalachian Spruce-Fir Ecosystem.* See also "The Balsam Woolly Adelgid and Spruce-Fir Forests: A Summary of Pertinent Information for the Great Smoky Mountains National Park," prepared as part of The Uplands Field Research Laboratory Volunteer-in-Parks Interpretation of Science Project, May 1983.

Future of Fraser fir: Ronald Hay, Christopher Eagar, Kristine Johnson, "Status of the Balsam Woolly Aphid in the Great Smoky Mountains National Park — 1976," University of Tennessee Department of Forestry, typescript in vertical files, Great Smoky Mountains National Park Library, Sugarlands Visitor Center.

"A faint echo": Keith Langdon, Division of Resource Management and Science, interview with author, Great Smoky Mountains National Park, 7 April 1992.

Effects on bird communities: Kerry N. Rabenold and Patricia P. Rabenold, "Change in an Avian Community After Loss of a Dominant Canopy Tree Species," Department of Biological Sciences, Purdue University, West Lafayette, typescript in vertical files, Great Smoky Mountains National Park Library, Sugarlands Visitor Center; also, Fred J. Alsop, III and Thomas F. Laughlin, "Censuses of a Breeding Bird Population in a Virgin Spruce-Fir Forest on Mt. Guyot, Great Smoky Mountains National Park Before and After Balsam Wooly Aphid Infestation," Department of Biological Sciences, East Tennessee State University, Johnson City, April 1986.

Air pollution-ozone: James Renfroe, plant physiologist, Uplands Field Research Laboratory, interview with author, Great Smoky Mountains National Park, 25 June 1992.

Acid deposition: "Acid Rain: A Summary of Pertinent Information for the Great Smoky Mountains National Park," Uplands Field Research Laboratory, 1987; Renfroe interview.

Keith R. Langdon and Kristine D. Johnson, "Alien Forest Insects and Diseases in Eastern USNPS Units: Impacts and Interventions," in *Exotic Species in U.S. National Parks: Diverse Facets of an Increasingly Pervasive Problem, The George Wright Forum,* Vol. 9, no. 1, 1992; "Summary of Forest Insect Disease Impacts in Great Smoky Mountains National Park," briefing statement, Great Smoky Mountains National Park Public Information Office, February 1991.; "Saving the Smokies: A Struggle for Balance," *Knoxville Journal* Special Report, 18 November 1991.

Chapter 12 The Range of Life

"Every cog and wheel": Aldo Leopold, *A Sand County Almanac: With Essays on Conservation from Round River* (New York: Sierra Club/Ballanatine Books, 1970).

Robert Whittaker's theories of biodiversity: Bryan G. Norton, "The Spiral of Life," *Wilderness,* Spring 1987; other definitions and discussions of biodiversity can be found in Hal Salwasser's "Roles for Land and Resource Managers in Conserving Biological Diversity" in *Challenges in the Conservation of Biological Resources,* ed. Daniel J. Decker et al. (Boulder: Westview Press, 1991).

Invisible diversity: Eugene Odum, "Natural Diversity as a Scientific Concept in Resource Management" in *Natural Diversity in Forest Ecosystems: Proceedings of the Workshop, Nov. 29-Dec. 1, 1982,* ed. James L. Cooley and June H. Cooley, Institute of Ecology, University of Georgia, Athens, April 1984.

Rate of extinctions: Charles C. Mann, "Extinction: Are Ecologists Crying Wolf?" *Science,* Vol. 253, 16 August 1991; Paul R. Ehrlich and Edward O. Wilson, "Biodiversity Studies: Science and Policy," *Science,* Vol. 253, 16 August 1991.

Estimates of species worldwide and reasons for preserving biodiversity: Ehrlich and Wilson, "Biodiversity Studies."

Biosphere reserves: Raymond Hermann and Peter White, *The Great Smoky Mountains National Park: Monitoring Environmental Impacts,* IUCN Bulletin, Vol. 13, nos. 7-8-9, July-Aug-Sept 1982.

Corridors and gap analysis: J. Michael Scott, Blair Csuti, and Steven Caicco, "Gap Analysis: Assessing Protection Needs" in *Landscape Linkages and Biodiversity,* ed. Wendy E. Hudson (Washington, D.C. and Covelo, Calif.: Defenders of Wildlife and Island Press, 1991); Reed F. Noss, "Landscape

Connectivity: Different Functions at Different Scales" in *Landscape Linkages and Biodiversity;* M. Rupert Cutler, "Meeting the Biodiversity Challenge Through Coordinated Land Use Planning," *Proceedings, Second Annual Southern Appalachian Man and the Biosphere Conference,* ed. Elizabeth R. Smith, Norris, Tenn.: Tennessee Valley Authority, 4-5 November 1991.

Estimate of old-growth forest in Smokies: Charlotte Pyle, *Vegetation Disturbance History of Great Smoky Mountains National Park: An Analysis of Archival Maps and Records,* Research/Resources Management Report SER-77, Atlanta: National Park Service, Southeast Region, October 1985; see also Mary Davis, "Old Growth in the East: A Preliminary Overview," *Earth First!* 1990.

Woody debris in streams: David G. Silsbee and Gary L. Larson, "A comparison of streams in logged and unlogged areas of Great Smoky Mountains National Park," *Hydrobiologia,* Vol. 102, 1988: 99-111.

Mimicing old-growth conditions: James R. Runkle, "Gap Dynamics of Old-Growth Eastern Forests: Management Implications," *Natural Areas* Vol. 11, no.1, 1991.

Map Credits

Inside Cover, Great Smoky Mountains National Park. Credit: Wendy Baylor

Chapter 1, Long-term landscape changes on Mount LeConte over the last 20,000 years. Credit: From "Dynamic landscapes of East Tennessee: an integration of paleoecology, geomorphology, and archaeology." University of Tennessee, Knoxville. Department of Geological Sciences, *Studies in Geology* 9: 191-220. Courtesy of Paul Delcourt

Chapter 4, Distribution of grassy balds. Credit: Grassy Balds of Great Smoky Mountains National Park. Research/Resources Management Report SER-58. National Park Service, Uplands Field Research Laboratory.

Chapter 9, Corporate logging, settlement, and other disturbance before establishment of Great Smoky Mountains National Park in 1934. Credit: Charlotte Pyle, Fig. 2 in Vegetation Disturbance History of Great Smoky Mountains National Park: An Analysis of Archival Maps and Records. Research/Resources Management Report SER-77. National Park Service Uplands Field Research Laboratory.

BIBLIOGRAPHY

Alsop, Fred J., III. 1991. *Birds of the Smokies.* Gatlinburg, Tenn.: Great Smoky Mountains Natural History Association.

Bates, Marston. 1960. *The Forest and the Sea.* New York: Time Incorporated.

Bernhardt, Peter. 1989. *Wily Violets & Underground Orchids: Revelations of a Botanist.* New York: William Morrow.

Bishop, Sherman C. 1943. *Handbook of Salamanders.* Ithaca, N.Y.: Comstock Publishing.

Bland, John. 1971. *Forests of Lilliput: The Realm of Mosses and Lichens.* Englewood Cliffs, N.J.: Prentice-Hall.

Borror, Donald J., and Richard E. White. 1970. *A Field Guide to the Insects.* Boston: Houghton Mifflin.

Brooks, Maurice. 1965. *The Appalachians.* Boston: Houghton Mifflin.

Campbell, Carlos C., William F. Hutson, and Aaron J. Sharp. 1984. *Great Smoky Mountains Wildflowers.* 4th ed. Knoxville: University of Tennessee Press.

Cobb, Boughton. 1956. *A Field Guide to the Ferns.* Boston: Houghton Mifflin.

Cochran, M. Ford. 1990. "Chestnuts: Back From the Brink." *National Geographic* 177:2 (February).

Delcourt, Hazel R., and Paul A. Delcourt. 1988. "Quaternary landscape ecology: Relevant scales in space and time." *Landscape Ecology 2:1:23-34.*

Doolittle, Jerome. 1975. *The Southern Appalachians.* New York: Time-Life Books.

Duellman, William E., and Linda Trueb. 1986. *Biology of Amphibians.* New York: McGraw-Hill.

Farb, Peter. 1963. *The Forest.* New York: Time-Life Books.

————. 1962. *The Insects.* New York: Time-Life Books.

Frome, Michael. 1980. *Strangers in High Places: The Story of the Great Smoky Mountains.* Rev. ed. Knoxville: University of Tennessee Press.

Fuller, Margaret. 1991. *Forest Fires: An Introduction to Wildland Fire Behavior, Management, Firefighting, and Prevention.* New York: John Wiley & Sons.

Hairston, Nelson G., Sr. 1987. *Community Ecology and Salamander Guilds.* Cambridge: Cambridge University Press.

Huheey, James E., and Arthur Stupka. 1967. *Amphibians and Reptiles of Great Smoky Mountains National Park.* Knoxville: University of Tennessee Press.

Huxley, T.H. [1880 D. Appleton] 1973. *The Crayfish: An Introduction to the Study of Zoology.* Reprint, with a foreword by S. A. Raymond. Cambridge: MIT Press.

Ingold, C.T. 1984. *The Biology of Fungi.* 5th ed. London: Hutchinson.

Johnsson, Robert G. 1984. *A Naturalist's Notebook: Great Smoky Mountains National Park.* Gatlinburg, Tenn.: Great Smoky Mountains Natural History

Association.

King, Philip B., Robert B. Neuman, and Jarvis B. Hadley. 1968. *Geology of the Great Smoky Mountains National Park, Tennessee and North Carolina.* Washington, D.C.: Government Printing Office. Geological Survey Professional Paper 587.

Kozlowski, T.T., and C.E. Ahlgren (eds.). 1974. *Fire and Ecosystems.* New York: Academic Press.

Kricher, John C. 1988. *A Field Guide to Eastern Forests.* Peterson Field Guide Series. Boston: Houghton Mifflin.

Lindsay, Mary. 1976. *History of the Grassy Balds in Great Smoky Mountains National Park.* Great Smoky Mountains National Park. Uplands Field Research Laboratory Management Report No. 4.

Line, Les, and Walter Henricks Hodge. 1978. *The Audubon Society Book of Wildflowers.* New York: Harry N. Abrams.

Linzey, Alicia V., and Donald W. Linzey. 1971. *Mammals of Great Smoky Mountains National Park.* Knoxville: University of Tennessee Press.

McCormick, Jack. 1966. *The Life of the Forest.* New York: McGraw-Hill.

McPhee, John. 1982. *In Suspect Terrain.* New York: Farrar, Straus, Giroux.

Moore, Harry L. 1988. *A Roadside Guide to the Geology of the Great Smoky Mountains National Park.* Knoxville: University of Tennessee Press.

Niering, William A. 1979. *The Audubon Society Field Guide to North American Wildflowers.* New York: Alfred A. Knopf.

Ogburn, Charlton. 1975. *The Southern Appalachians: A Wilderness Quest.* New York: William Morrow.

Page, Jake, and The Editors of Time-Life Books. 1983. *Forest.* Planet Earth Series. Alexandria, Va.: Time-Life Books.

Rennicke, Jeff. 1991. *The Smoky Mountain Black Bear: Spirit of the Hills.* Gatlinburg, Tenn.: Great Smoky Mountains Natural History Association.

Segerberg, Osborn, Jr. 1971. *Where Have All the Flowers, Fishes, Birds, Trees, Water, and Air Gone?* New York: David McKay.

Shelton, Napier. 1981. *Great Smoky Mountains.* Washington, D.C.: Department of the Interior. National Park Service Handbook 112.

Simbeck, Damien J. 1990. "Distribution of the Fishes of the Great Smoky Mountains National Park." Master's thesis, University of Tennessee, Knoxville.

Stokes, Donald W. 1983. *A Guide to Observing Insect Lives.* Boston: Little, Brown.

Stolz, Judith, and Judith Schnell (eds.). 1991. *Trout.* Harrisburg, Pa.: Stackpole Books.

Stupka, Arthur. 1964. *Trees, Shrubs, and Woody Vines of Great Smoky Mountains National Park.* Knoxville: University of Tennessee Press.

Sutton, Ann, and Myron Sutton. 1985. *Eastern Forests.* The Audubon Society Nature Guide Series. New York: Alfred A. Knopf.

Tate, Jane. 1984. *Techniques for Controlling Wild Hogs in Great Smoky Mountains National Park: Proceedings of a Workshop, November 29-30, 1983.* Atlanta: National Park Service, Southeast Region. Research/Resources Management Report SER-72.

Terres, John K. 1980. *The Audubon Society Encyclopedia of North American Birds.* New York: Alfred A. Knopf.

Waring, Richard H., and William H. Schlesinger. 1985. *Forest Ecosystems: Concepts and Management.* Orlando: Academic Press.

Weber, Nancy Smith, and Alexander H. Smith. 1985. *A Field Guide to Southern Mushrooms.* Ann Arbor: University of Michigan Press.

White, Peter S. (ed.). 1984. *The Southern Appalachian Spruce-Fir Ecosystem: Its Biology and Threats.* Atlanta: National Park Service, Southeast Region. Research/Resources Management Report SER-71.

Whittaker, Robert H. 1975. *Communities and Ecosystems.* New York: Macmillan.

INDEX